THE WICKED + THE DIVINE

VOL. 7, MOTHERING INVENTION

GILLEN

M^cKELVIE

WILSON

COWLES

KIERON GILLEN
WRITER

JAMIE McKELVIE
ARTIST

MATTHEW WILSON
COLOURIST

CLAYTON COWLES
LETTERER

SERGIO SERRANO
DESIGNER

CHRISSY WILLIAMS
EDITOR

DEE CUNNIFFE
FLATTER

THE WICKED + THE DIVINE, VOL. 7, MOTHERING INVENTION
First printing. October 2018.
ISBN: 978-1-5343-0840-4
Published by Image Comics Inc.
Office of publication: 2701 NW Vaughn St., Suite 780, Portland, OR 97210.

For information regarding the CPSIA on this printed material call: 203-595-3636
and provide reference # RICH – 813516. Representation: Law Offices of Harris M.
Miller II, P.C. (rights.inquiries@gmail.com).

This book was designed by Sergio Serrano, based on a design by Hannah
Donovan and Jamie McKelvie, and set into type by Sergio Serrano in Edmonton,
Canada. The text face is Gotham, designed and issued by Hoefler & Co. in 2000.
The paper is Liberty 60 matte.

GILLEN McKELVIE WILSON COWLES

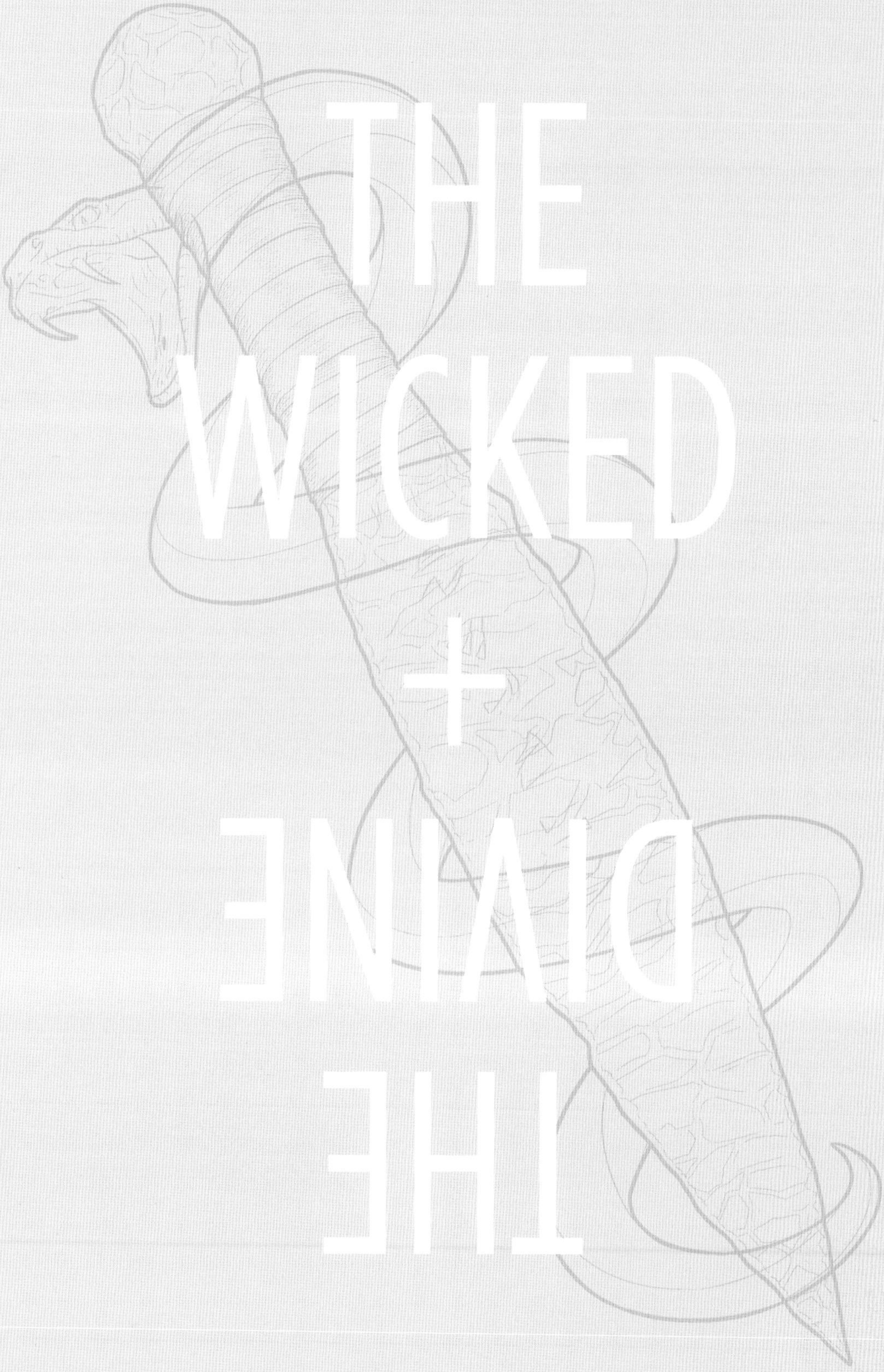

THE WICKED + THE DIVINE

VOL. 7: MOTHERING INVENTION

THE
WICKED
+
THE DIVINE

PREVIOUSLY...

Every ninety years twelve gods return as young people. They are loved. They are hated. In two years, they are all dead. It's happening now. It's happening again.

Since Persephone murdered Ananke to avenge her family, and the Pantheon covered it up, it's gone from bad to abyssal horror. In the aftermath of the horror, Persephone and Cassandra discover a secret room in Valhalla — where Woden (actually academic David Blake) was trapping Mimir (actually his son Jon Blake). Unfortunately, Woden traps them all in the divinity-negating cage he was keeping Jon in. Oh, and Jon's a living head.

Persephone. Ascended fangirl Laura. Blames self for murder of her family by Ananke.

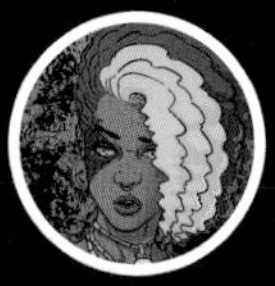

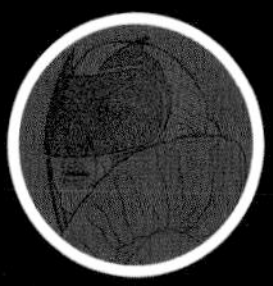

Ananke. Murderous manipulative ~~immortal~~ god of destiny. A bad 'un.

THE PANTHEON

Lucifer. Underworld god. Framed for murder. Apparently killed, actually living head.

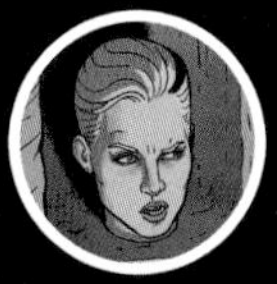

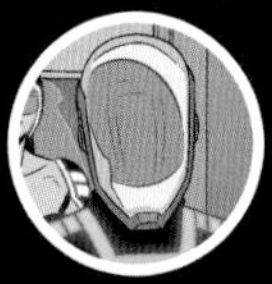

Woden. Shithead 'god'. Was Ananke's secret semi-willing assistant. Gains abilities through living head of son.

Baphomet. Punderworld god. The Morrigan's lover. Cheated with Persephone. Beaten by Morrigan.

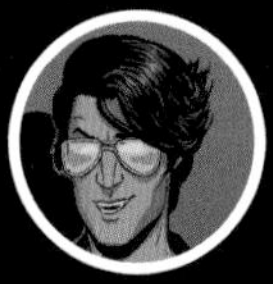

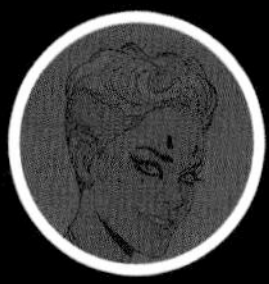

Sakhmet. Feline war god. Ate her dad. Went on rampage. Was killed in lover Persephone's home.

The Morrigan. Triple-formed underworld god. Ignored alert when she realised Persephone was in danger.

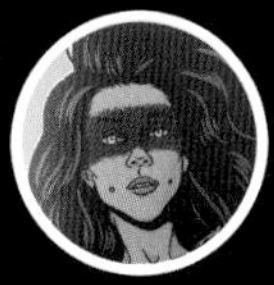

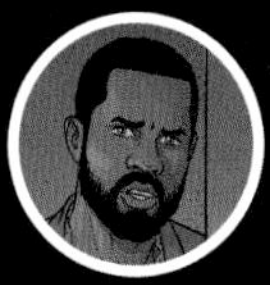

Baal. Storm god. Ex-lover of Inanna and Persephone. The Great Darkness killed his dad.

Dionysus. Hivemind dancefloor god. Doesn't sleep. Burned out powers. Now brain dead in hospital.

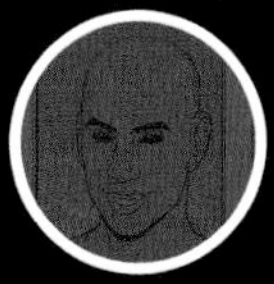

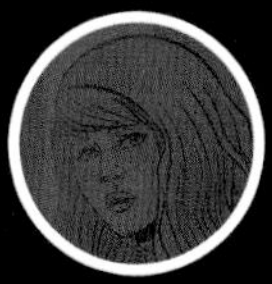

Amaterasu. Sun god. Accidentally prompted Sakhmet's killing spree. Eventually killed by Sakhmet.

The Norns. Cynical journo Cass and crew tried for months to understand Ananke's Machine. Failed entirely.

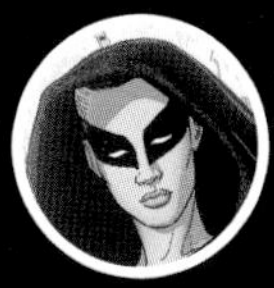

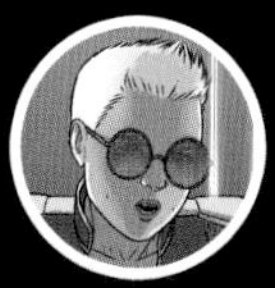

Minerva. Wisdom god. Attempted to steal Sakhmet's head and failed. Claimed "she is Ananke". WTF?

Inanna. Queen of heaven. Ex-lover of Baal. Seemingly murdered, actually living head.

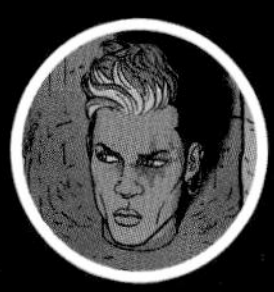

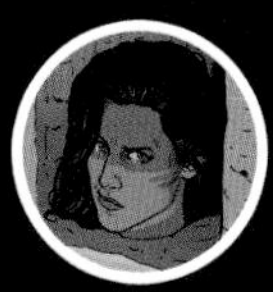

Tara. Apparently secretly killed by Ananke in assisted suicide, actually a living head.

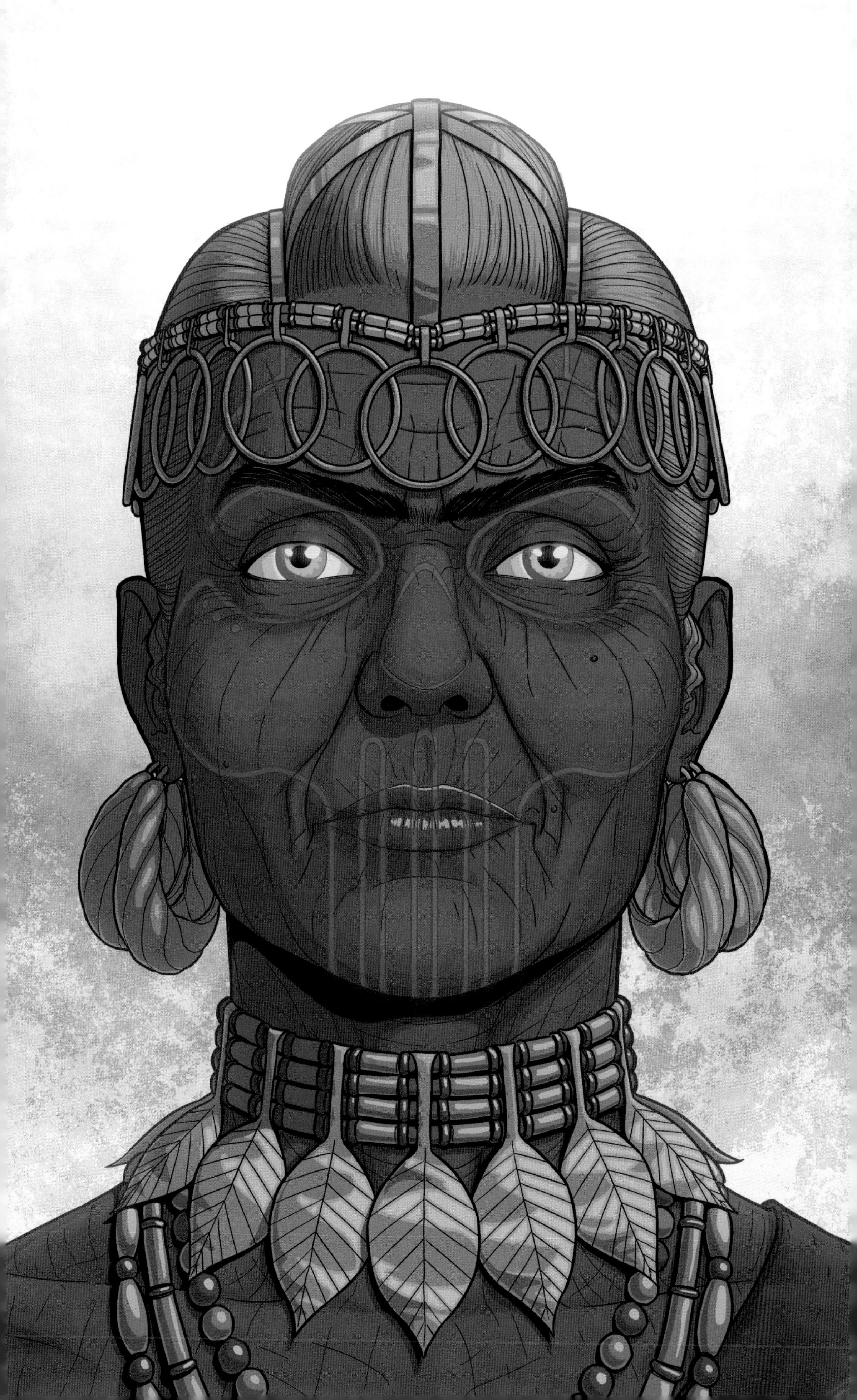

It's nearly 6,000 years ago.
It's never happened before.

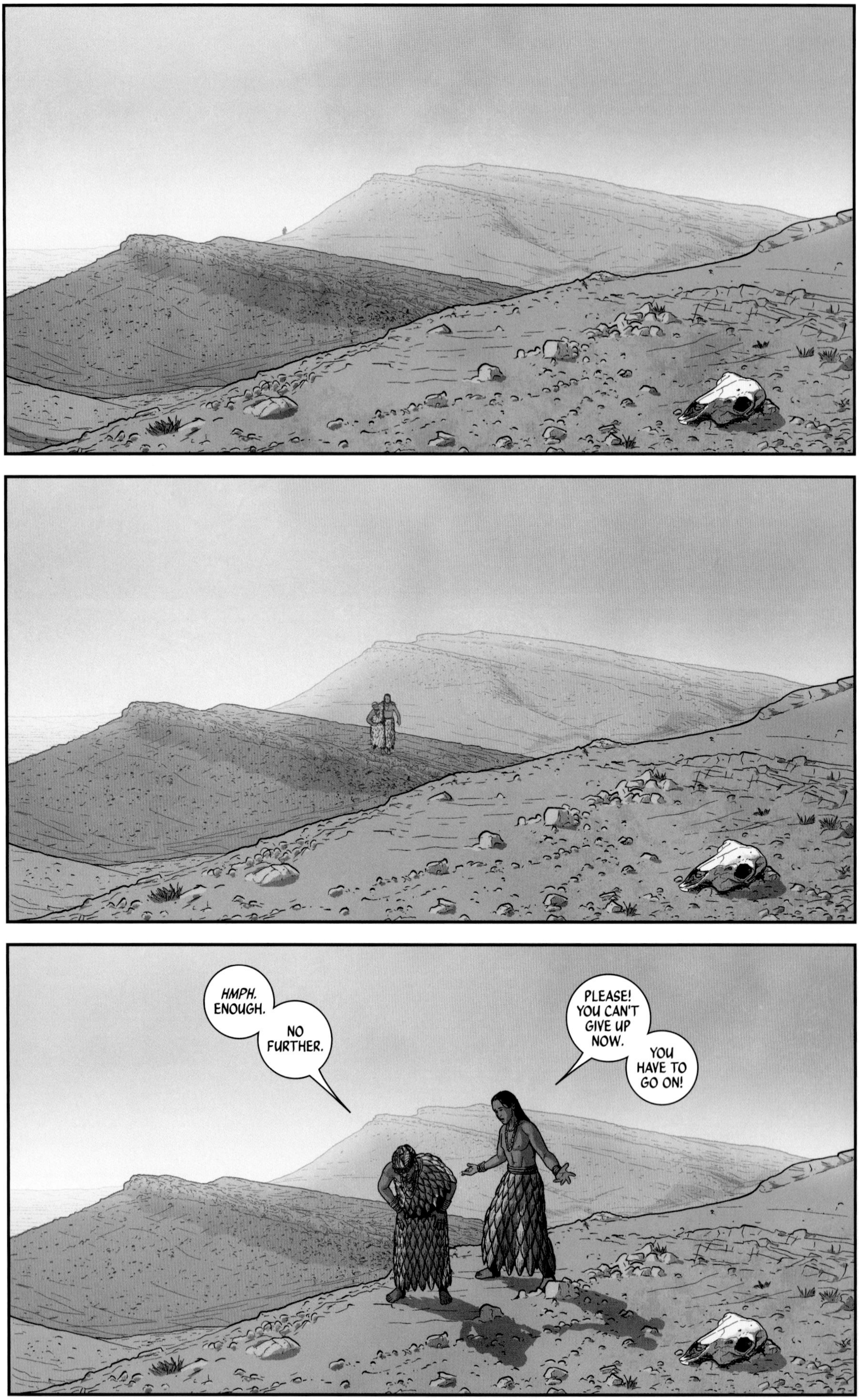
HMPH. ENOUGH.
NO FURTHER.
PLEASE! YOU CAN'T GIVE UP NOW.
YOU HAVE TO GO ON!

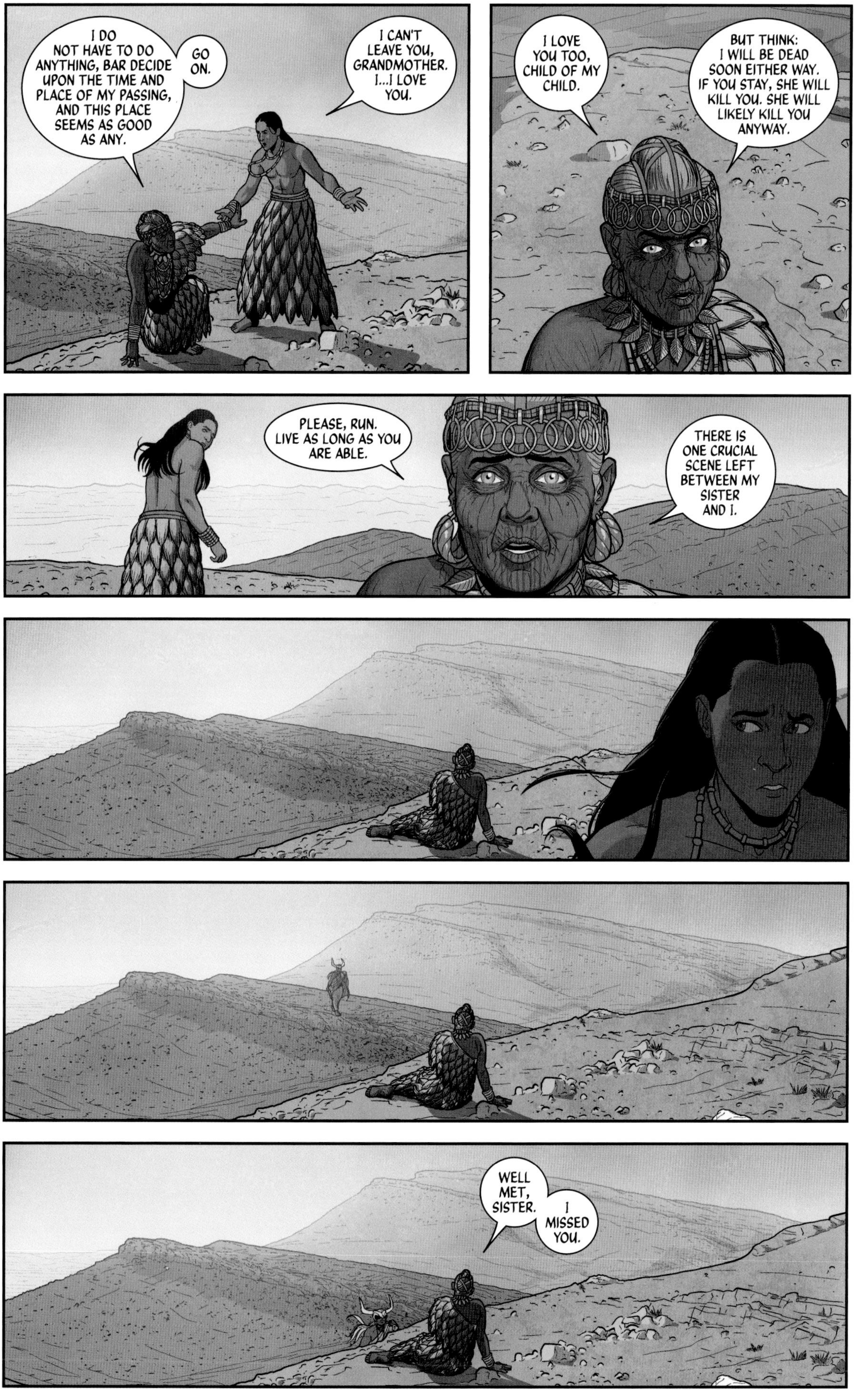
I DO NOT HAVE TO DO ANYTHING, BAR DECIDE UPON THE TIME AND PLACE OF MY PASSING, AND THIS PLACE SEEMS AS GOOD AS ANY.
GO ON.
I CAN'T LEAVE YOU, GRANDMOTHER. I...I LOVE YOU.
I LOVE YOU TOO, CHILD OF MY CHILD.
BUT THINK: I WILL BE DEAD SOON EITHER WAY. IF YOU STAY, SHE WILL KILL YOU. SHE WILL LIKELY KILL YOU ANYWAY.
PLEASE, RUN. LIVE AS LONG AS YOU ARE ABLE.
THERE IS ONE CRUCIAL SCENE LEFT BETWEEN MY SISTER AND I.
WELL MET, SISTER.
I MISSED YOU.

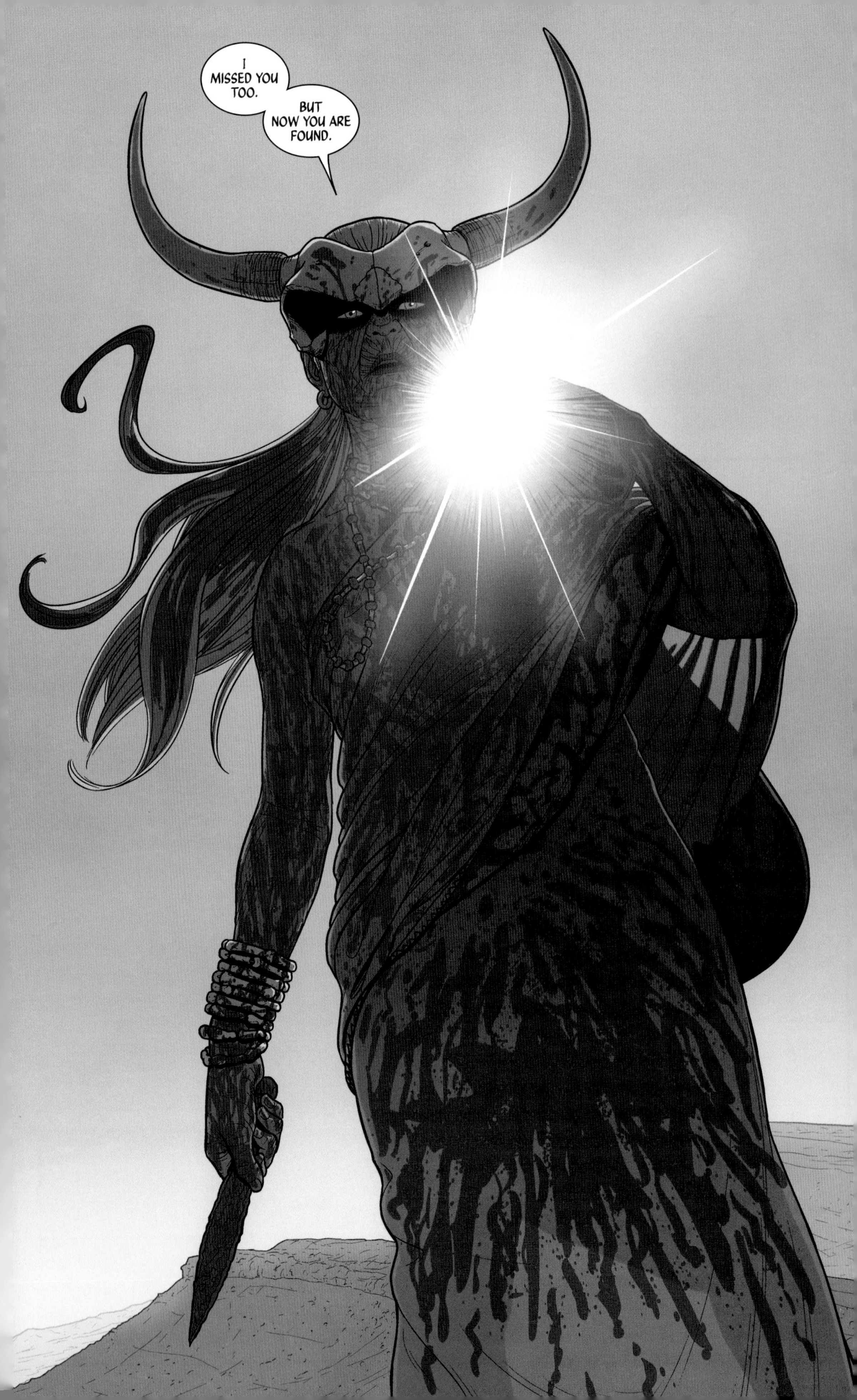
I MISSED YOU TOO.
BUT NOW YOU ARE FOUND.

YOUR LOAD IS QUIETER THAN I'D HAVE THOUGHT.

THEY WOULD NOT BE SILENT.

IN MY GRAND DESIGN, I WILL NOT SUFFER ANY CRITICISM.

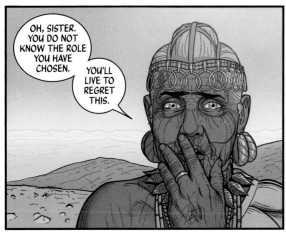

OH, SISTER. YOU DO NOT KNOW THE ROLE YOU HAVE CHOSEN.

YOU'LL LIVE TO REGRET THIS.

PERHAPS.

BUT I WILL *LIVE* TO REGRET IT.

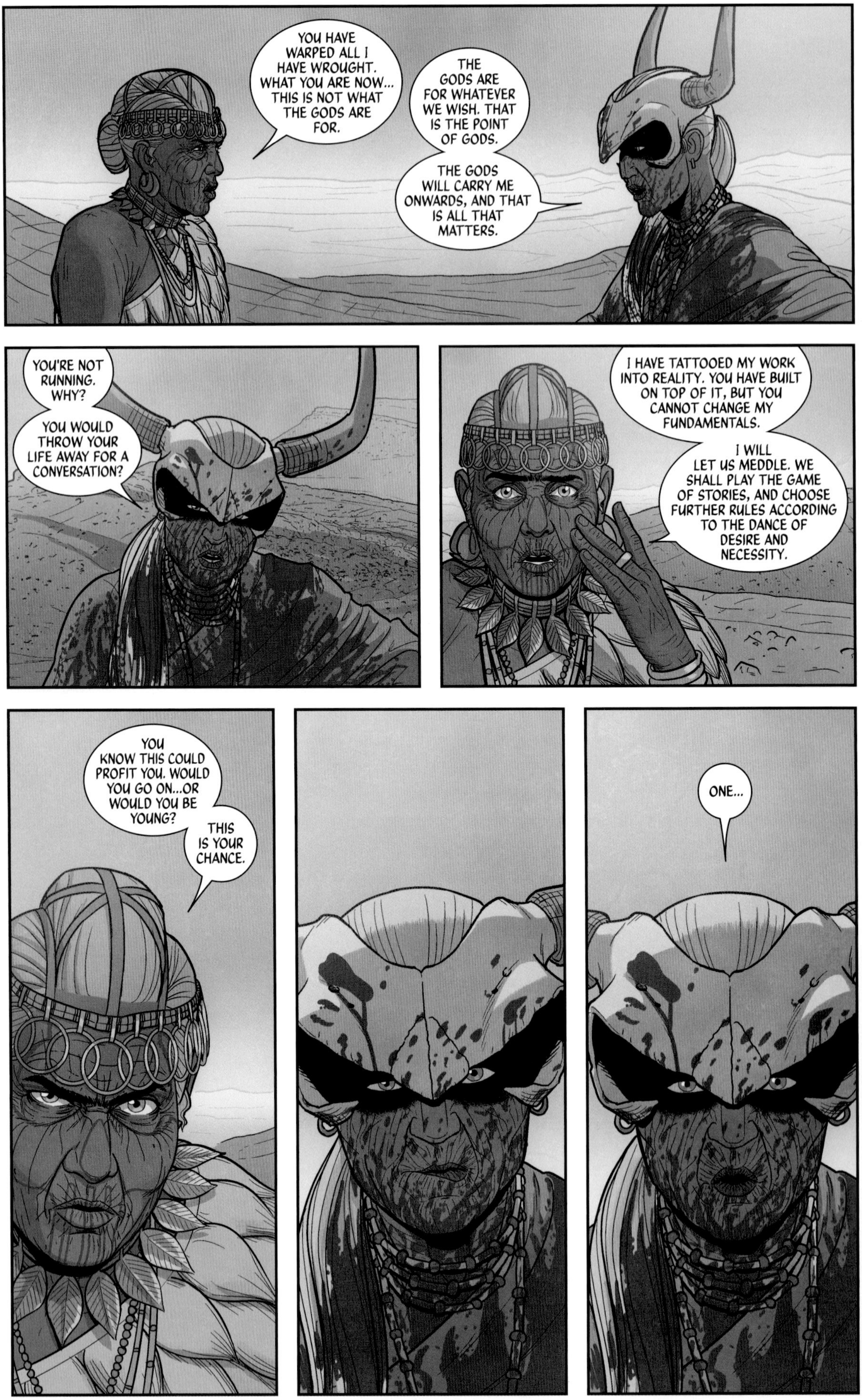
YOU HAVE WARPED ALL I HAVE WROUGHT. WHAT YOU ARE NOW... THIS IS NOT WHAT THE GODS ARE FOR.
THE GODS ARE FOR WHATEVER WE WISH. THAT IS THE POINT OF GODS.
THE GODS WILL CARRY ME ONWARDS, AND THAT IS ALL THAT MATTERS.
YOU'RE NOT RUNNING. WHY?
YOU WOULD THROW YOUR LIFE AWAY FOR A CONVERSATION?
I HAVE TATTOOED MY WORK INTO REALITY. YOU HAVE BUILT ON TOP OF IT, BUT YOU CANNOT CHANGE MY FUNDAMENTALS.
I WILL LET US MEDDLE. WE SHALL PLAY THE GAME OF STORIES, AND CHOOSE FURTHER RULES ACCORDING TO THE DANCE OF DESIRE AND NECESSITY.
YOU KNOW THIS COULD PROFIT YOU. WOULD YOU GO ON...OR WOULD YOU BE YOUNG?
THIS IS YOUR CHANCE.
ONE...

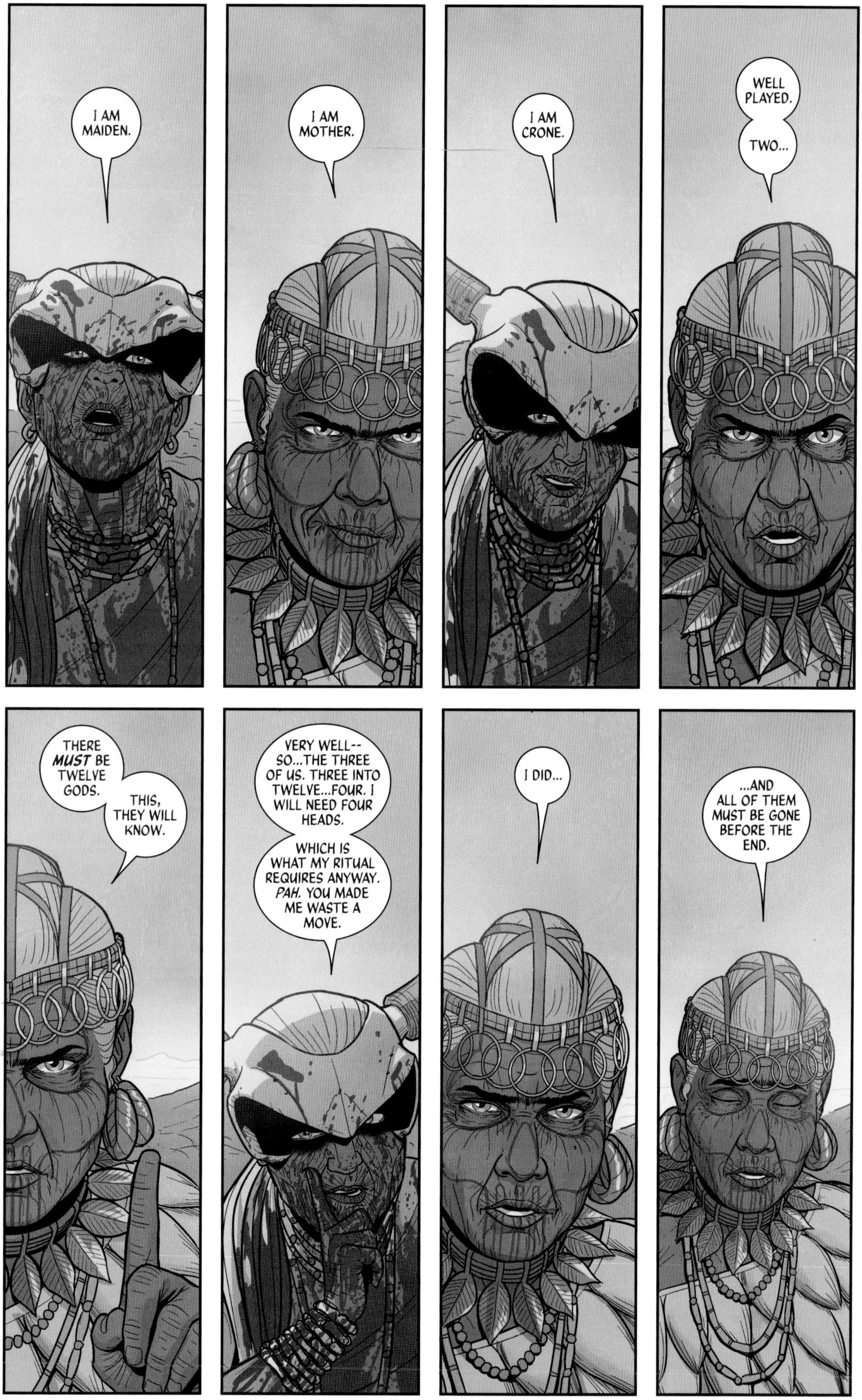
I AM MAIDEN.
I AM MOTHER.
I AM CRONE.
WELL PLAYED.
TWO...
THERE MUST BE TWELVE GODS.
THIS, THEY WILL KNOW.
VERY WELL-- SO...THE THREE OF US. THREE INTO TWELVE...FOUR. I WILL NEED FOUR HEADS.
WHICH IS WHAT MY RITUAL REQUIRES ANYWAY. PAH. YOU MADE ME WASTE A MOVE.
I DID...
...AND ALL OF THEM MUST BE GONE BEFORE THE END.

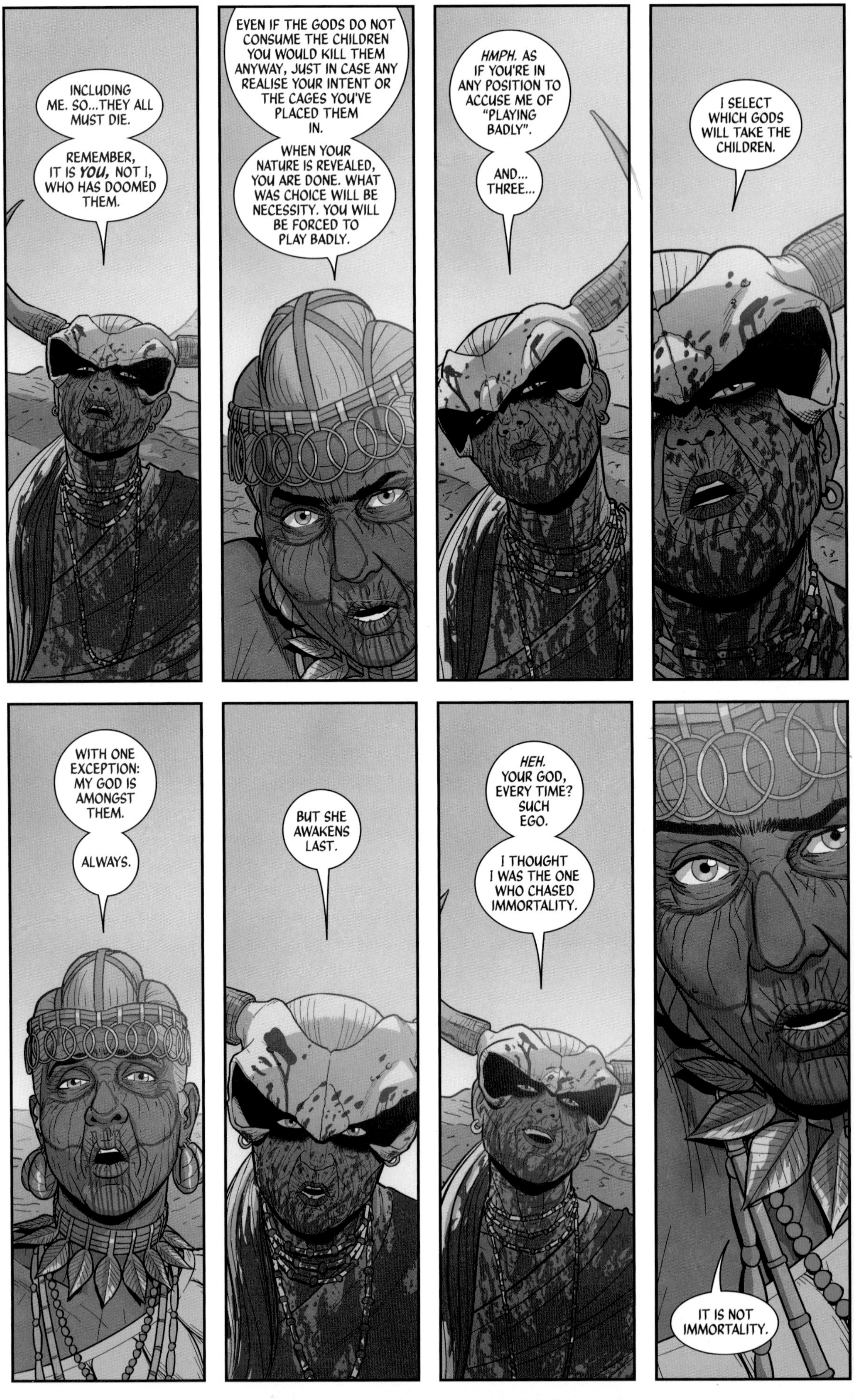
INCLUDING ME. SO...THEY ALL MUST DIE.
REMEMBER, IT IS *YOU,* NOT I, WHO HAS DOOMED THEM.
EVEN IF THE GODS DO NOT CONSUME THE CHILDREN YOU WOULD KILL THEM ANYWAY, JUST IN CASE ANY REALISE YOUR INTENT OR THE CAGES YOU'VE PLACED THEM IN.
WHEN YOUR NATURE IS REVEALED, YOU ARE DONE. WHAT WAS CHOICE WILL BE NECESSITY. YOU WILL BE FORCED TO PLAY BADLY.
HMPH. AS IF YOU'RE IN ANY POSITION TO ACCUSE ME OF "PLAYING BADLY".
AND... THREE...
I SELECT WHICH GODS WILL TAKE THE CHILDREN.
WITH ONE EXCEPTION: MY GOD IS AMONGST THEM.
ALWAYS.
BUT SHE AWAKENS LAST.
HEH. YOUR GOD, EVERY TIME? SUCH EGO.
I THOUGHT I WAS THE ONE WHO CHASED IMMORTALITY.
IT IS NOT IMMORTALITY.

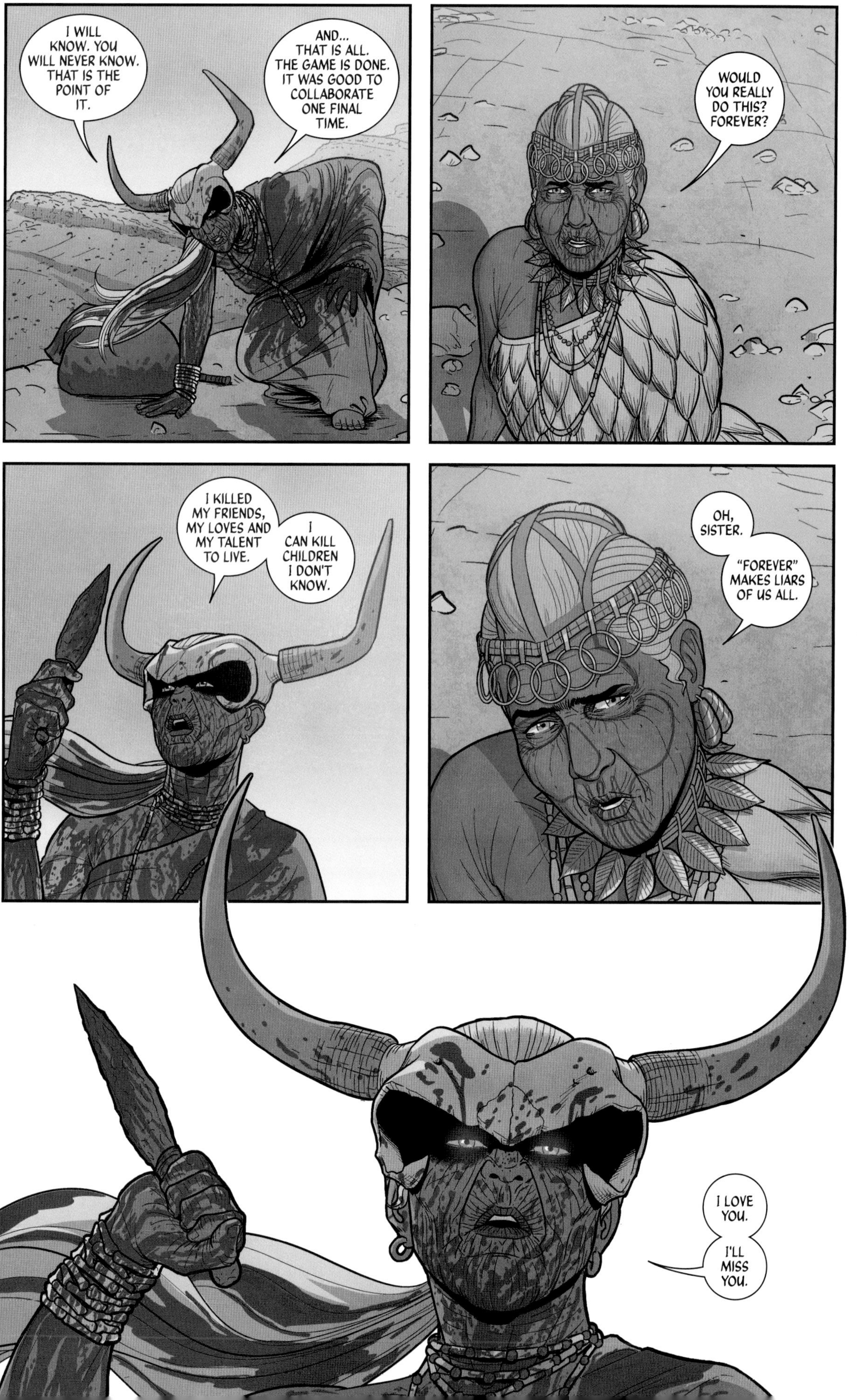
I WILL KNOW. YOU WILL NEVER KNOW. THAT IS THE POINT OF IT.
AND... THAT IS ALL. THE GAME IS DONE. IT WAS GOOD TO COLLABORATE ONE FINAL TIME.
WOULD YOU REALLY DO THIS? FOREVER?
I KILLED MY FRIENDS, MY LOVES AND MY TALENT TO LIVE.
I CAN KILL CHILDREN I DON'T KNOW.
OH, SISTER.
"FOREVER" MAKES LIARS OF US ALL.
I LOVE YOU.
I'LL MISS YOU.

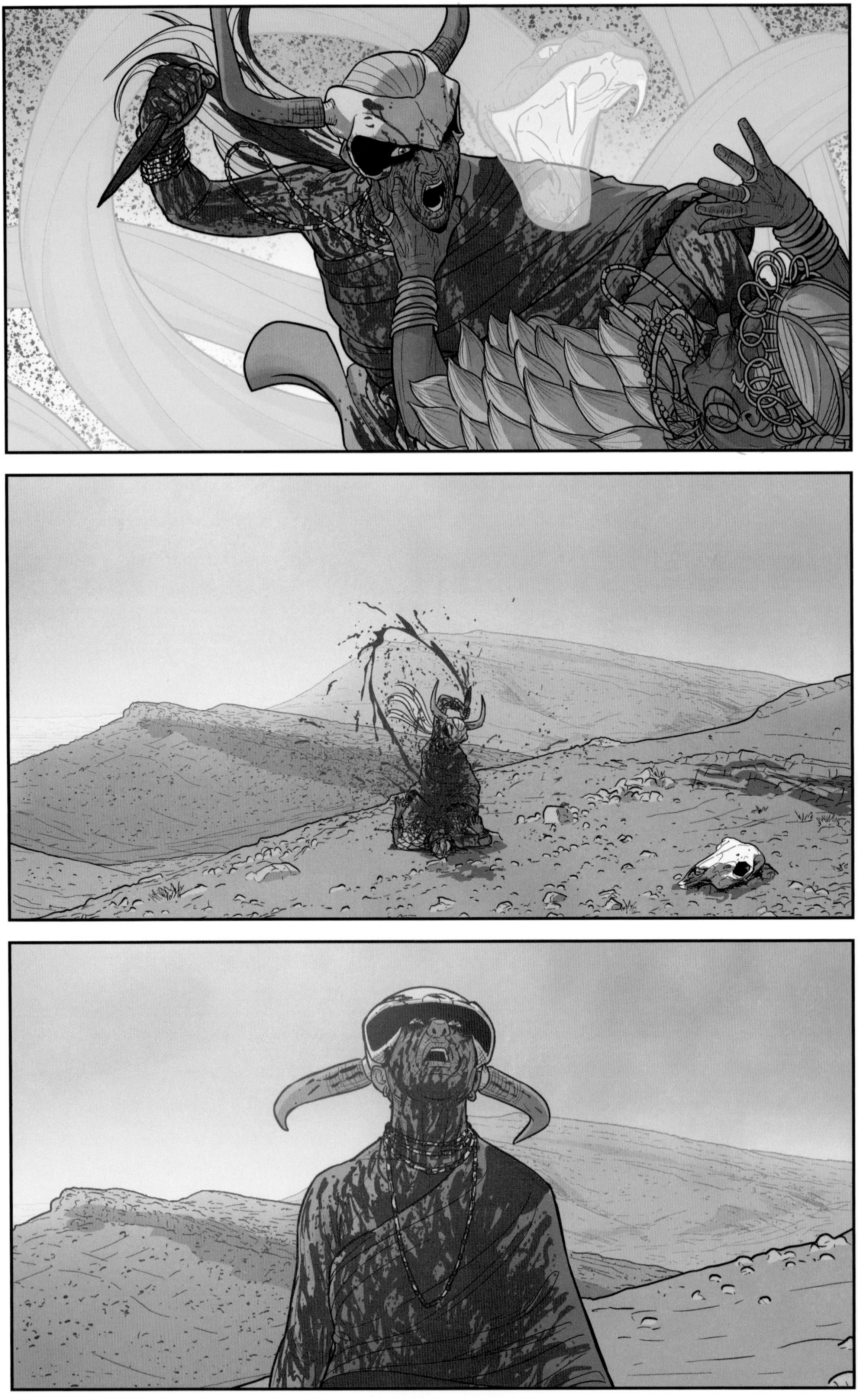

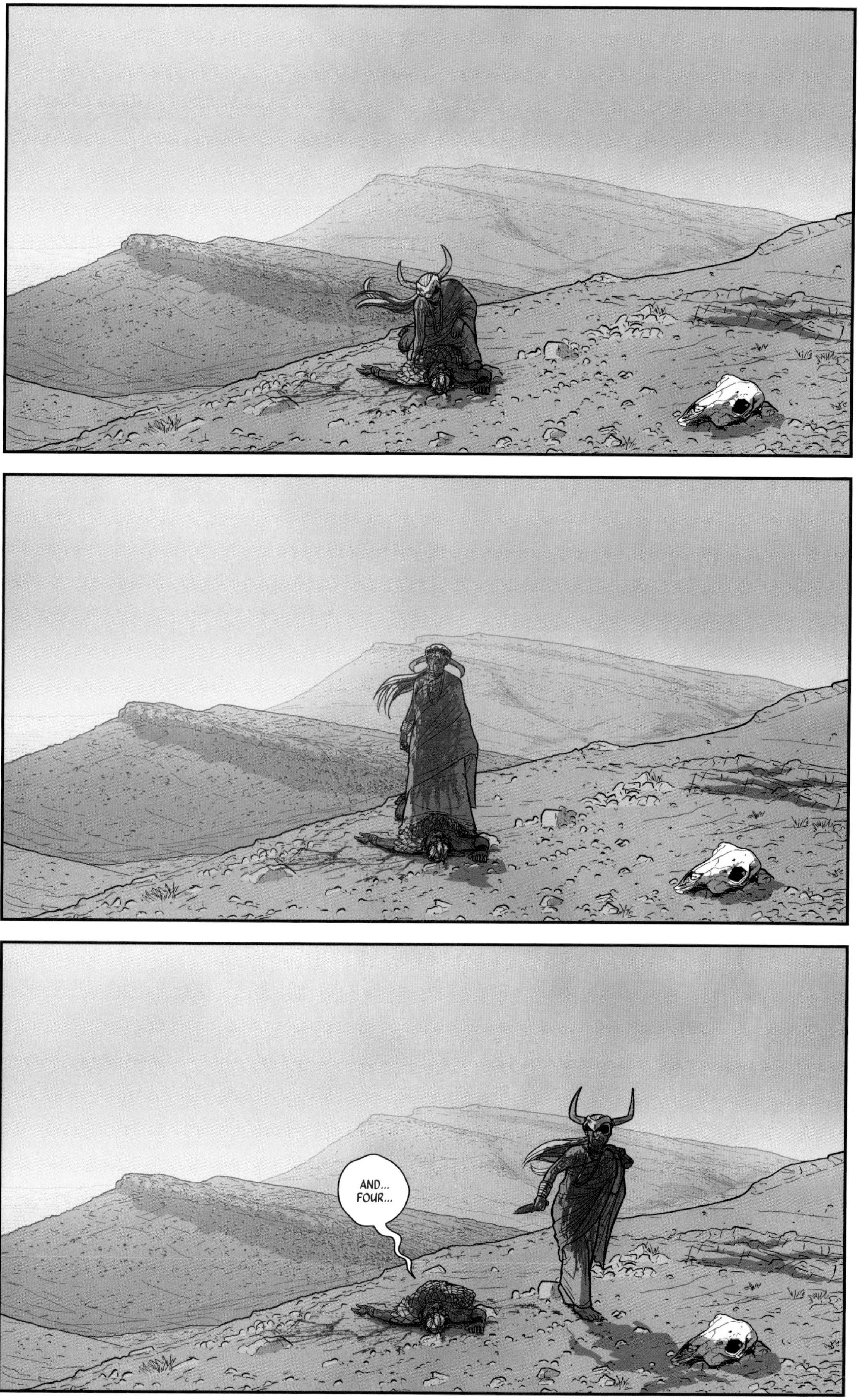
AND... FOUR...

1, 2, 3, 4

9 MARCH 2015

IT'S A SIMPLE QUESTION, SKULD.

I MEAN, WE ALL KNOW THAT SHE'S BEYONCÉ.

BUT WHICH OF US IS KELLY AND WHO'S... THE OTHER ONE?

PUT IT THIS WAY, VERDANDI. THE PRESS MAKE THE EFFORT TO TYPE URDR'S WEIRD ACCENT PROPERLY. THINK THEY'RE GOING TO DO YOUR "Ð" TOO?

I MEAN, YOU--

WELL, I GUESS THAT ANSWERS THE QUESTION...

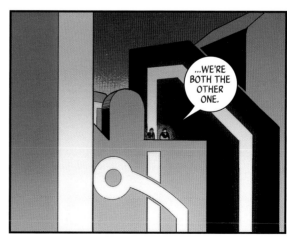

...WE'RE BOTH THE OTHER ONE.

I MISSED YOU

9 MARCH 2015

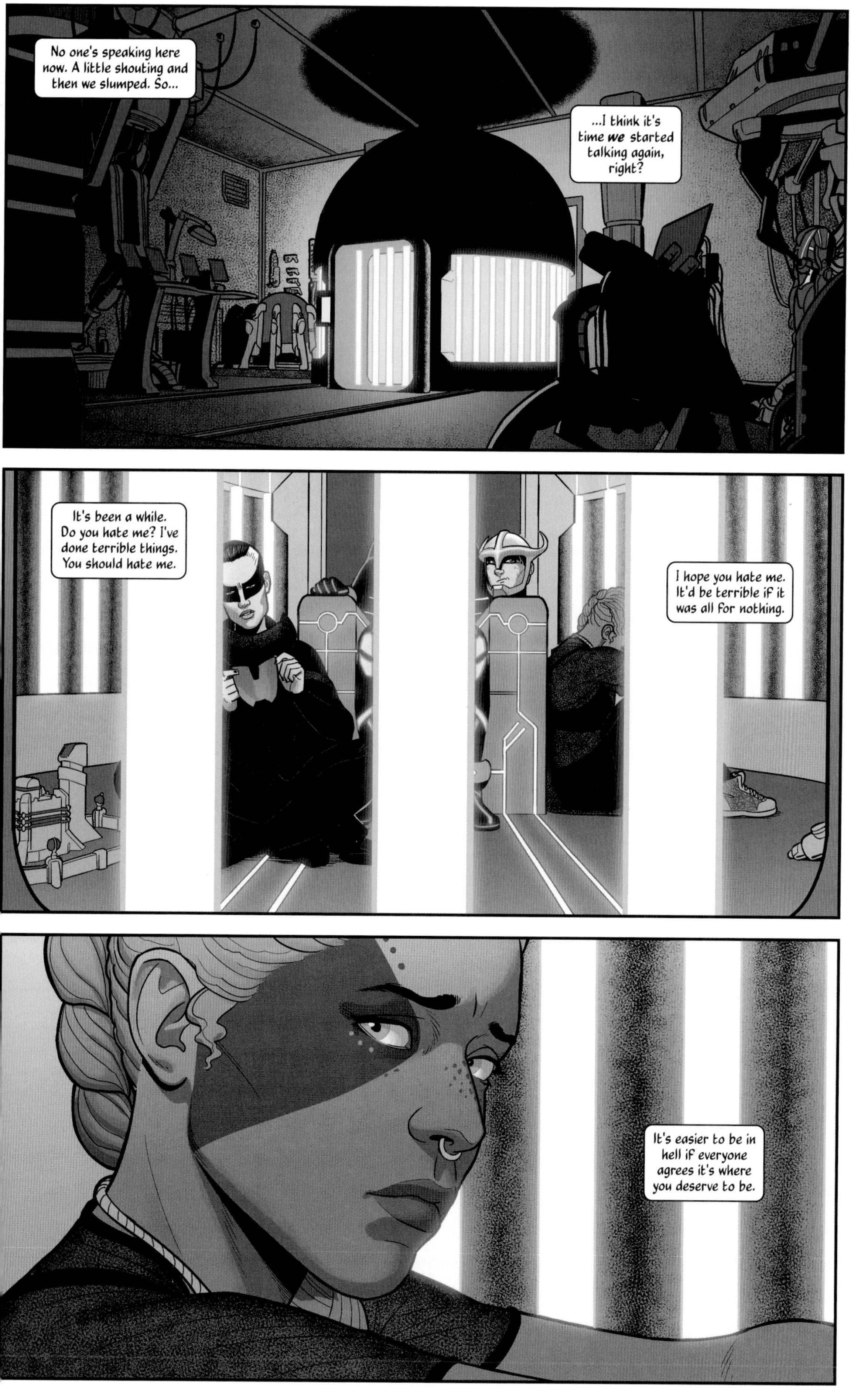
No one's speaking here now. A little shouting and then we slumped. So...
...I think it's time we started talking again, right?
It's been a while. Do you hate me? I've done terrible things. You should hate me.
I hope you hate me. It'd be terrible if it was all for nothing.
It's easier to be in hell if everyone agrees it's where you deserve to be.

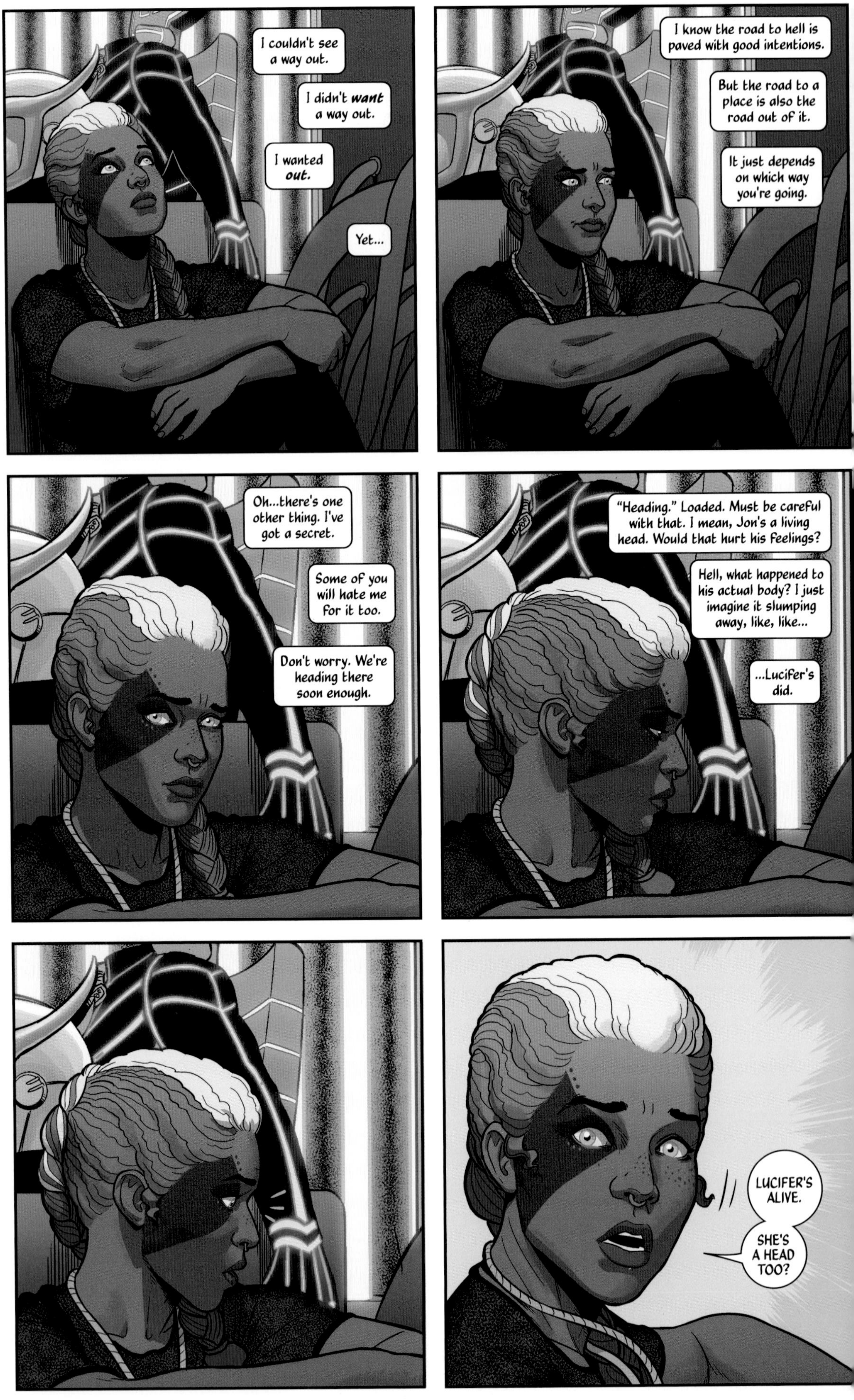
I couldn't see a way out.
I didn't *want* a way out.
I wanted **out.**
Yet...
I know the road to hell is paved with good intentions.
But the road to a place is also the road out of it.
It just depends on which way you're going.
Oh...there's one other thing. I've got a secret.
Some of you will hate me for it too.
Don't worry. We're heading there soon enough.
"Heading." Loaded. Must be careful with that. I mean, Jon's a living head. Would that hurt his feelings?
Hell, what happened to his actual body? I just imagine it slumping away, like, like...
...Lucifer's did.
LUCIFER'S ALIVE.
SHE'S A HEAD TOO?

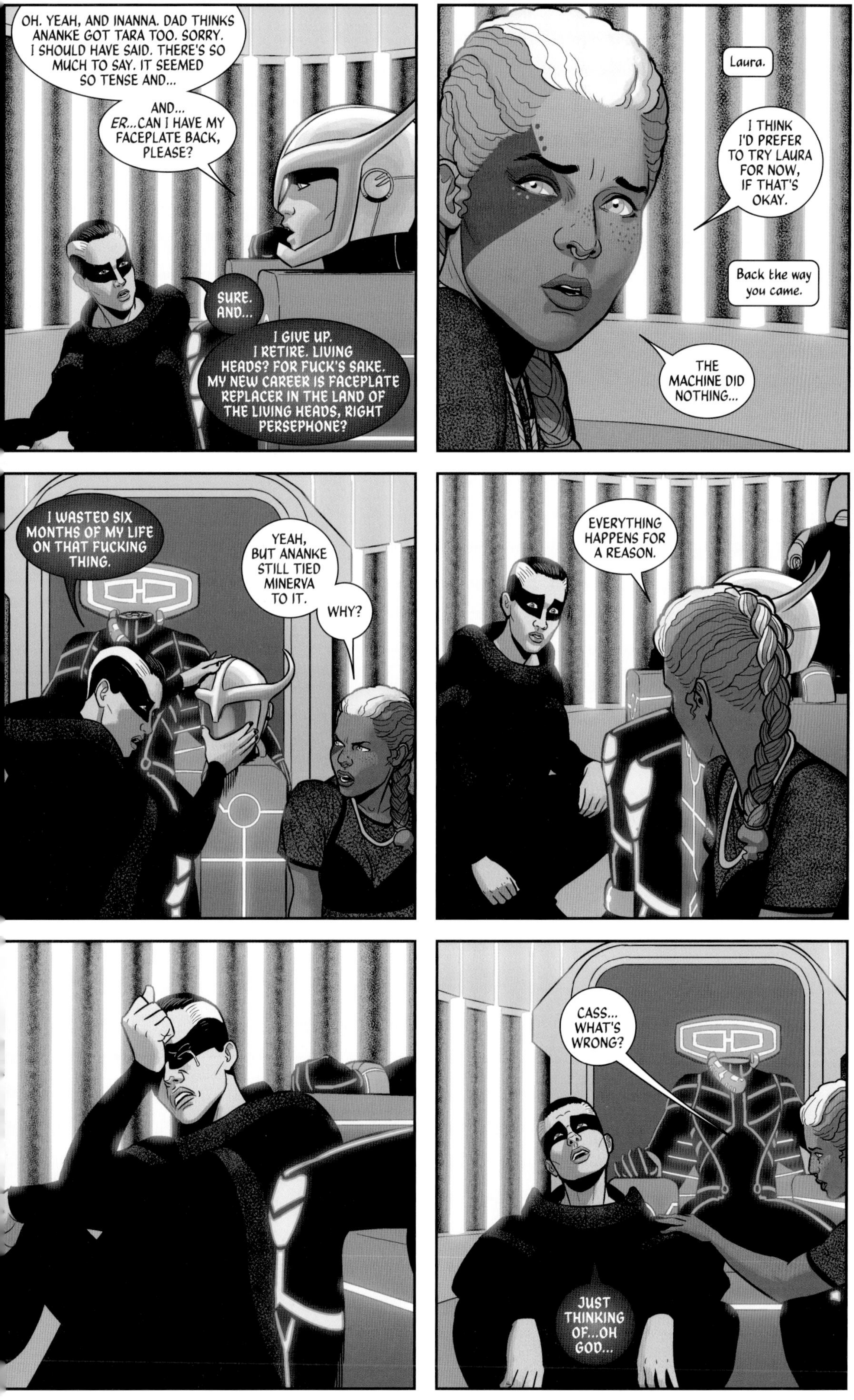
OH. YEAH, AND INANNA. DAD THINKS ANANKE GOT TARA TOO. SORRY. I SHOULD HAVE SAID. THERE'S SO MUCH TO SAY. IT SEEMED SO TENSE AND...
AND... ER...CAN I HAVE MY FACEPLATE BACK, PLEASE?
SURE. AND...
I GIVE UP. I RETIRE. LIVING HEADS? FOR FUCK'S SAKE. MY NEW CAREER IS FACEPLATE REPLACER IN THE LAND OF THE LIVING HEADS, RIGHT PERSEPHONE?
Laura.
I THINK I'D PREFER TO TRY LAURA FOR NOW, IF THAT'S OKAY.
Back the way you came.
THE MACHINE DID NOTHING...
I WASTED SIX MONTHS OF MY LIFE ON THAT FUCKING THING.
YEAH, BUT ANANKE STILL TIED MINERVA TO IT.
WHY?
EVERYTHING HAPPENS FOR A REASON.
CASS... WHAT'S WRONG?
JUST THINKING OF...OH GOD...

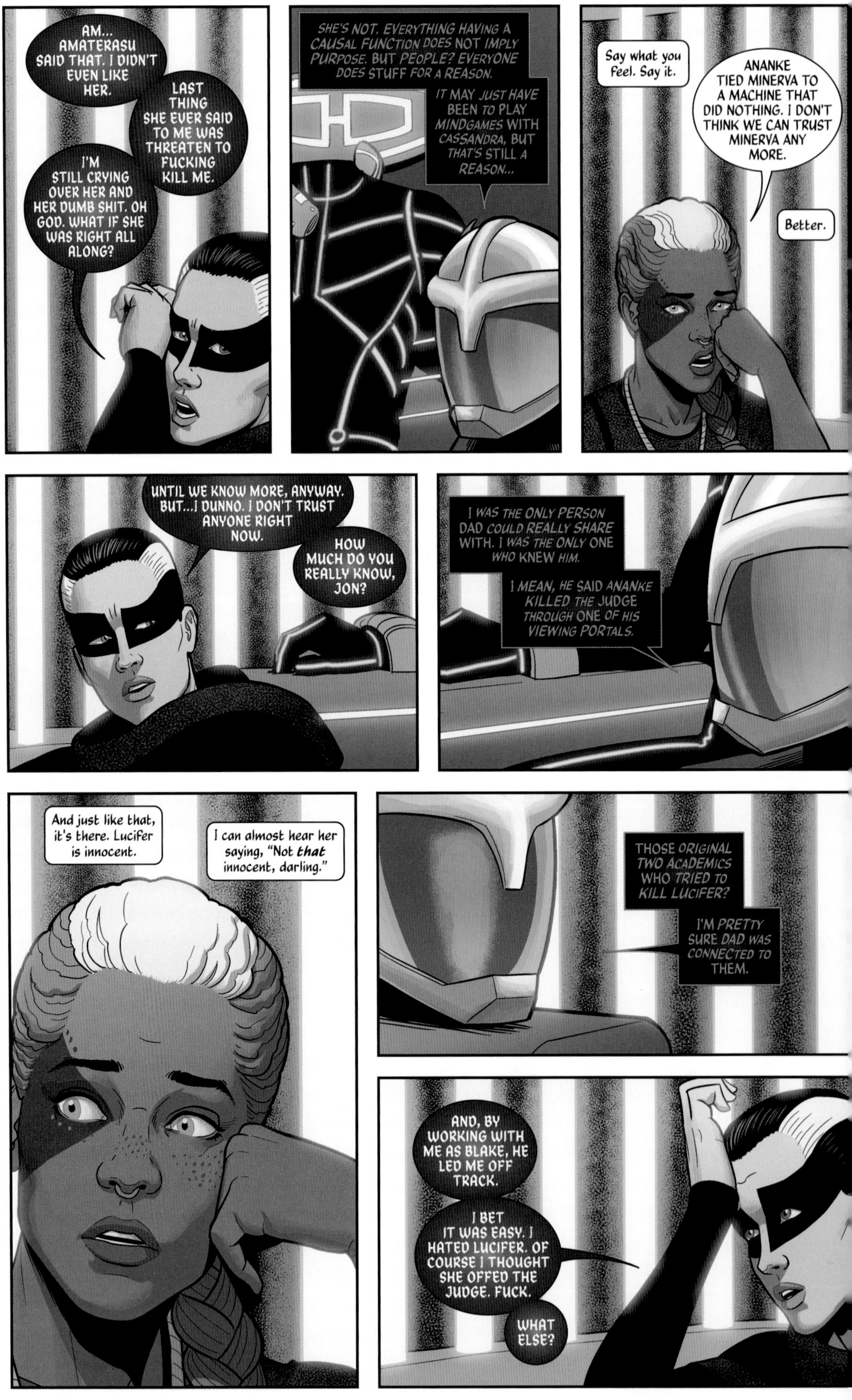

AM... AMATERASU SAID THAT. I DIDN'T EVEN LIKE HER.
LAST THING SHE EVER SAID TO ME WAS THREATEN TO FUCKING KILL ME.
I'M STILL CRYING OVER HER AND HER DUMB SHIT. OH GOD. WHAT IF SHE WAS RIGHT ALL ALONG?
SHE'S NOT. EVERYTHING HAVING A CAUSAL FUNCTION DOES NOT IMPLY PURPOSE. BUT PEOPLE? EVERYONE DOES STUFF FOR A REASON.
IT MAY JUST HAVE BEEN TO PLAY MINDGAMES WITH CASSANDRA, BUT THAT'S STILL A REASON...
Say what you feel. Say it.
ANANKE TIED MINERVA TO A MACHINE THAT DID NOTHING. I DON'T THINK WE CAN TRUST MINERVA ANY MORE.
Better.
UNTIL WE KNOW MORE, ANYWAY. BUT...I DUNNO. I DON'T TRUST ANYONE RIGHT NOW.
HOW MUCH DO YOU REALLY KNOW, JON?
I WAS THE ONLY PERSON DAD COULD REALLY SHARE WITH. I WAS THE ONLY ONE WHO KNEW HIM.
I MEAN, HE SAID ANANKE KILLED THE JUDGE THROUGH ONE OF HIS VIEWING PORTALS.
And just like that, it's there. Lucifer is innocent.
I can almost hear her saying, "Not that innocent, darling."
THOSE ORIGINAL TWO ACADEMICS WHO TRIED TO KILL LUCIFER?
I'M PRETTY SURE DAD WAS CONNECTED TO THEM.
AND, BY WORKING WITH ME AS BLAKE, HE LED ME OFF TRACK.
I BET IT WAS EASY. I HATED LUCIFER. OF COURSE I THOUGHT SHE OFFED THE JUDGE. FUCK.
WHAT ELSE?

ANANKE WANTED *FOUR* HEADS.

I HAVE NO IDEA WHY. NEITHER DID DAD. AT LEAST, HE NEVER TOLD ME.

DAD *WAS NERVOUS* THAT SHE MIGHT TAKE ME TO FINISH THE SET. HE DIDN'T WANT THAT...

I THINK HE DOESN'T REALLY UNDERSTAND. HE THINKS *HE CAN SAVE ME*, EVEN NOW.

HE'D HAVE THE MIDLIFE CRISIS TO END ALL MIDLIFE CRISES FOR A COUPLE OF YEARS AND THEN...TRY AND COME OUT THE OTHER SIDE? HE'S DOING BAD STUFF, BUT HE'S NOT BAD...

I think that's what bad people are.

People doing bad stuff, right now.

I THINK YOU'RE MORE GROWN UP THAN YOUR DAD.

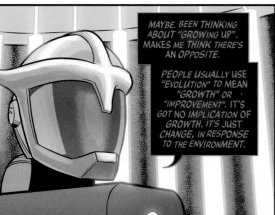

MAYBE. BEEN THINKING ABOUT "GROWING UP". MAKES ME THINK THERE'S AN OPPOSITE.

PEOPLE USUALLY USE "EVOLUTION" TO MEAN "GROWTH" OR "IMPROVEMENT". IT'S GOT NO IMPLICATION OF GROWTH. IT'S JUST CHANGE, IN RESPONSE TO THE ENVIRONMENT.

TO THINK *OTHERWISE* IS BASED ON THE CHAIN OF *BEING* IDEA WITH US AT THE TOP AND EVERYTHING ELSE BENEATH US.

CHANGE *IS* JUST CHANGE. IT'S NEITHER GOOD NOR BAD. IT SIMPLY IS.

ER...IT'S BEEN A WHILE SINCE I'VE REALLY TALKED TO ANYONE.

DON'T WORRY. I'M STILL TRYING TO WORK OUT HOW YOU EVEN *CAN* TALK.

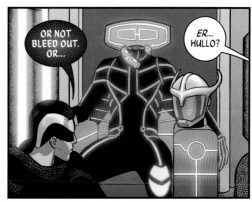

OR NOT BLEED OUT. OR...

ER... HULLO?

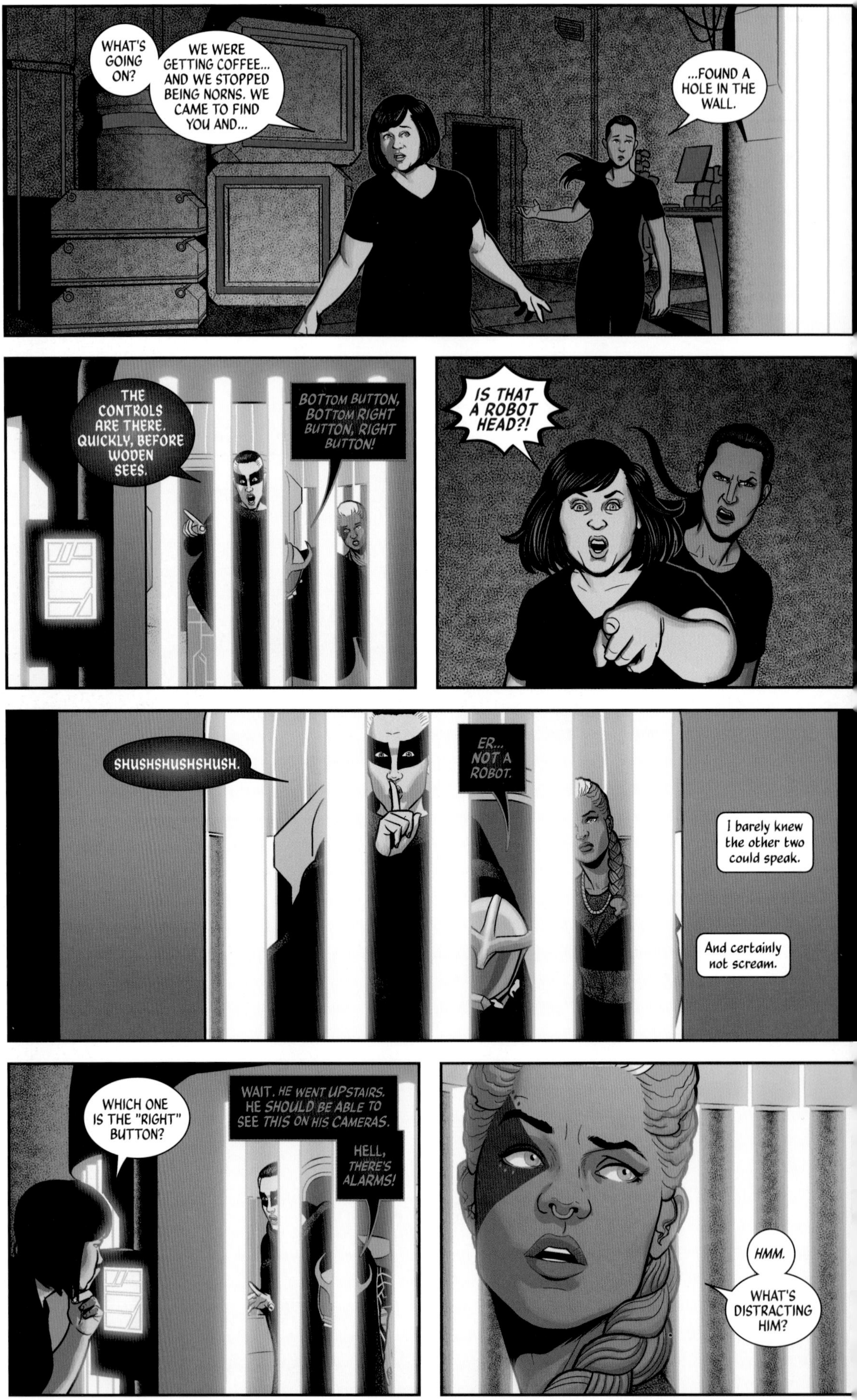
WHAT'S GOING ON?
WE WERE GETTING COFFEE... AND WE STOPPED BEING NORNS. WE CAME TO FIND YOU AND...
...FOUND A HOLE IN THE WALL.
THE CONTROLS ARE THERE. QUICKLY, BEFORE WODEN SEES.
BOTTOM BUTTON, BOTTOM RIGHT BUTTON, RIGHT BUTTON!
IS THAT A ROBOT HEAD?!
SHUSHSHUSHSHUSH.
ER... NOT A ROBOT.
I barely knew the other two could speak.
And certainly not scream.
WHICH ONE IS THE "RIGHT" BUTTON?
WAIT. HE WENT UPSTAIRS. HE SHOULD BE ABLE TO SEE THIS ON HIS CAMERAS.
HELL, THERE'S ALARMS!
HMM.
WHAT'S DISTRACTING HIM?

10 MINUTES EARLIER.

OKAY. LET'S SEE WHAT WE'VE GOT...

ACCESS OWLY'S UPLOAD. 22:05 TO 22:10 HOURS, YESTERDAY. LOCALISE PEAKS OF DATA.

GREAT. SO...

MINERVA'S GOGGLES UPLOAD. SAME TIME.

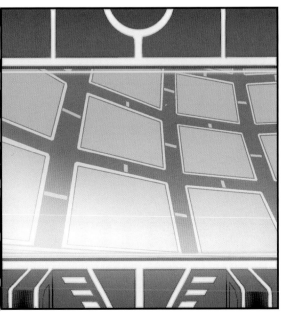

SHE LEFT THEM ON HER FUCKING DESK. THANKS, MINERVA.

RIGHT... HOW ABOUT...

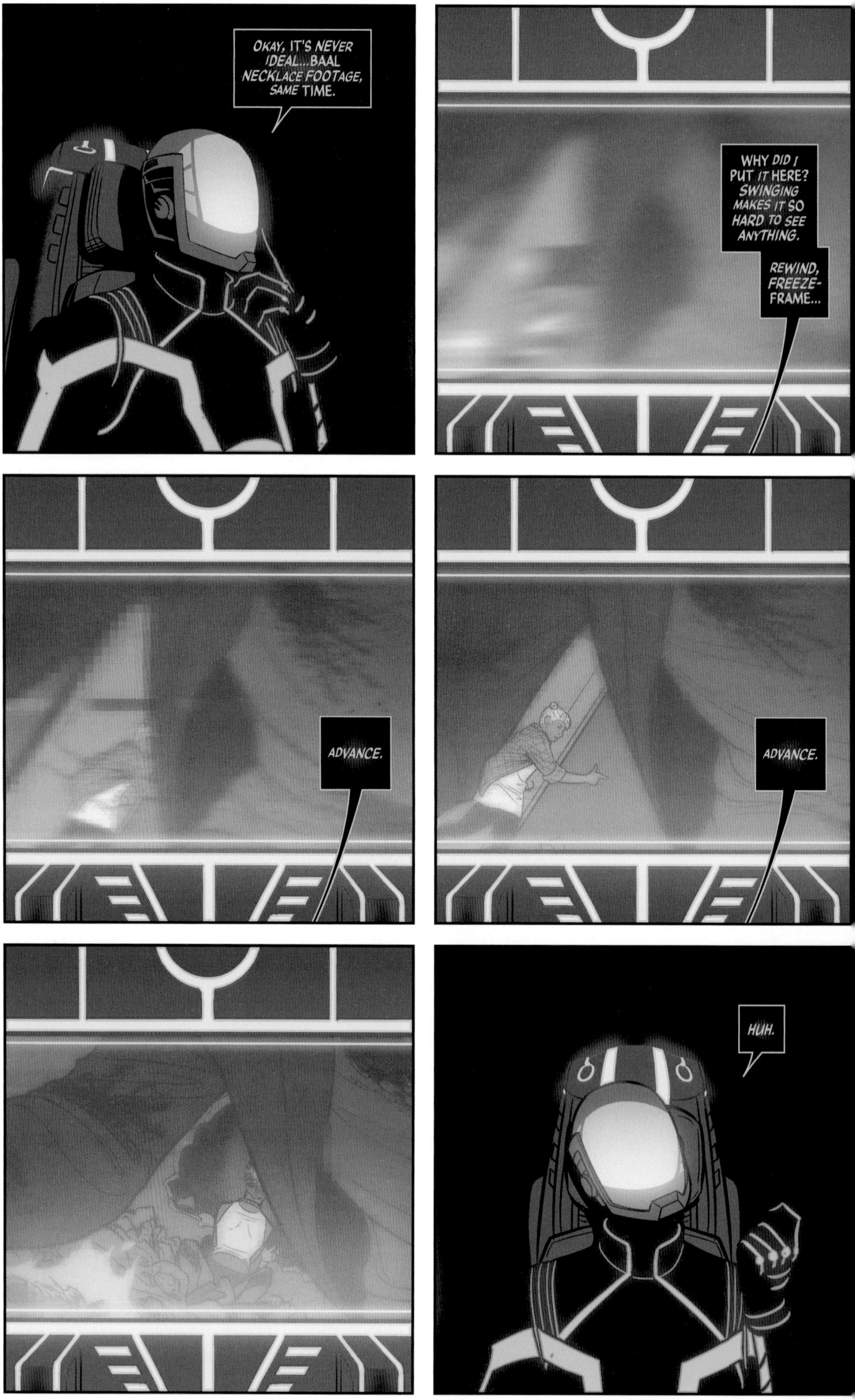
OKAY, IT'S NEVER IDEAL...BAAL NECKLACE FOOTAGE, SAME TIME.
WHY DID I PUT IT HERE? SWINGING MAKES IT SO HARD TO SEE ANYTHING.
REWIND, FREEZE-FRAME...
ADVANCE.
ADVANCE.
HUH.

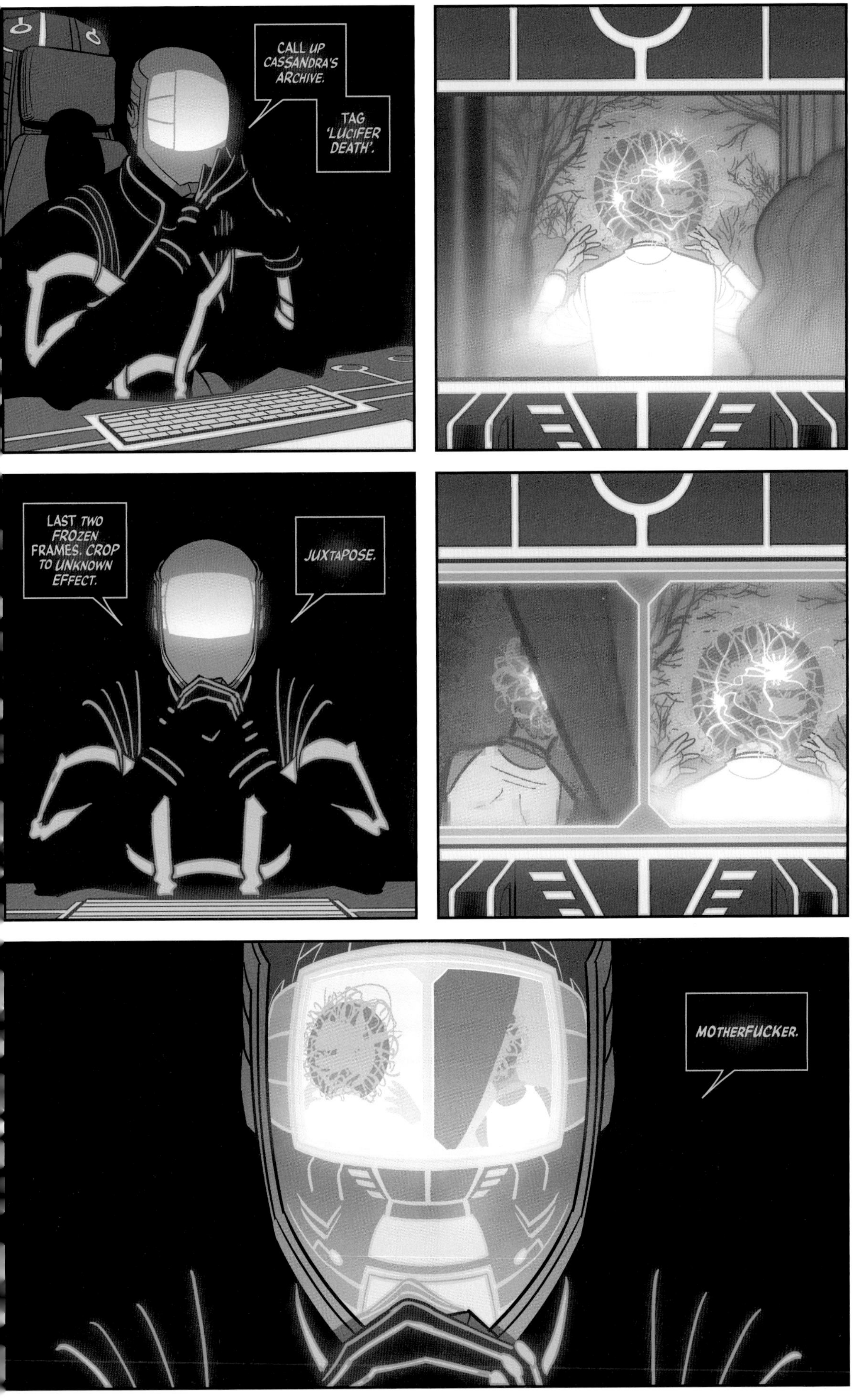
CALL UP CASSANDRA'S ARCHIVE.
TAG 'LUCIFER DEATH'.
LAST TWO FROZEN FRAMES. CROP TO UNKNOWN EFFECT.
JUXTAPOSE.
MOTHERFUCKER.

THE GRACE
OF LOVING
MACHINES

9 MARCH 2015

THE
WICKED
+
THE DIVINE

35

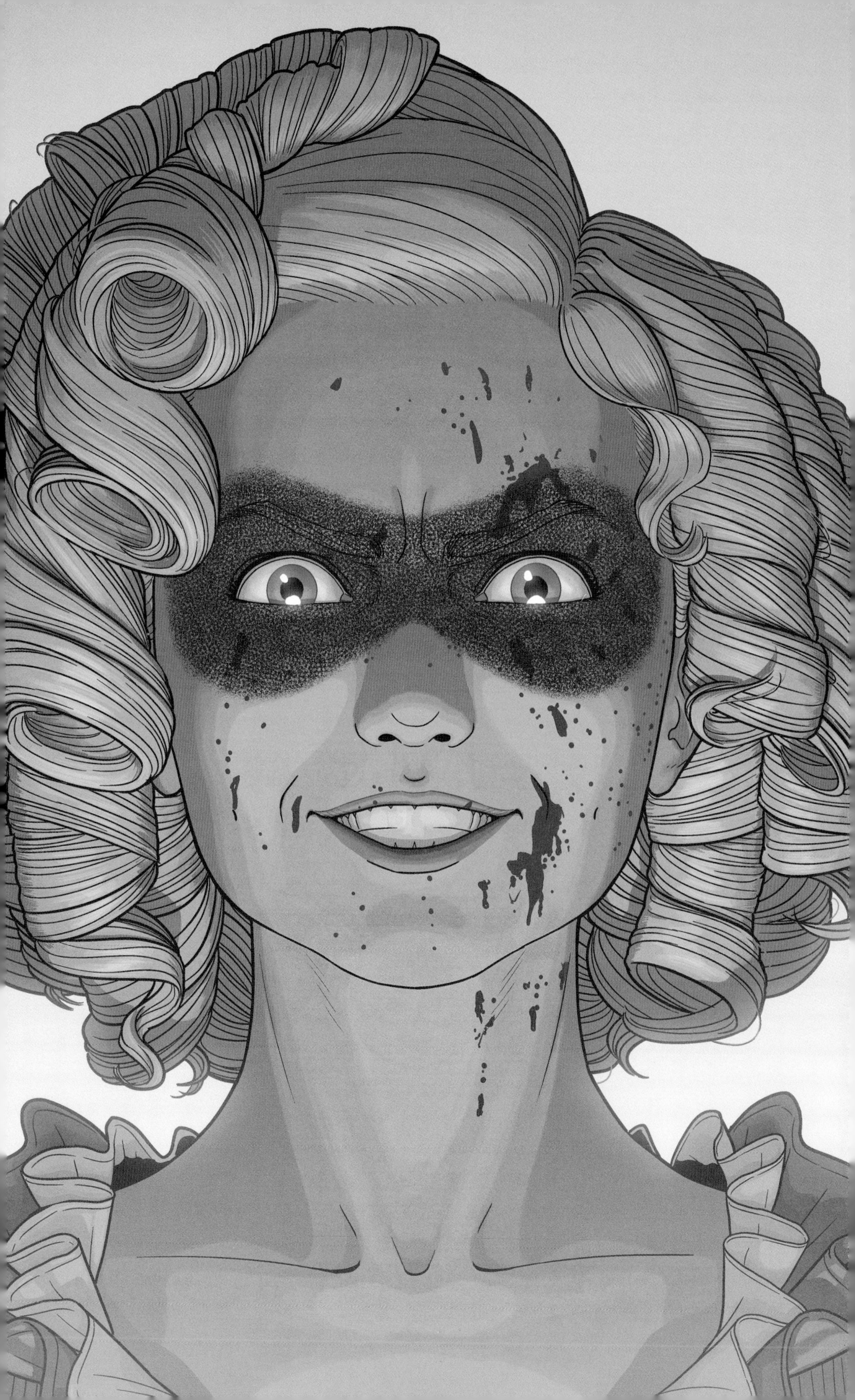

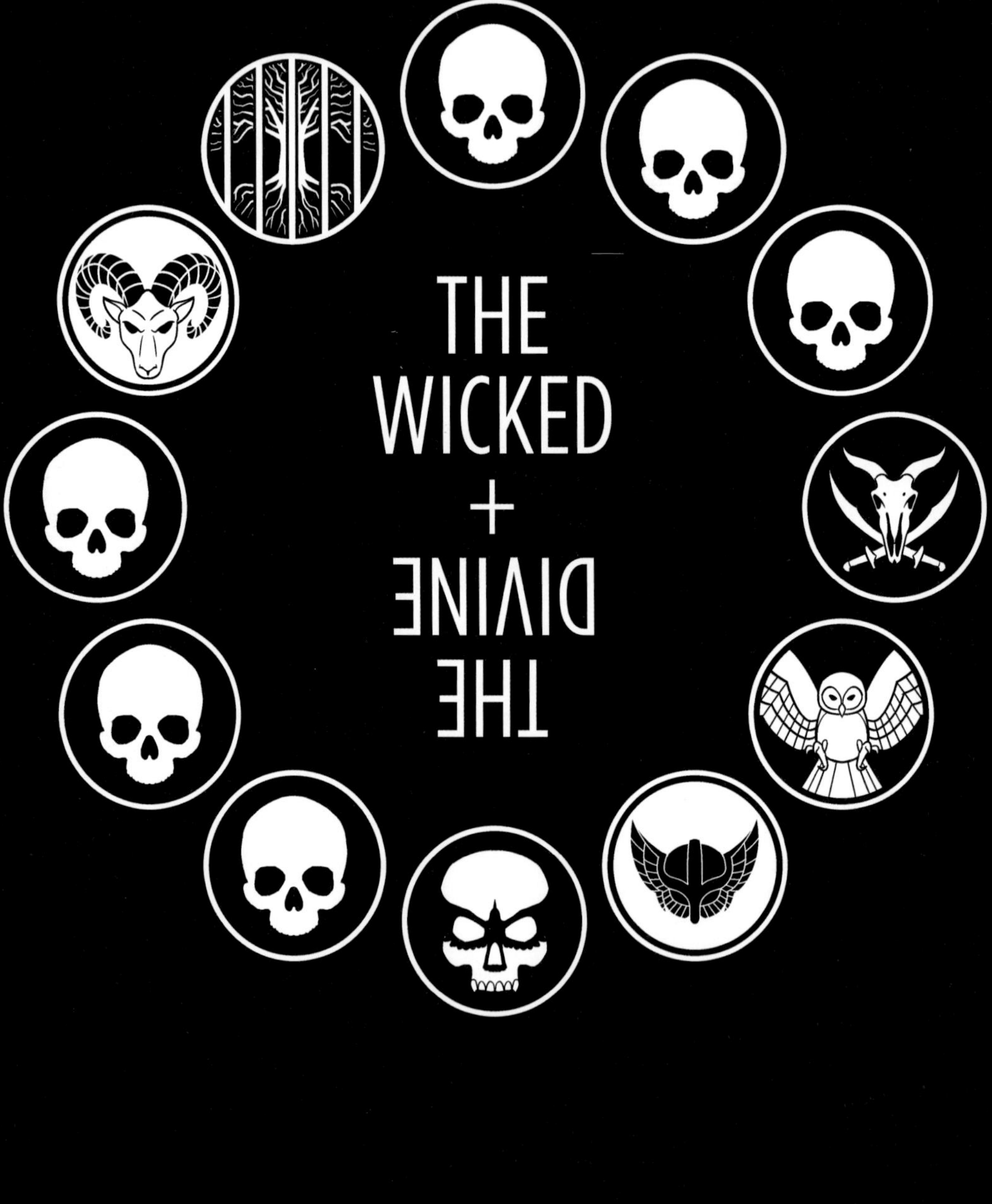
THE
WICKED
+
THE
DIVINE

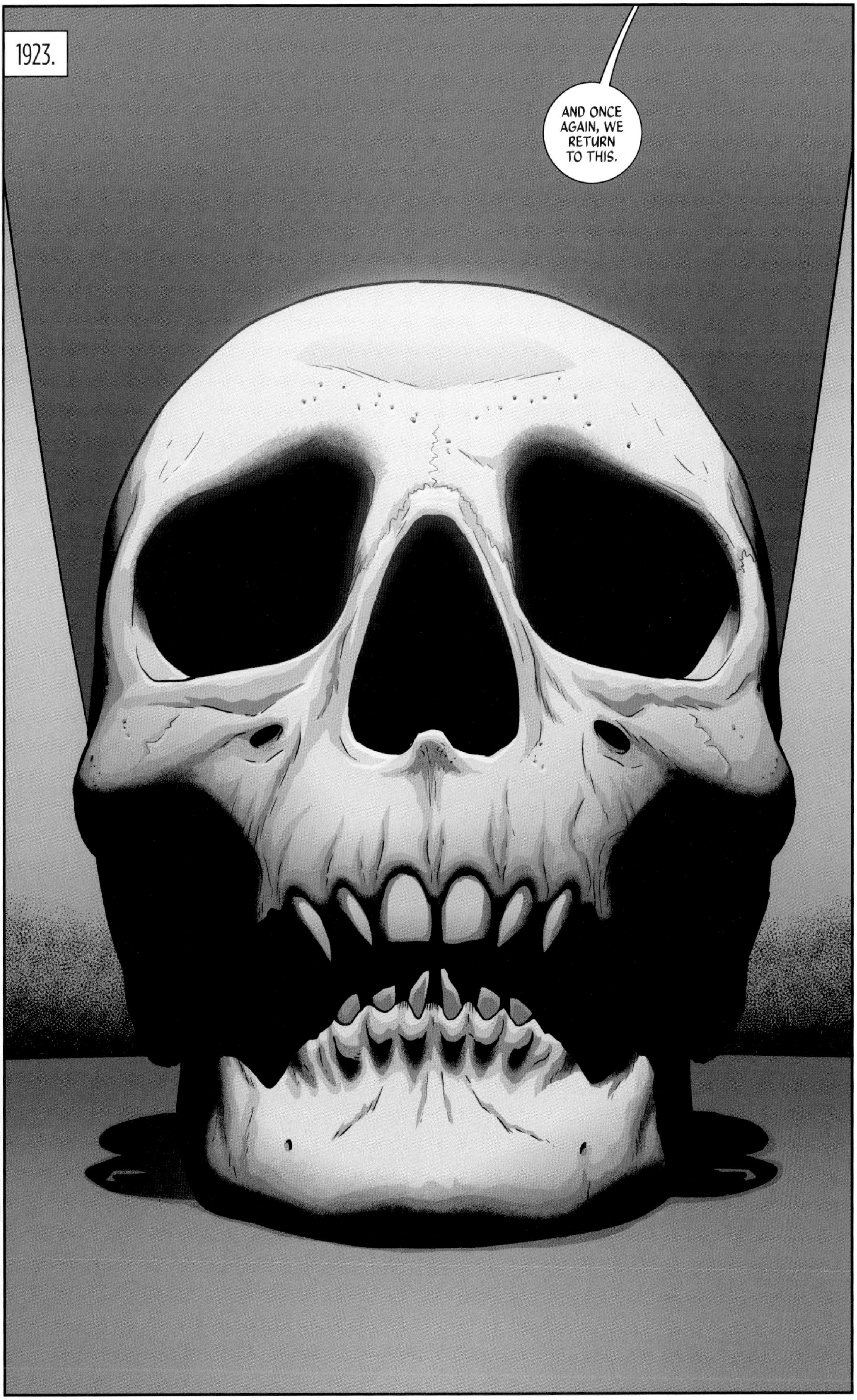
1923.
AND ONCE AGAIN, WE RETURN TO THIS.

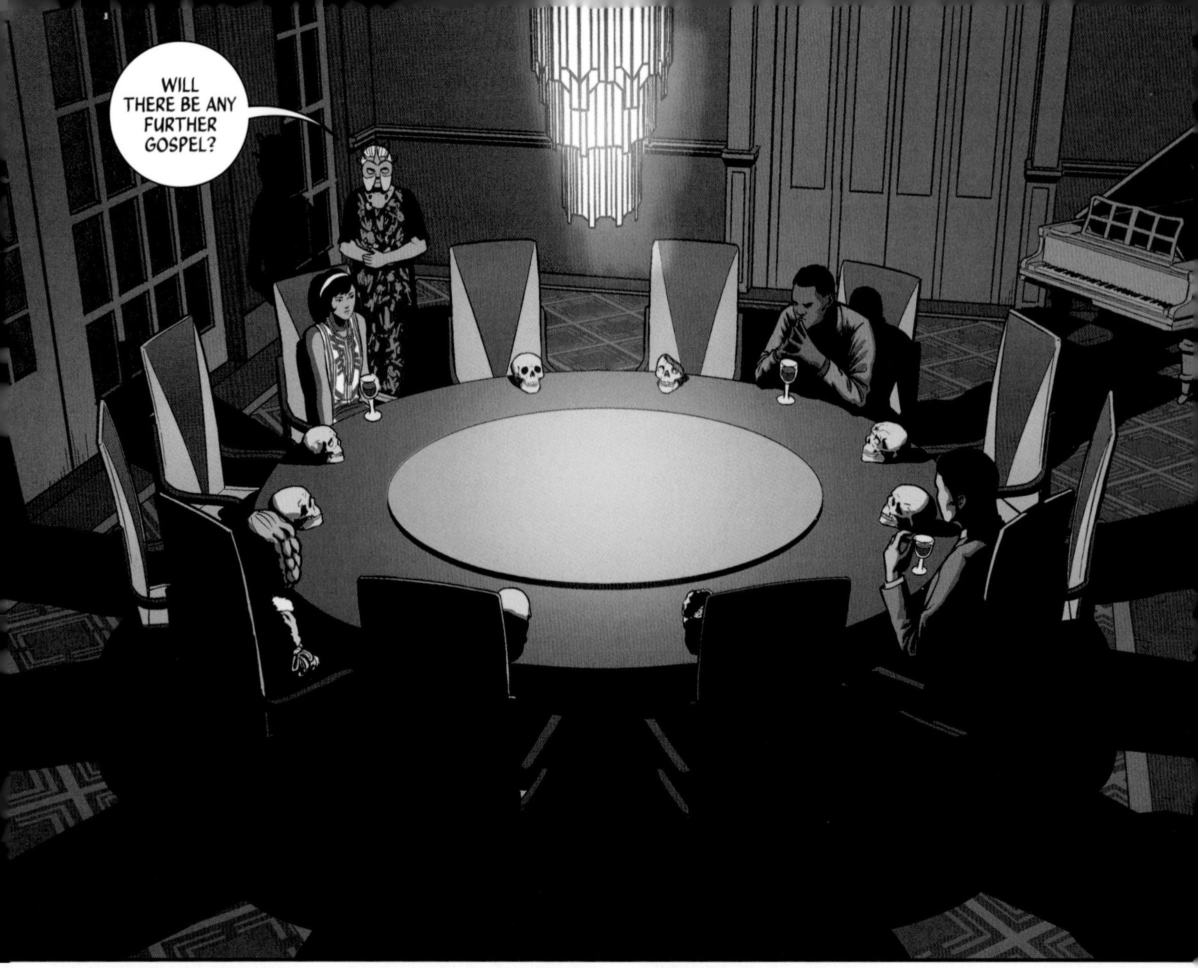
WILL THERE BE ANY FURTHER GOSPEL?

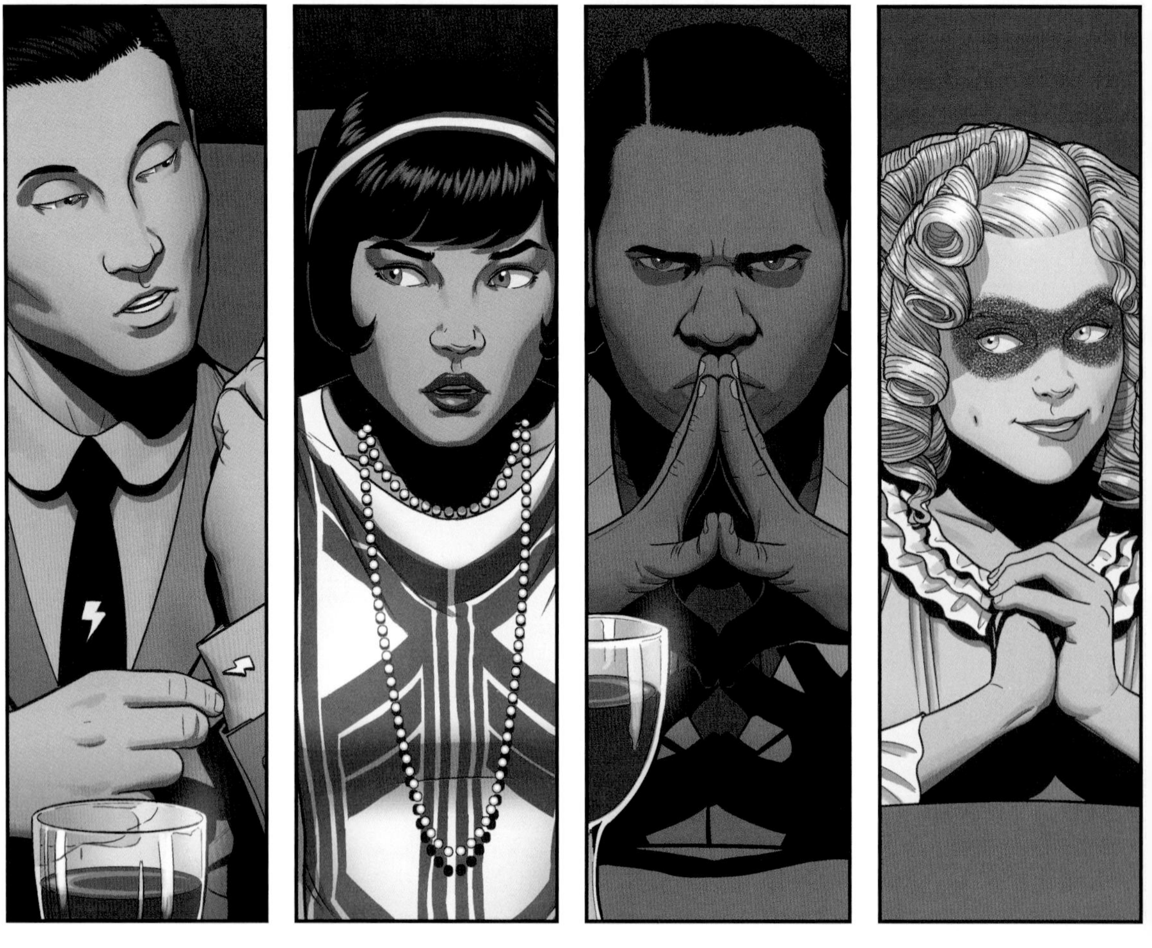

THEN I'LL GO.

ONCE AGAIN, IT'S BEEN A PLEASURE.

I LOVE YOU.

I LOVE YOU ALL.

I'LL MISS YOU.

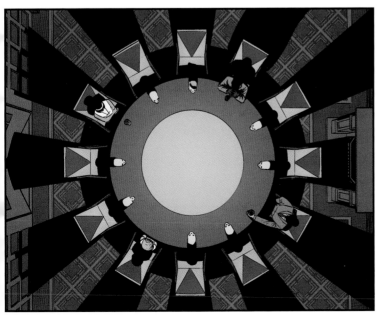

SO...

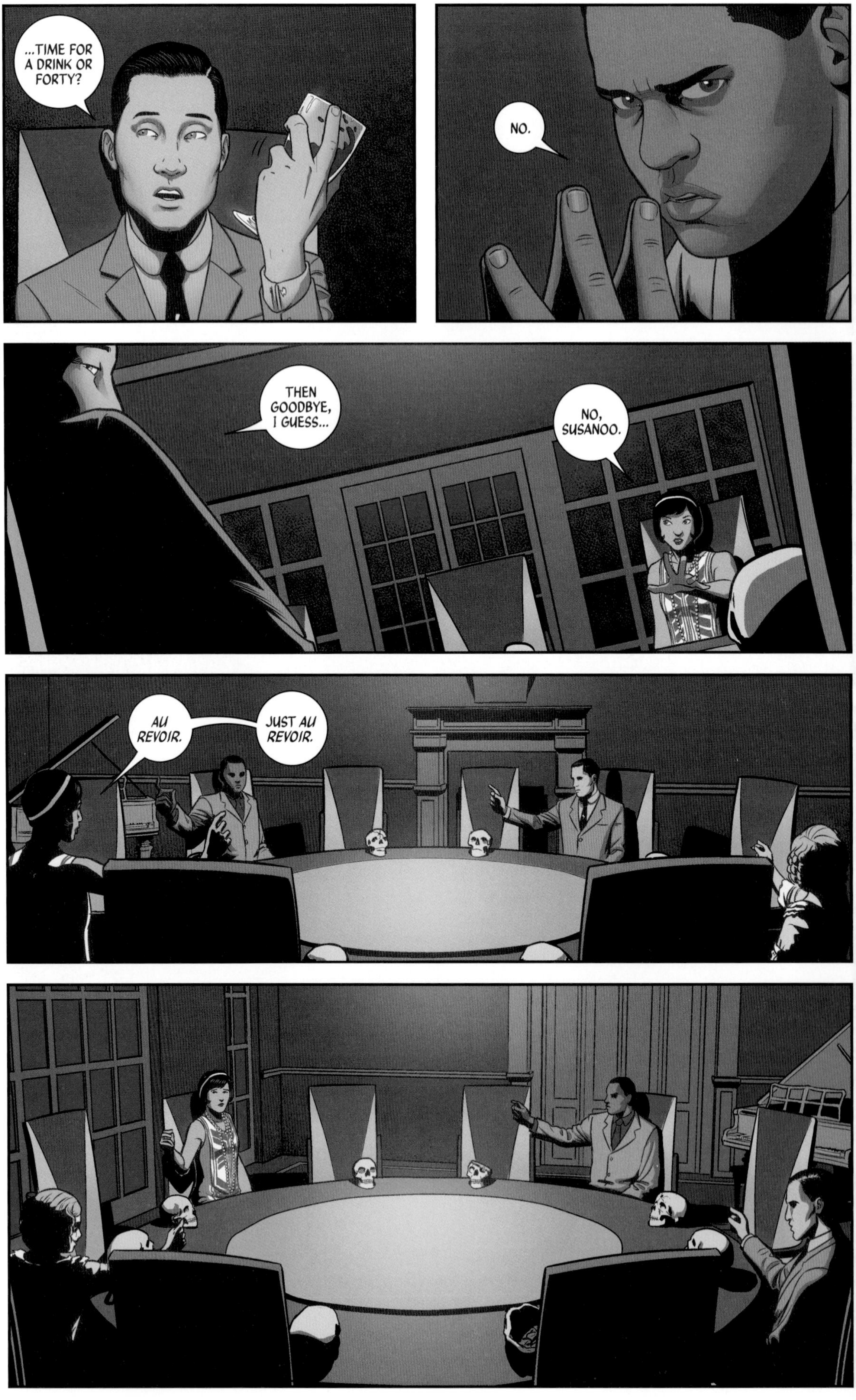
...TIME FOR A DRINK OR FORTY?
NO.
THEN GOODBYE, I GUESS...
NO, SUSANOO.
AU REVOIR.
JUST AU REVOIR.

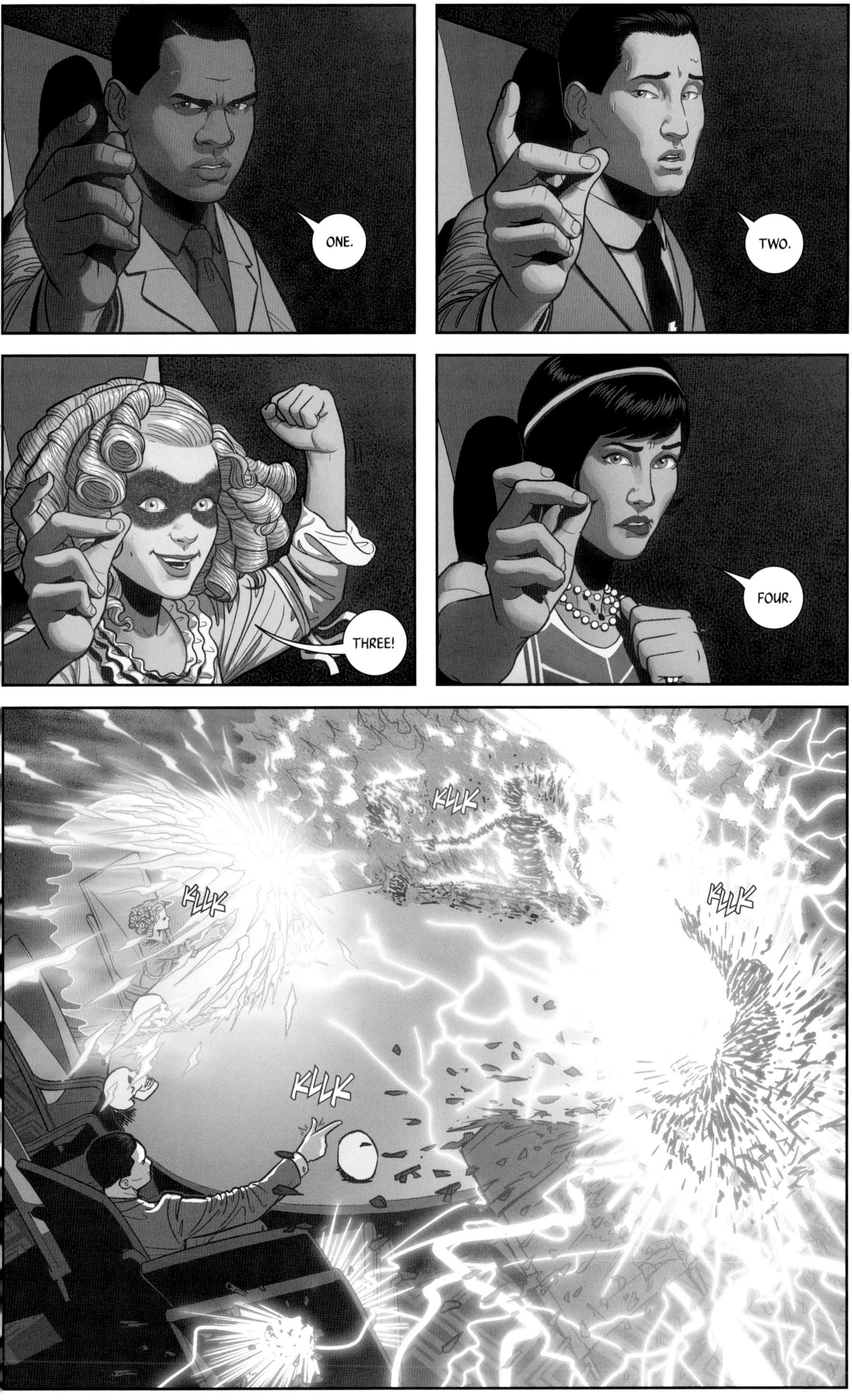
ONE.
TWO.
THREE!
FOUR.
KLLK
KLLK
KLLK
KLLK

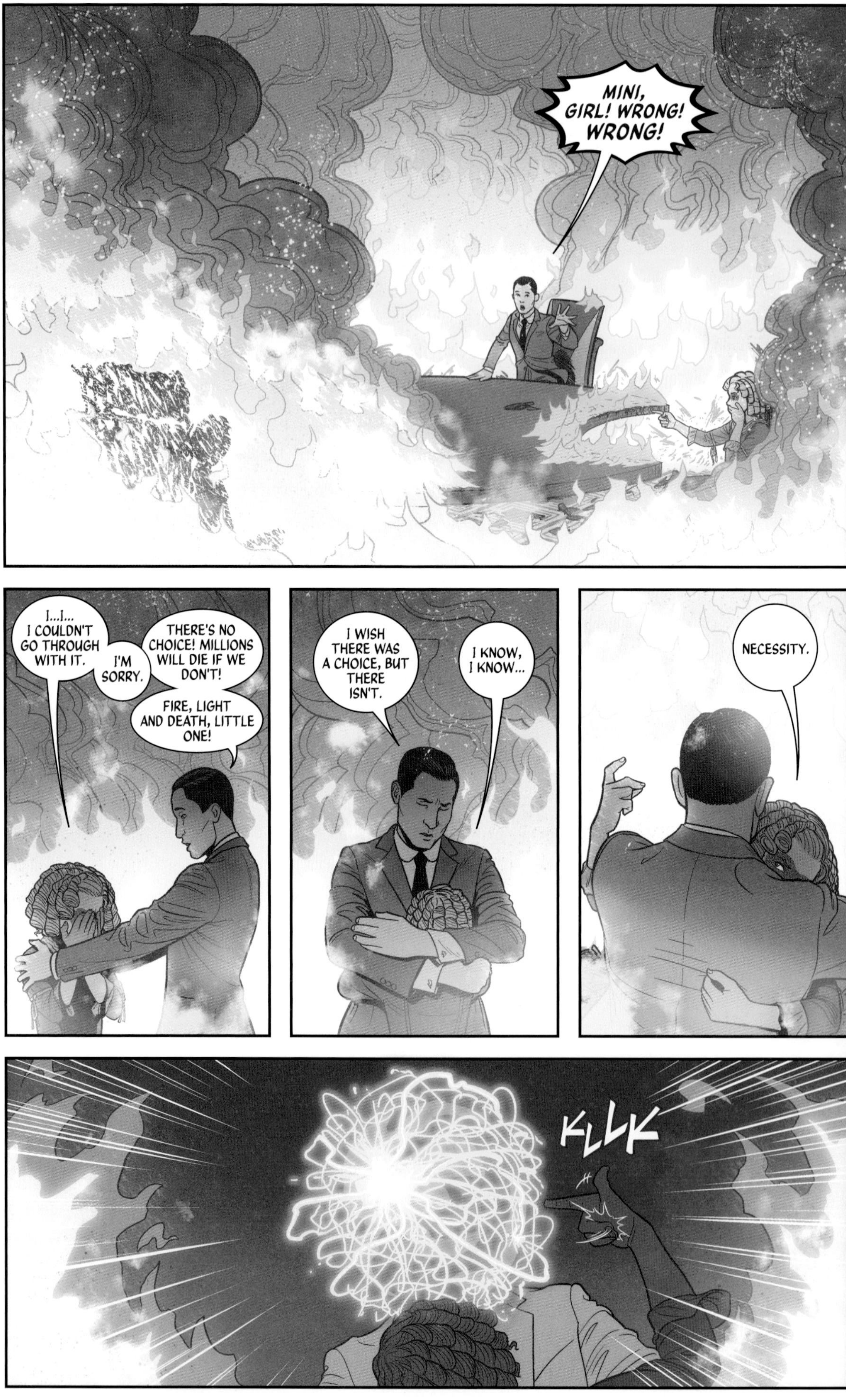
MINI, GIRL! WRONG! WRONG!
I...I... I COULDN'T GO THROUGH WITH IT.
I'M SORRY.
THERE'S NO CHOICE! MILLIONS WILL DIE IF WE DON'T!
FIRE, LIGHT AND DEATH, LITTLE ONE!
I WISH THERE WAS A CHOICE, BUT THERE ISN'T.
I KNOW, I KNOW...
NECESSITY.
KLLK

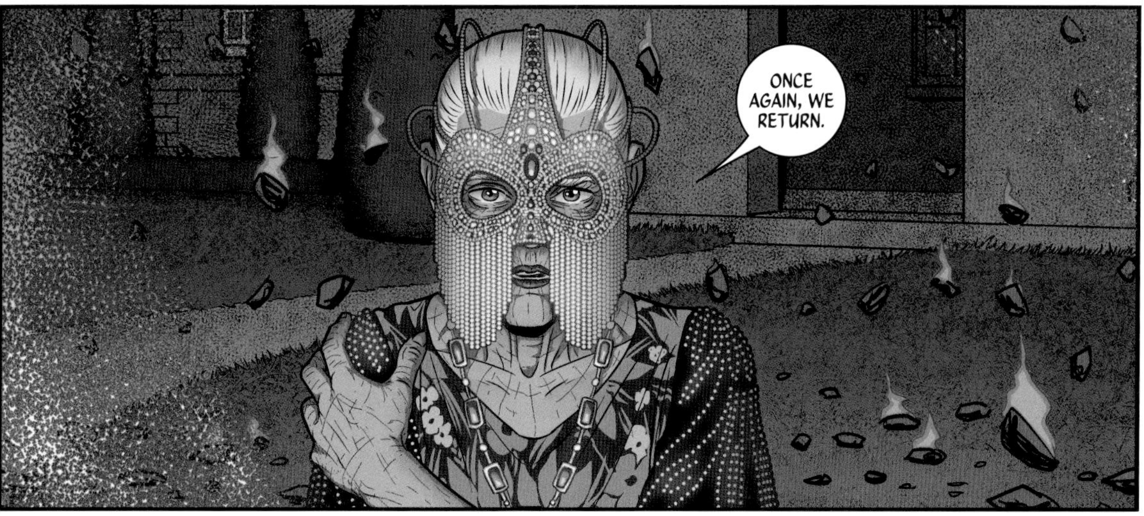
ONCE AGAIN, WE RETURN.

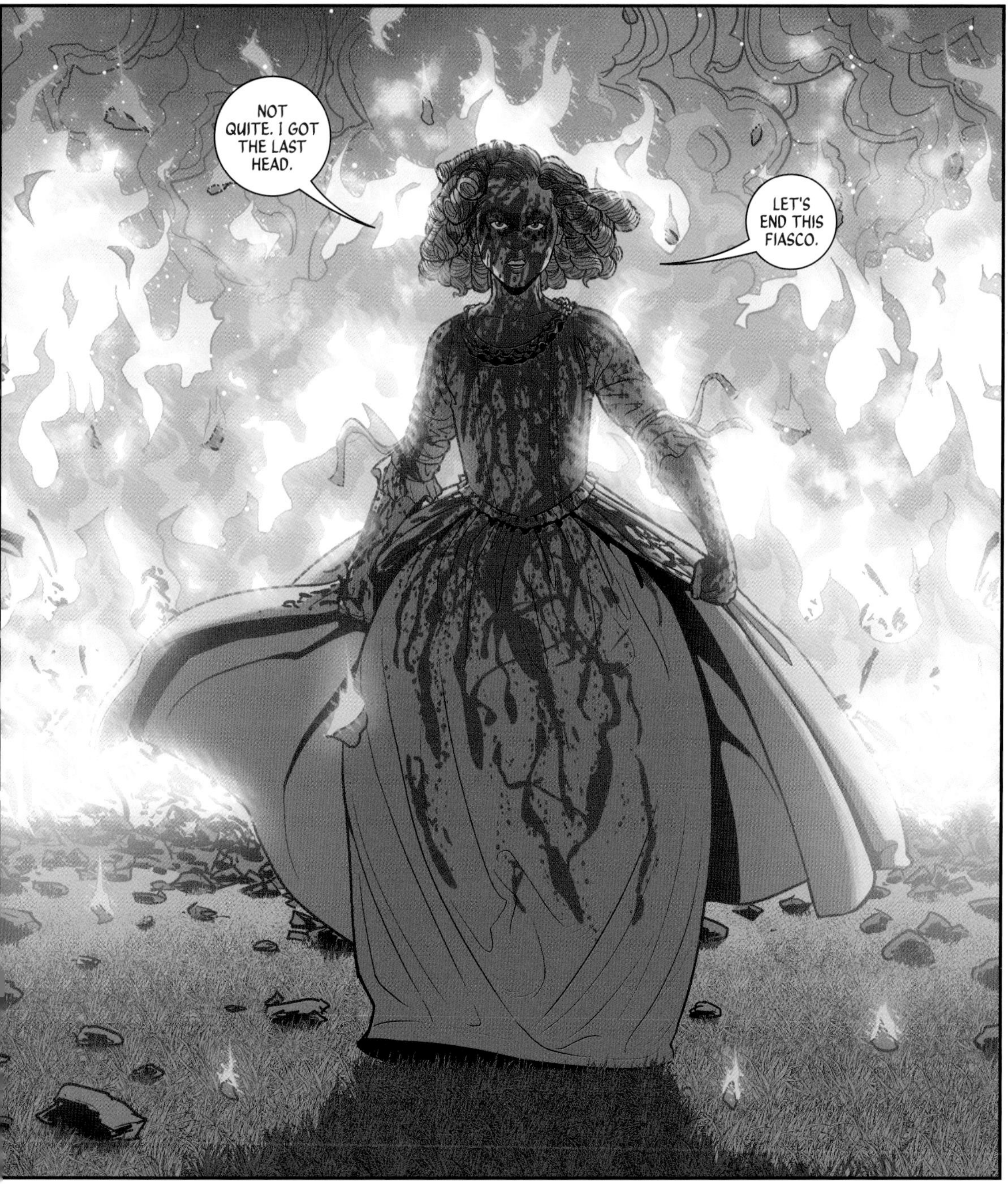
NOT QUITE. I GOT THE LAST HEAD.
LET'S END THIS FIASCO.

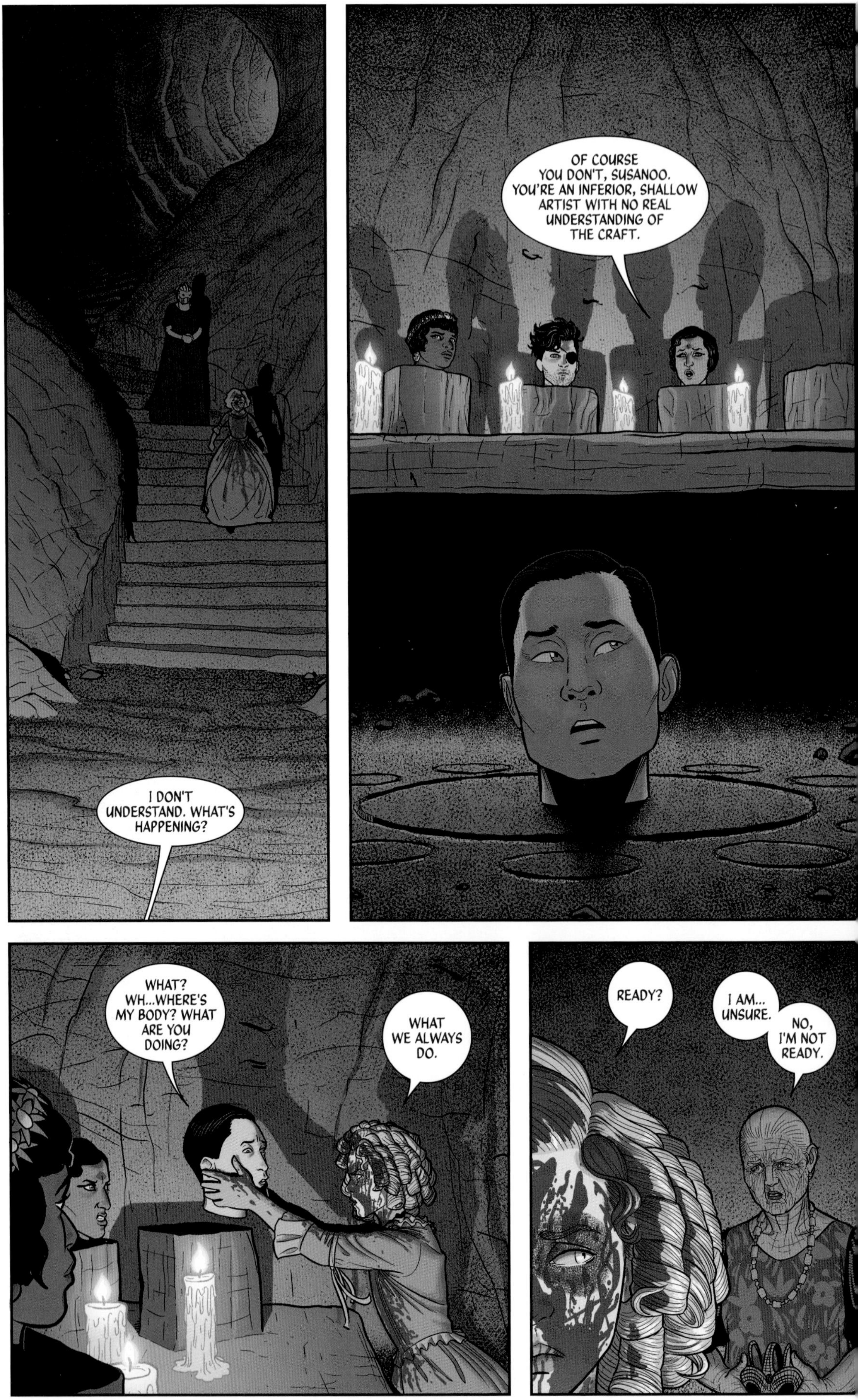
I DON'T UNDERSTAND. WHAT'S HAPPENING?
OF COURSE YOU DON'T, SUSANOO. YOU'RE AN INFERIOR, SHALLOW ARTIST WITH NO REAL UNDERSTANDING OF THE CRAFT.
WHAT? WH...WHERE'S MY BODY? WHAT ARE YOU DOING?
WHAT WE ALWAYS DO.
READY?
I AM... UNSURE.
NO, I'M NOT READY.

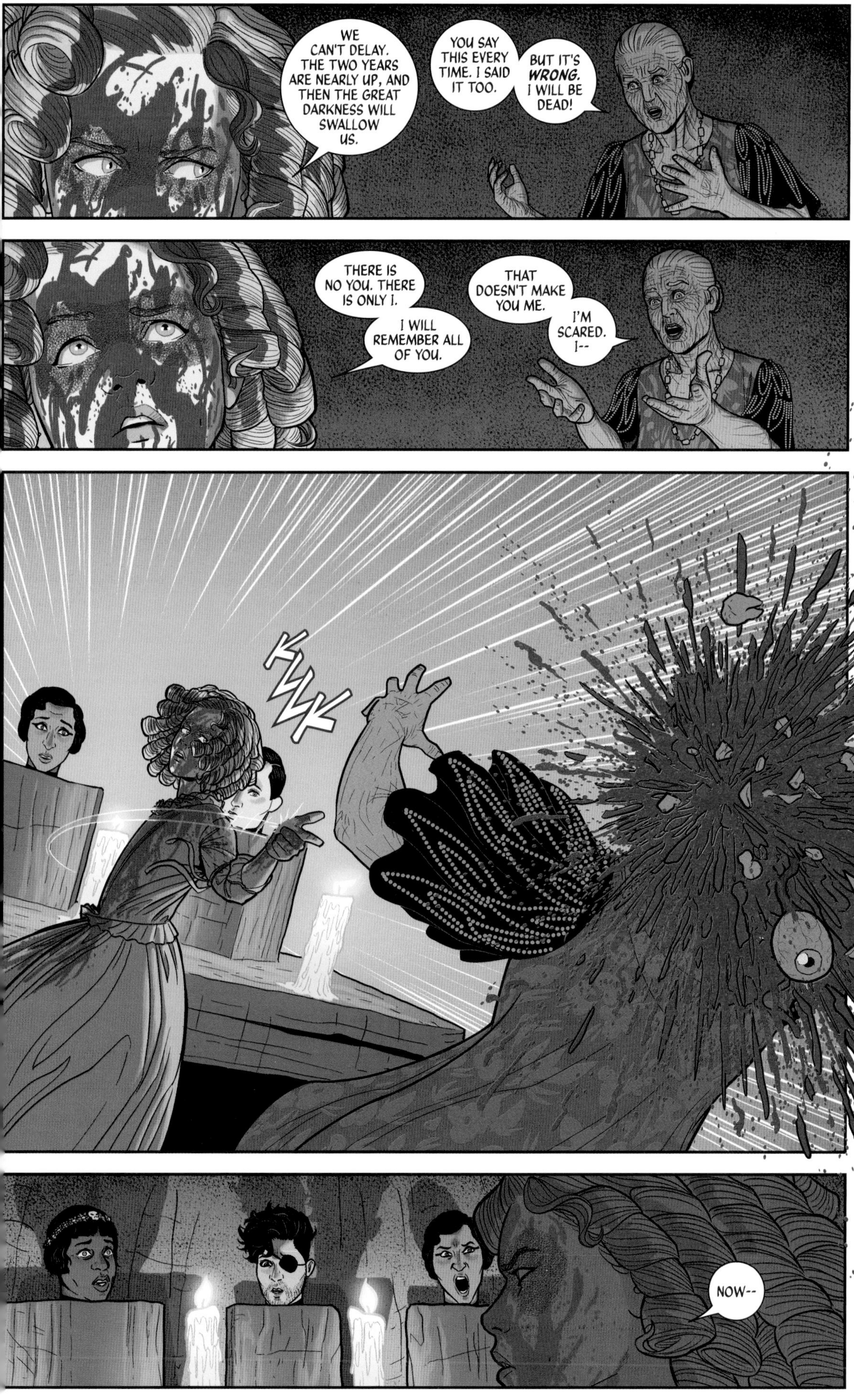
WE CAN'T DELAY. THE TWO YEARS ARE NEARLY UP, AND THEN THE GREAT DARKNESS WILL SWALLOW US.
YOU SAY THIS EVERY TIME. I SAID IT TOO.
BUT IT'S **WRONG.** I WILL BE DEAD!
THERE IS NO YOU. THERE IS ONLY I.
I WILL REMEMBER ALL OF YOU.
THAT DOESN'T MAKE YOU ME.
I'M SCARED. I--
KLLK
NOW--

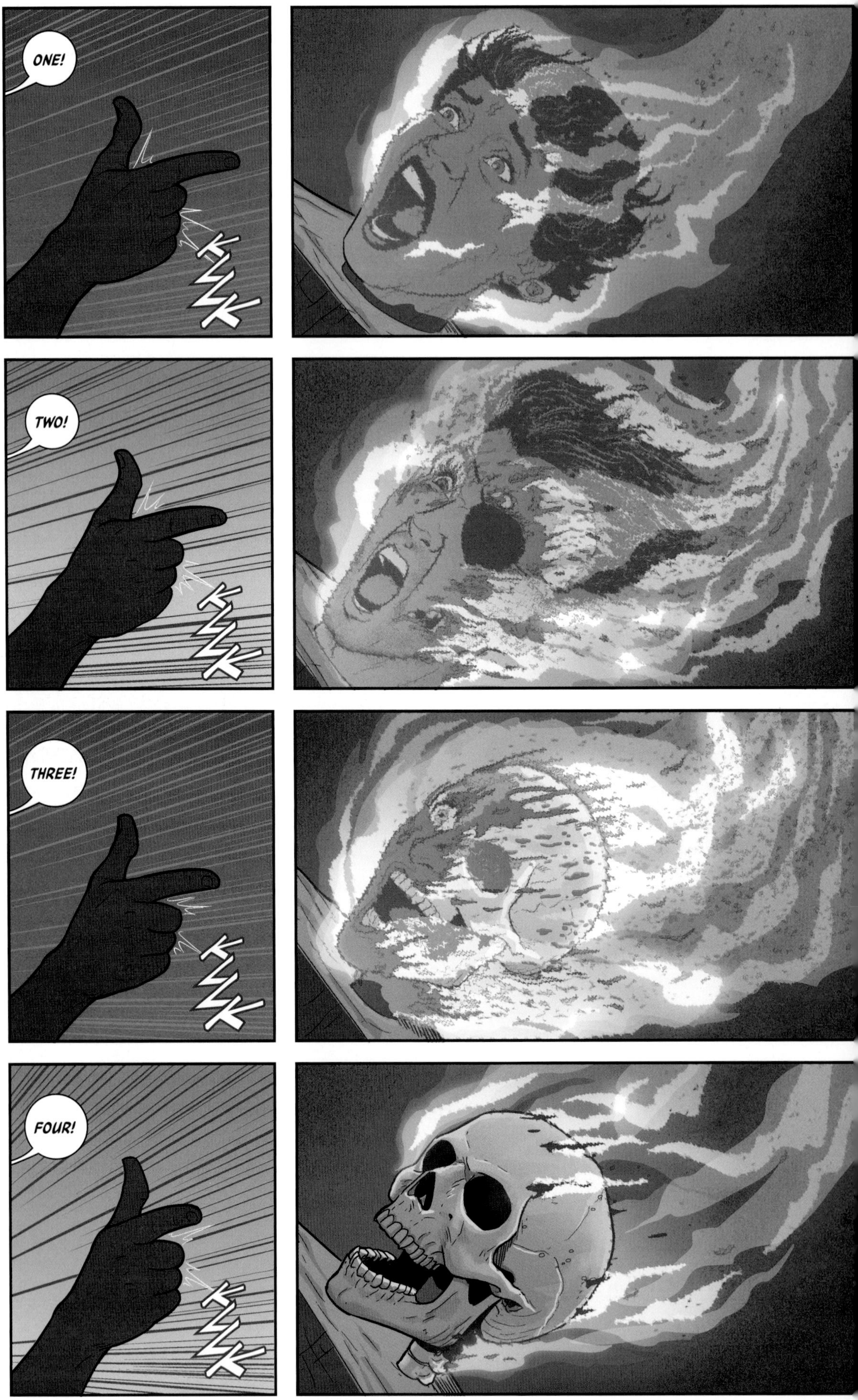
ONE!
KLIK
TWO!
KLIK
THREE!
KLIK
FOUR!
KLIK

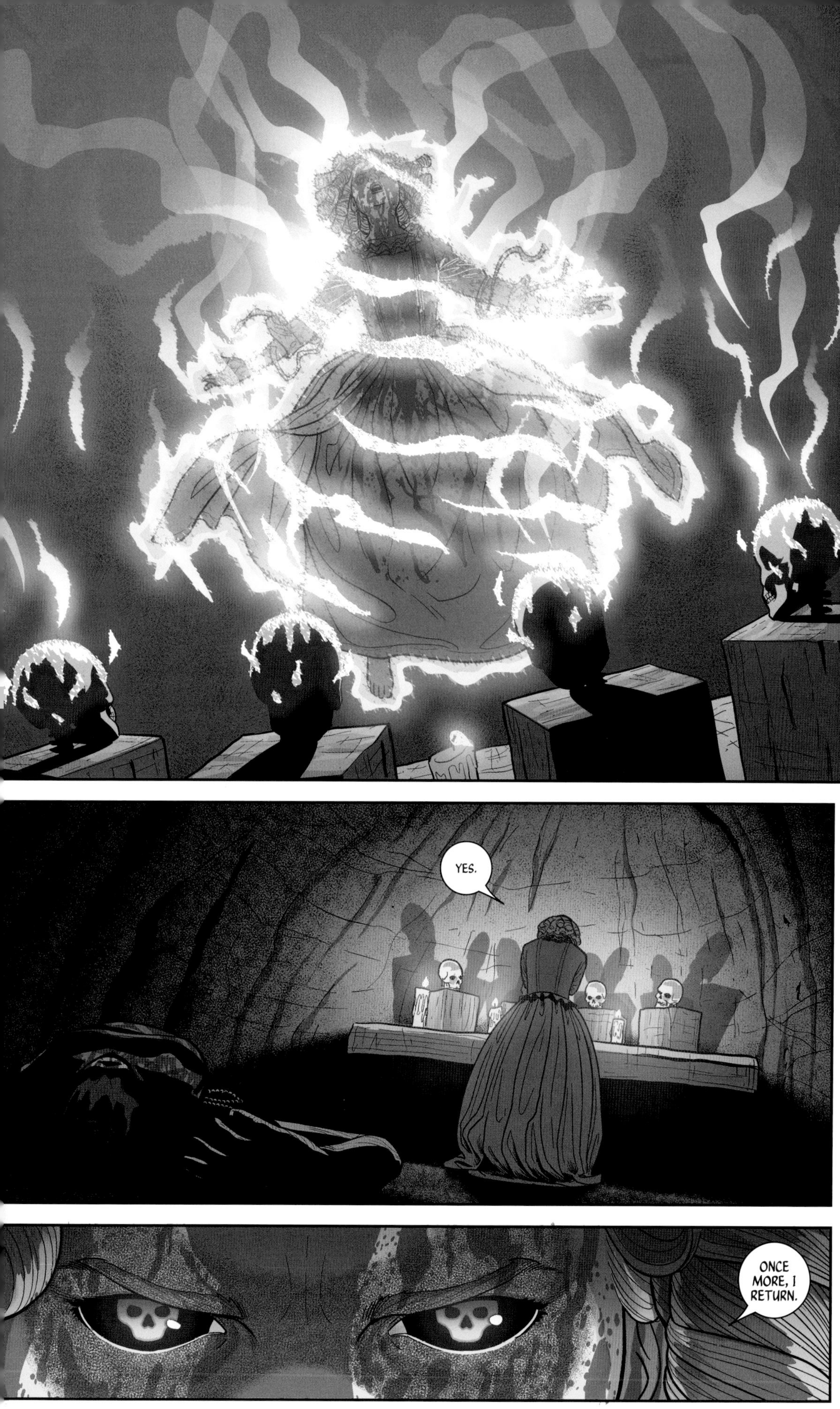
YES.
ONCE MORE, I RETURN.

1-2-3-4!

9 MARCH 2015

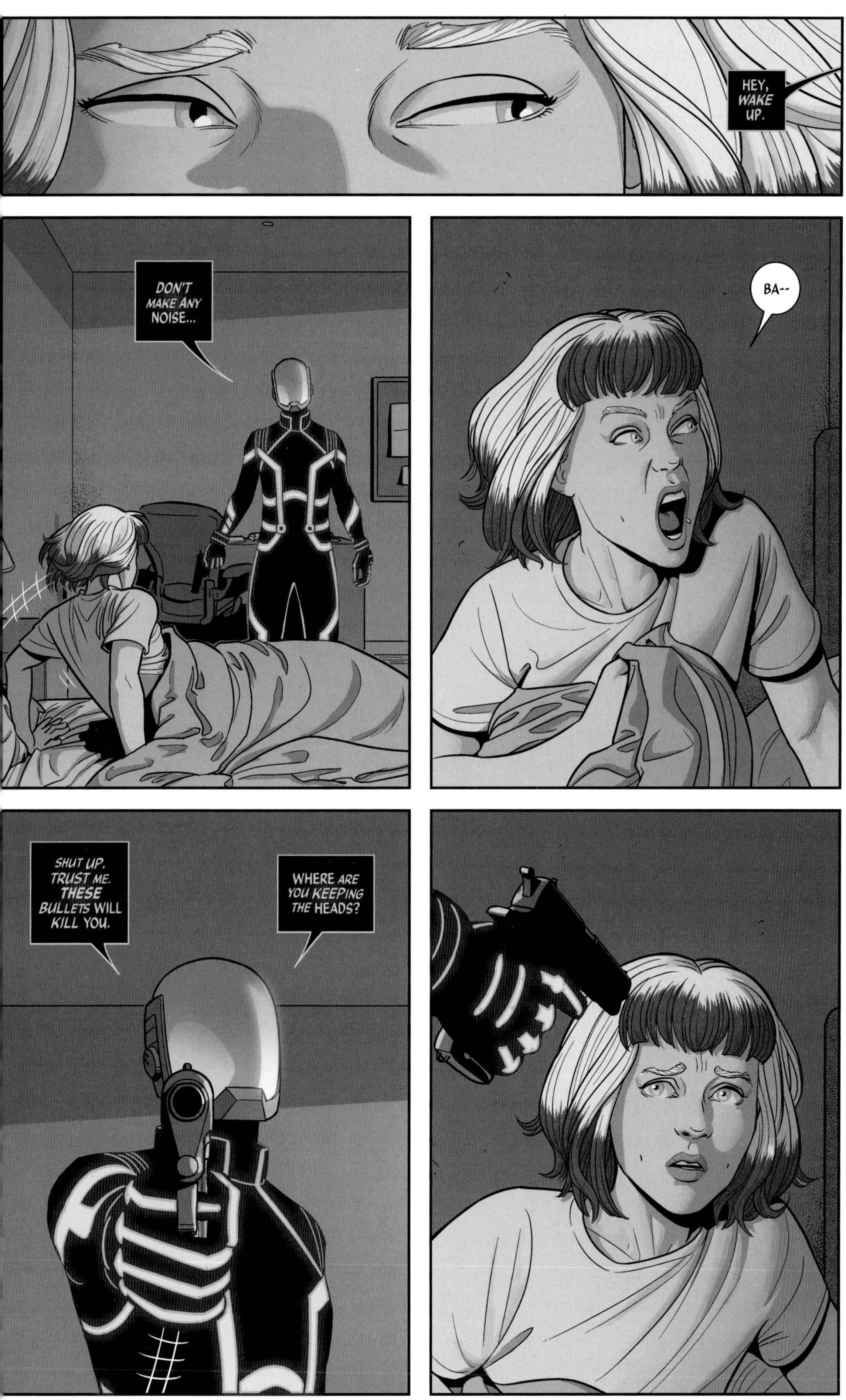
HEY, WAKE UP.
DON'T MAKE ANY NOISE...
BA--
SHUT UP. TRUST ME. THESE BULLETS WILL KILL YOU.
WHERE ARE YOU KEEPING THE HEADS?

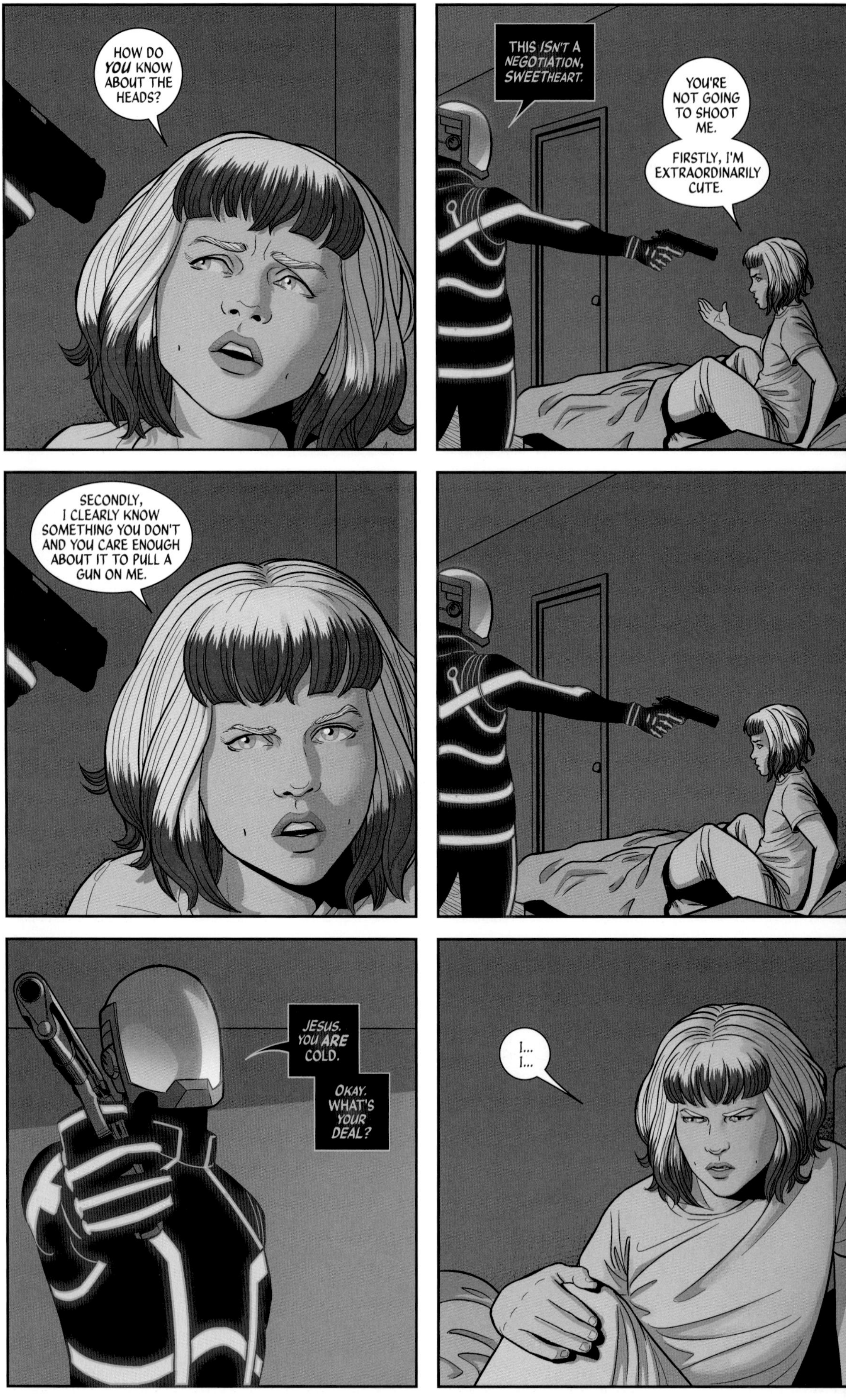
HOW DO YOU KNOW ABOUT THE HEADS?
THIS ISN'T A NEGOTIATION, SWEETHEART.
YOU'RE NOT GOING TO SHOOT ME.
FIRSTLY, I'M EXTRAORDINARILY CUTE.
SECONDLY, I CLEARLY KNOW SOMETHING YOU DON'T AND YOU CARE ENOUGH ABOUT IT TO PULL A GUN ON ME.
JESUS. YOU ARE COLD.
OKAY. WHAT'S YOUR DEAL?
I... I...

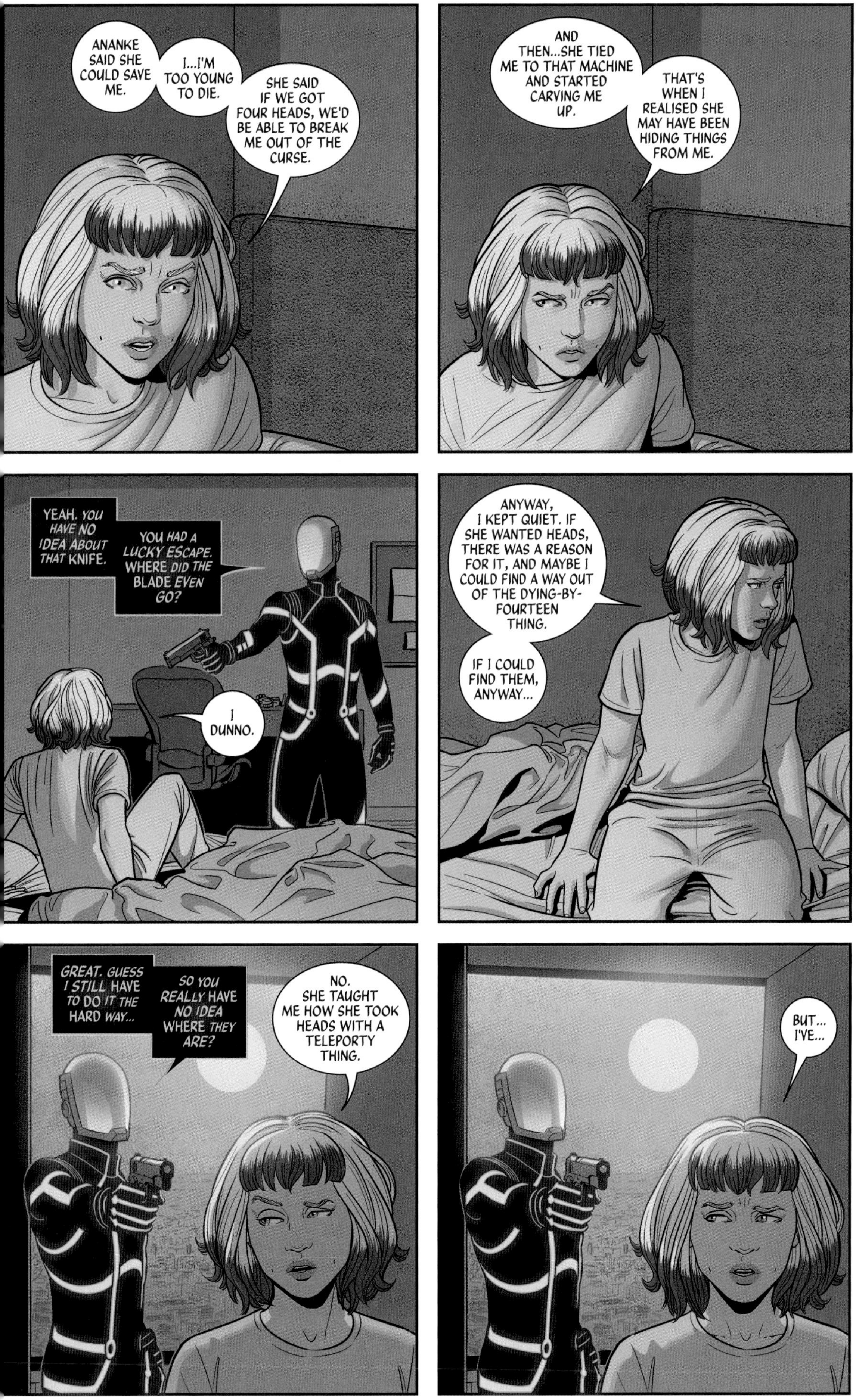

ANANKE SAID SHE COULD SAVE ME.
I...I'M TOO YOUNG TO DIE.
SHE SAID IF WE GOT FOUR HEADS, WE'D BE ABLE TO BREAK ME OUT OF THE CURSE.
AND THEN...SHE TIED ME TO THAT MACHINE AND STARTED CARVING ME UP.
THAT'S WHEN I REALISED SHE MAY HAVE BEEN HIDING THINGS FROM ME.
YEAH. YOU HAVE NO IDEA ABOUT THAT KNIFE.
YOU HAD A LUCKY ESCAPE. WHERE DID THE BLADE EVEN GO?
I DUNNO.
ANYWAY, I KEPT QUIET. IF SHE WANTED HEADS, THERE WAS A REASON FOR IT, AND MAYBE I COULD FIND A WAY OUT OF THE DYING-BY-FOURTEEN THING.
IF I COULD FIND THEM, ANYWAY...
GREAT. GUESS I STILL HAVE TO DO IT THE HARD WAY...
SO YOU REALLY HAVE NO IDEA WHERE THEY ARE?
NO. SHE TAUGHT ME HOW SHE TOOK HEADS WITH A TELEPORTY THING.
BUT... I'VE...

...ONLY JUST DARED TO DO IT. I THOUGHT I COULD TRACE ITS ROUTE SOMEHOW? BUT I COULDN'T.

PLUS... I THINK I KILLED SAKHMET.

NO *IDEA* IF YOU GOT *HER* HEAD *SAFELY* OR *NOT*, BUT I SAW YOU GIVING IT A SHOT.

HEY... HOW DO YOU EVEN KNOW ABOUT THE HEADS?

WHAT DO YOU MEAN "DO IT THE HARD WAY"?

WHAT DO *YOU* WANT THEM FOR?

SO MANY QUESTIONS, AND THE ANSWERS ARE MOSTLY "NONE OF YOUR BUSINESS". AND--

BLEEP

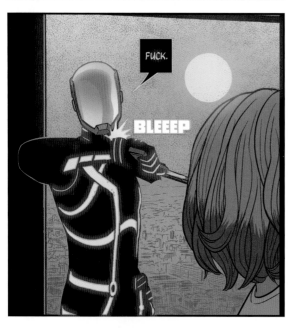

FUCK.

BLEEEP

SORRY, MINI. THIS ISN'T WHAT I WANTED, BUT--

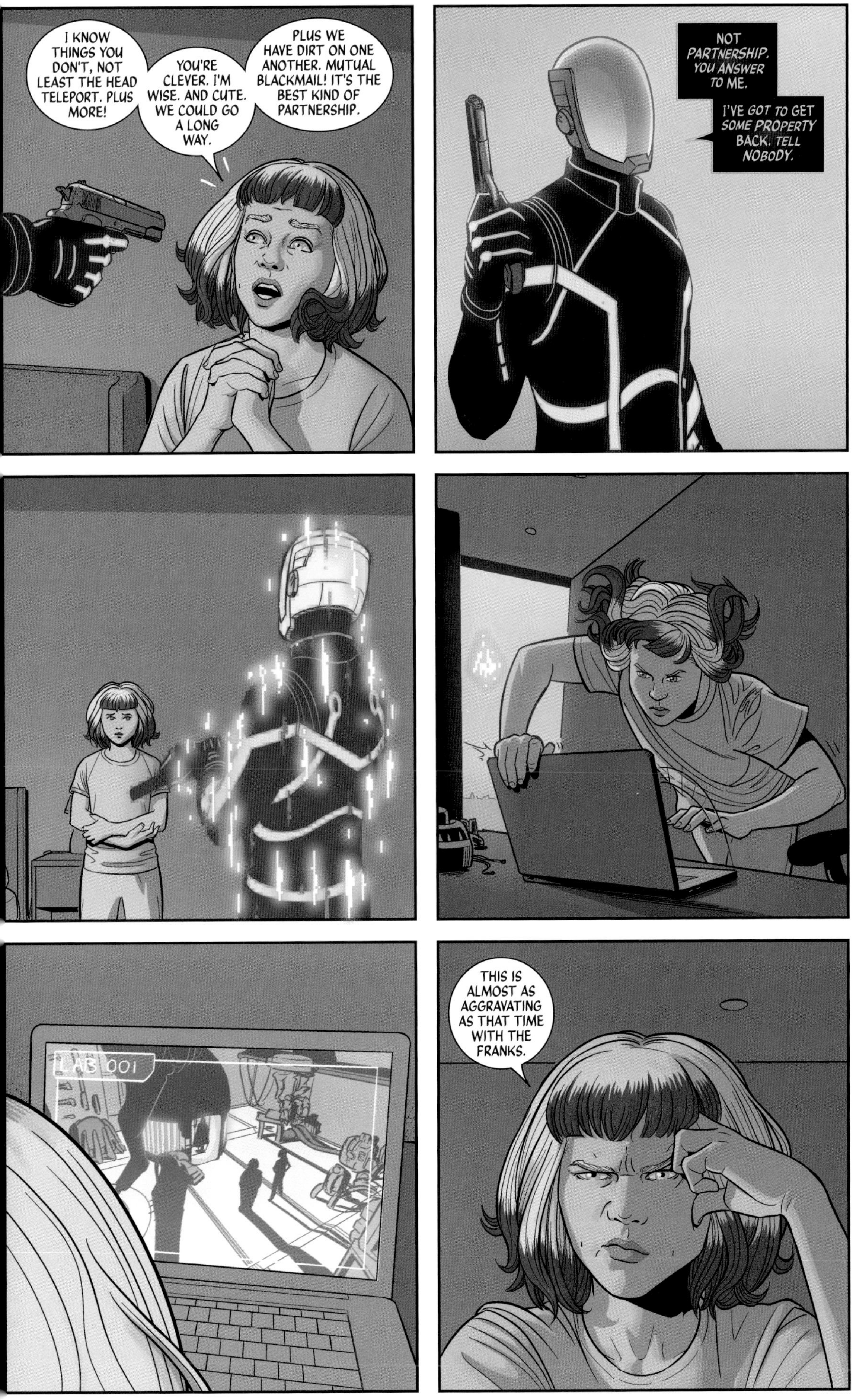
I KNOW THINGS YOU DON'T, NOT LEAST THE HEAD TELEPORT. PLUS MORE!
YOU'RE CLEVER. I'M WISE. AND CUTE. WE COULD GO A LONG WAY.
PLUS WE HAVE DIRT ON ONE ANOTHER. MUTUAL BLACKMAIL! IT'S THE BEST KIND OF PARTNERSHIP.
NOT *PARTNERSHIP*. YOU *ANSWER* TO ME.
I'VE *GOT TO* GET SOME *PROPERTY* BACK. *TELL NOBODY*.
LAB 001
THIS IS ALMOST AS AGGRAVATING AS THAT TIME WITH THE FRANKS.

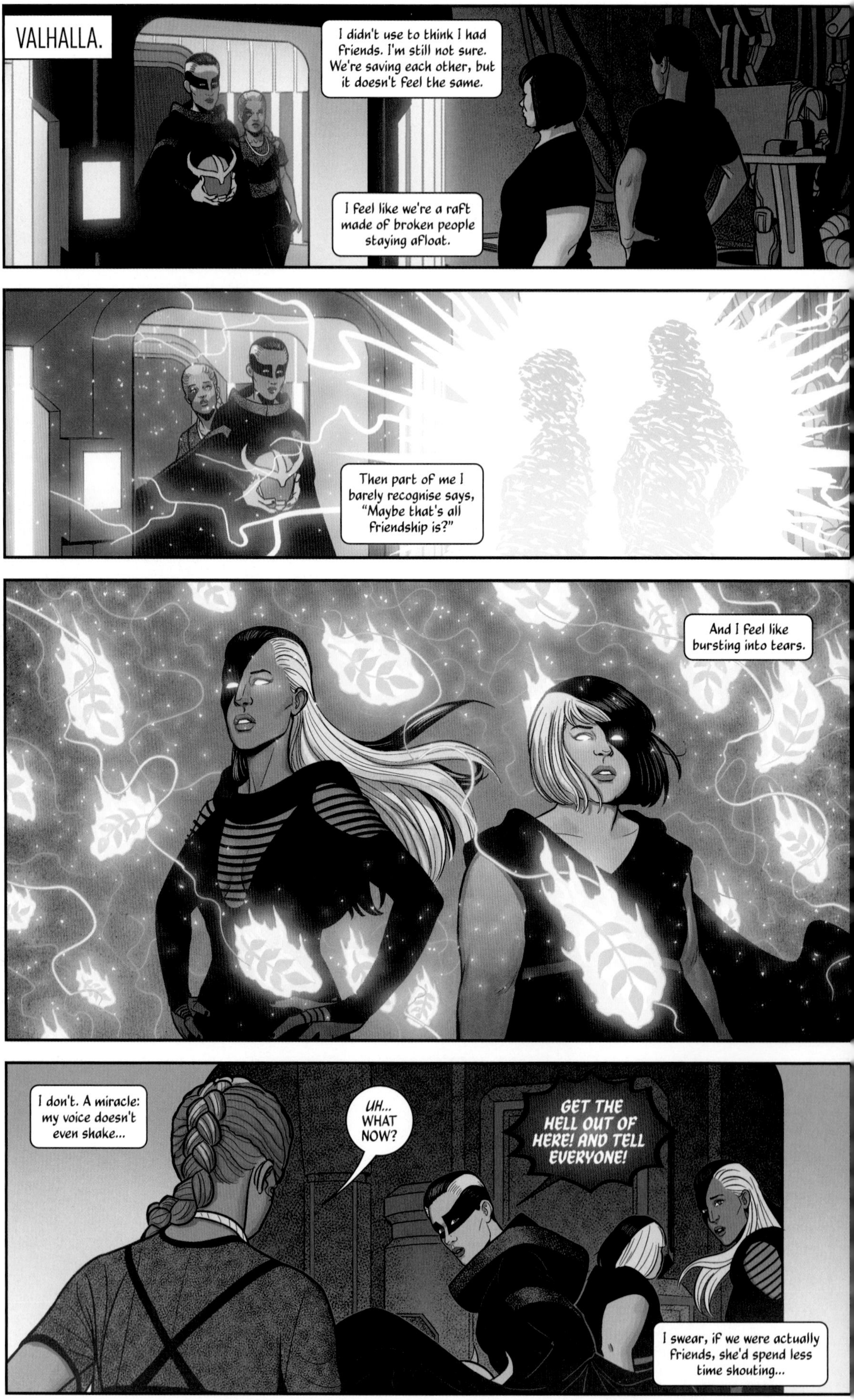
VALHALLA.
I didn't use to think I had friends. I'm still not sure. We're saving each other, but it doesn't feel the same.
I feel like we're a raft made of broken people staying afloat.
Then part of me I barely recognise says, "Maybe that's all friendship is?"
And I feel like bursting into tears.
I don't. A miracle: my voice doesn't even shake...
UH... WHAT NOW?
GET THE HELL OUT OF HERE! AND TELL EVERYONE!
I swear, if we were actually friends, she'd spend less time shouting...

...but "getting out of here" is an A+ idea.

CAN...CAN YOU OPEN MY FACEPLATE?

NEVER WAS A FRESH AIR SORT...

BUT YOU'LL BE AMAZED WHAT YOU MISS WHEN YOU'RE TRAPPED UNDERGROUND.

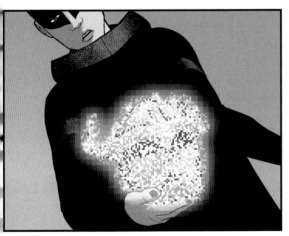

YOU DON'T ESCAPE THAT EASILY, JON.

QUICKLY! BACK TO THE LAB!

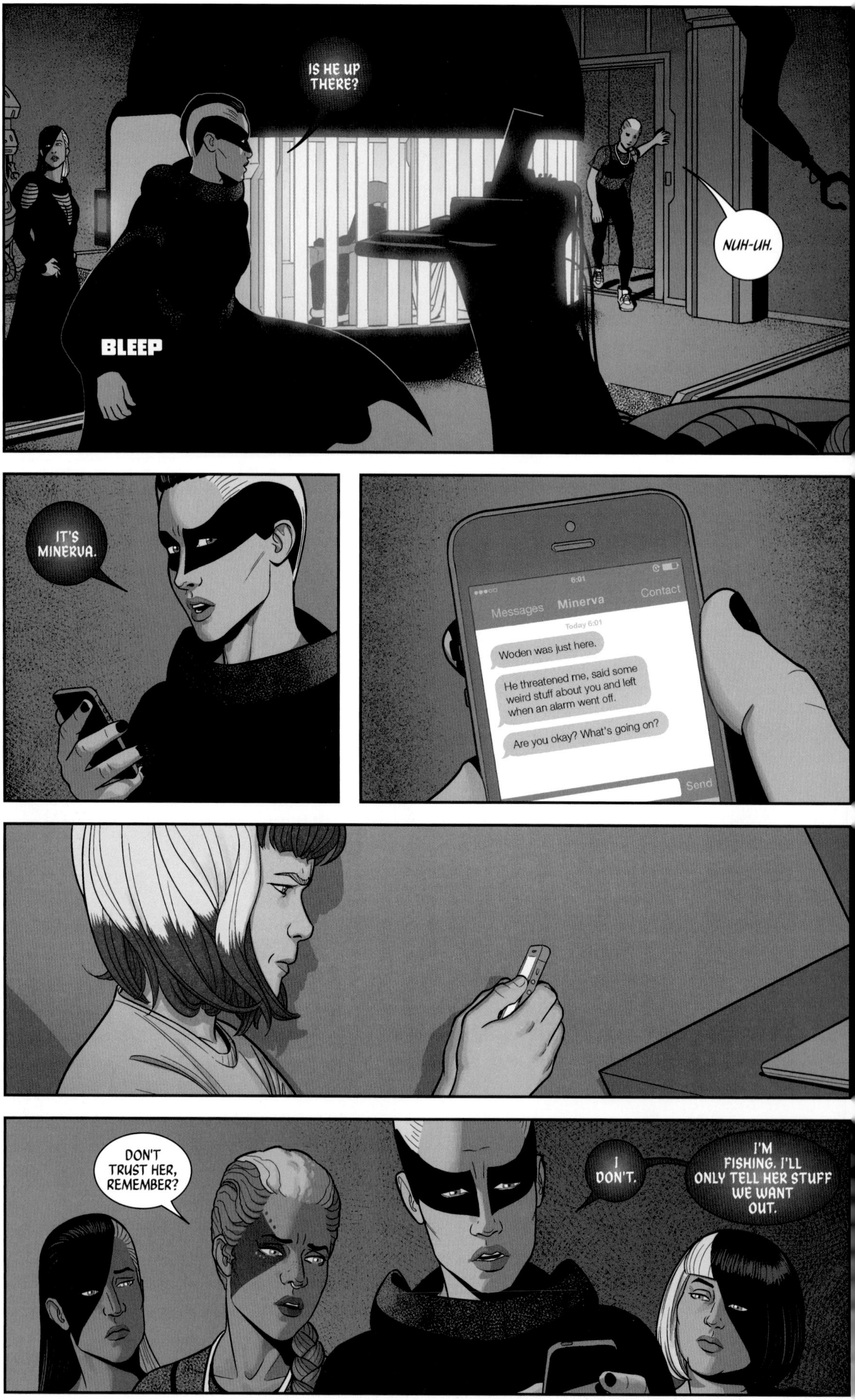
IS HE UP THERE?
NUH-UH.
BLEEP
IT'S MINERVA.
6:01
Messages Minerva Contact
Today 6:01
Woden was just here.
He threatened me, said some weird stuff about you and left when an alarm went off.
Are you okay? What's going on?
Send
DON'T TRUST HER, REMEMBER?
I DON'T.
I'M FISHING. I'LL ONLY TELL HER STUFF WE WANT OUT.

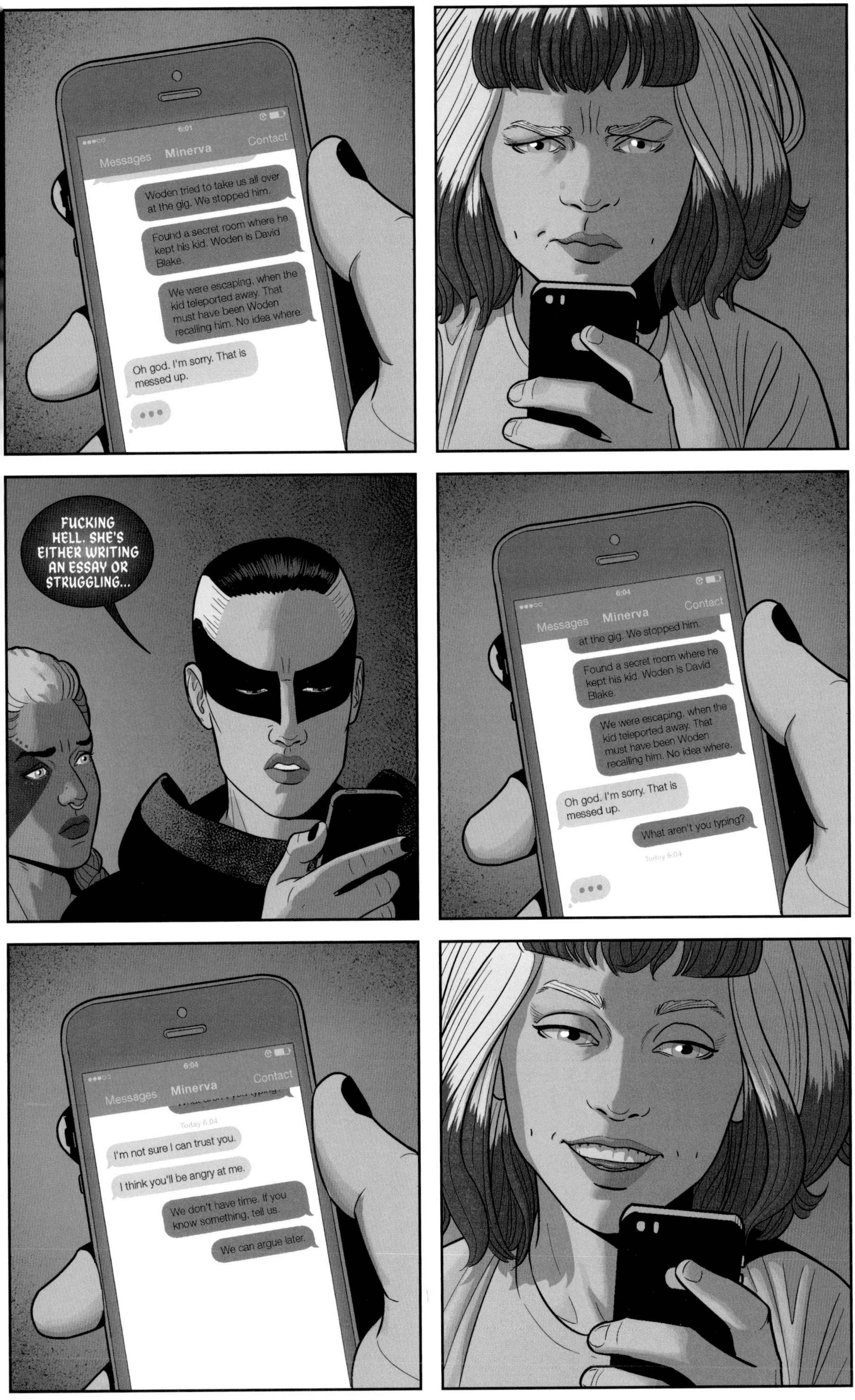
6:01
Messages
Minerva
Contact
Woden tried to take us all over at the gig. We stopped him.
Found a secret room where he kept his kid. Woden is David Blake.
We were escaping, when the kid teleported away. That must have been Woden recalling him. No idea where.
Oh god. I'm sorry. That is messed up.
FUCKING HELL. SHE'S EITHER WRITING AN ESSAY OR STRUGGLING...
6:04
Messages
Minerva
Contact
at the gig. We stopped him.
Found a secret room where he kept his kid. Woden is David Blake.
We were escaping, when the kid teleported away. That must have been Woden recalling him. No idea where.
Oh god. I'm sorry. That is messed up.
What aren't you typing?
Today 6:04
6:04
Messages
Minerva
Contact
Today 6:04
I'm not sure I can trust you.
I think you'll be angry at me.
We don't have time. If you know something, tell us.
We can argue later.

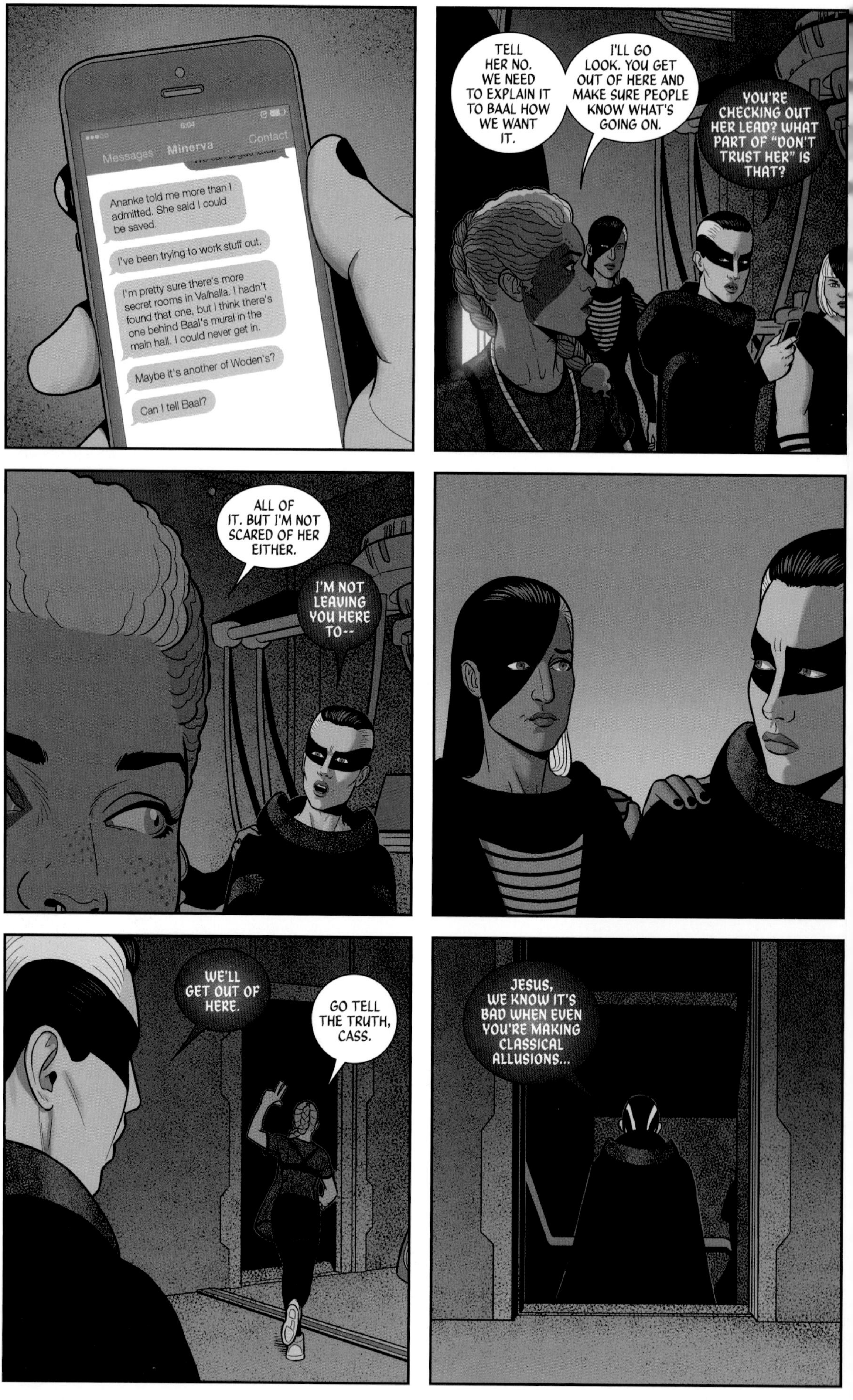
6:04
Messages
Minerva
Contact
Ananke told me more than I admitted. She said I could be saved.
I've been trying to work stuff out.
I'm pretty sure there's more secret rooms in Valhalla. I hadn't found that one, but I think there's one behind Baal's mural in the main hall. I could never get in.
Maybe it's another of Woden's?
Can I tell Baal?
TELL HER NO. WE NEED TO EXPLAIN IT TO BAAL HOW WE WANT IT.
I'LL GO LOOK. YOU GET OUT OF HERE AND MAKE SURE PEOPLE KNOW WHAT'S GOING ON.
YOU'RE CHECKING OUT HER LEAD? WHAT PART OF "DON'T TRUST HER" IS THAT?
ALL OF IT. BUT I'M NOT SCARED OF HER EITHER.
I'M NOT LEAVING YOU HERE TO--
WE'LL GET OUT OF HERE.
GO TELL THE TRUTH, CASS.
JESUS, WE KNOW IT'S BAD WHEN EVEN YOU'RE MAKING CLASSICAL ALLUSIONS...

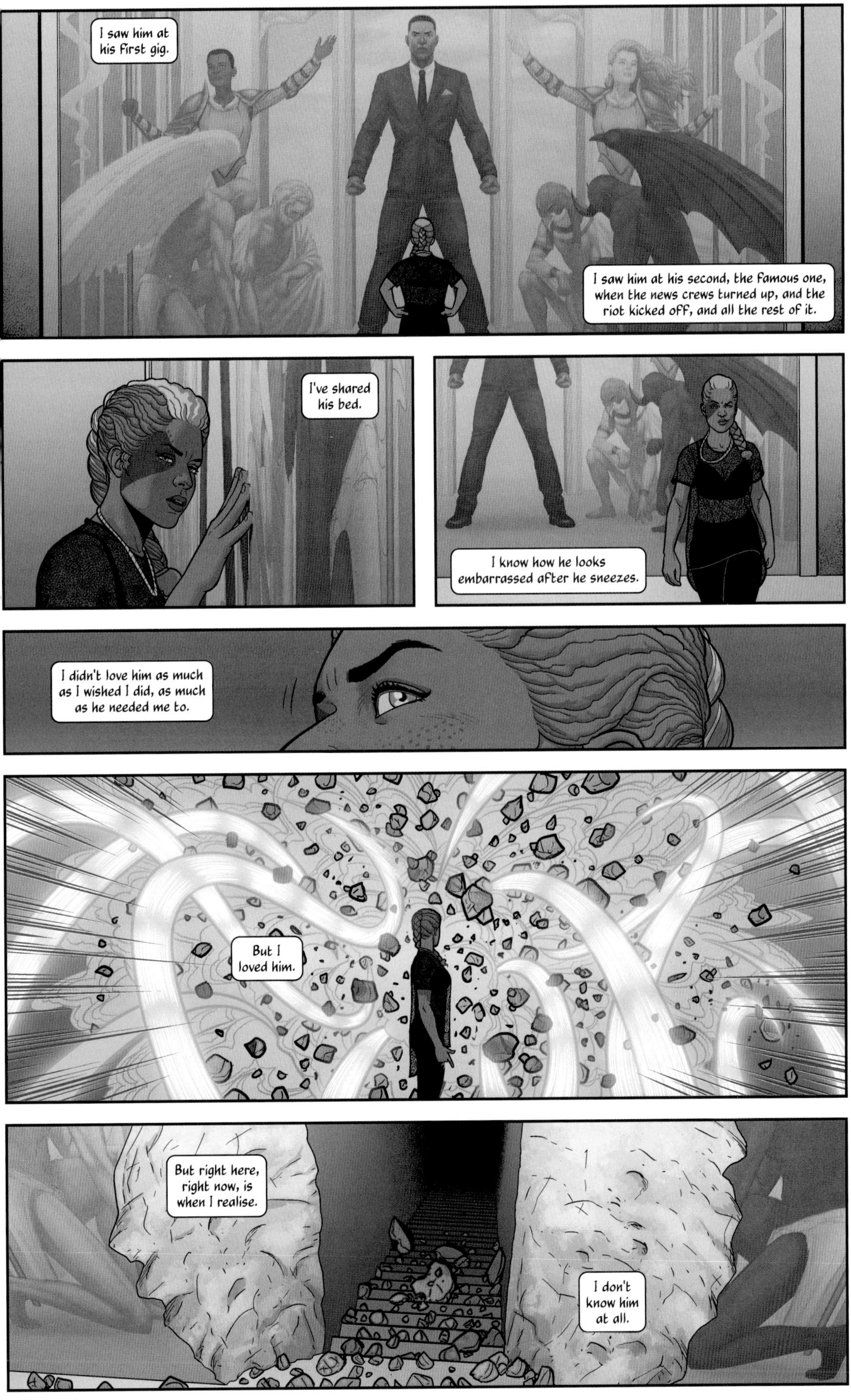
I saw him at his first gig.
I saw him at his second, the famous one, when the news crews turned up, and the riot kicked off, and all the rest of it.
I've shared his bed.
I know how he looks embarrassed after he sneezes.
I didn't love him as much as I wished I did, as much as he needed me to.
But I loved him.
But right here, right now, is when I realise.
I don't know him at all.

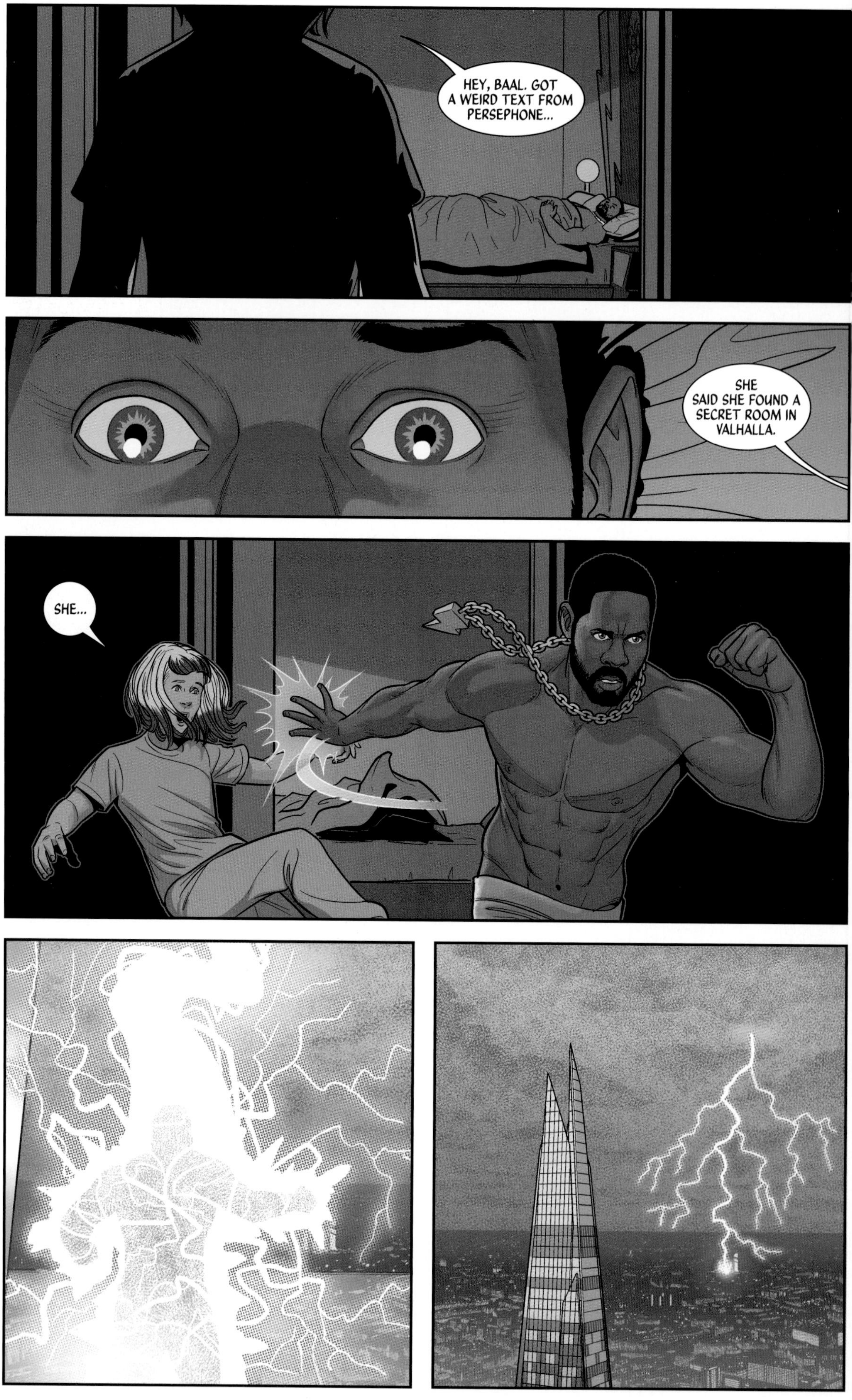
HEY, BAAL. GOT A WEIRD TEXT FROM PERSEPHONE...
SHE SAID SHE FOUND A SECRET ROOM IN VALHALLA.
SHE...

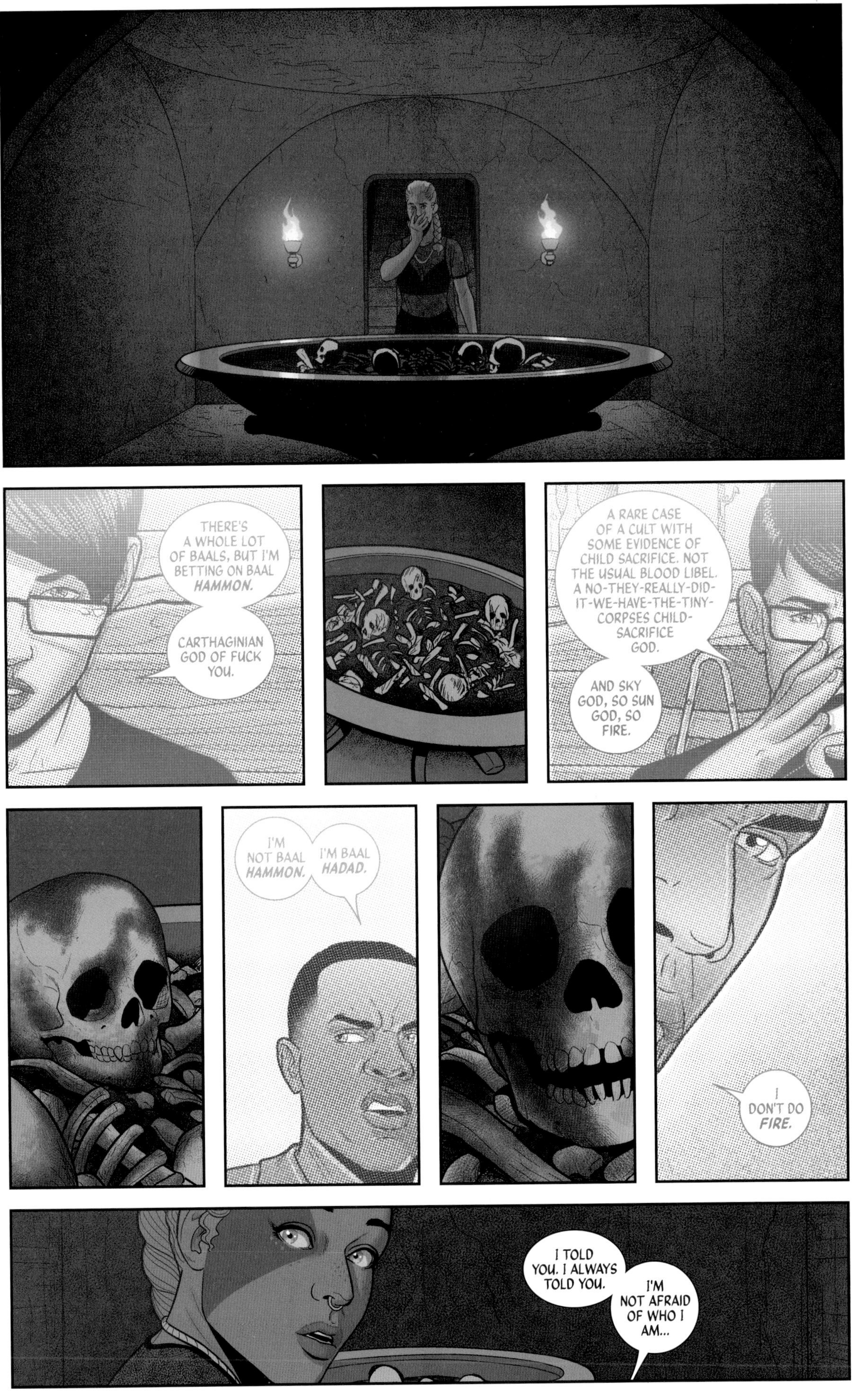
THERE'S A WHOLE LOT OF BAALS, BUT I'M BETTING ON BAAL HAMMON.
CARTHAGINIAN GOD OF FUCK YOU.
A RARE CASE OF A CULT WITH SOME EVIDENCE OF CHILD SACRIFICE. NOT THE USUAL BLOOD LIBEL. A NO-THEY-REALLY-DID-IT-WE-HAVE-THE-TINY-CORPSES CHILD-SACRIFICE GOD.
AND SKY GOD, SO SUN GOD, SO FIRE.
I'M NOT BAAL HAMMON.
I'M BAAL HADAD.
I DON'T DO FIRE.
I TOLD YOU. I ALWAYS TOLD YOU.
I'M NOT AFRAID OF WHO I AM...

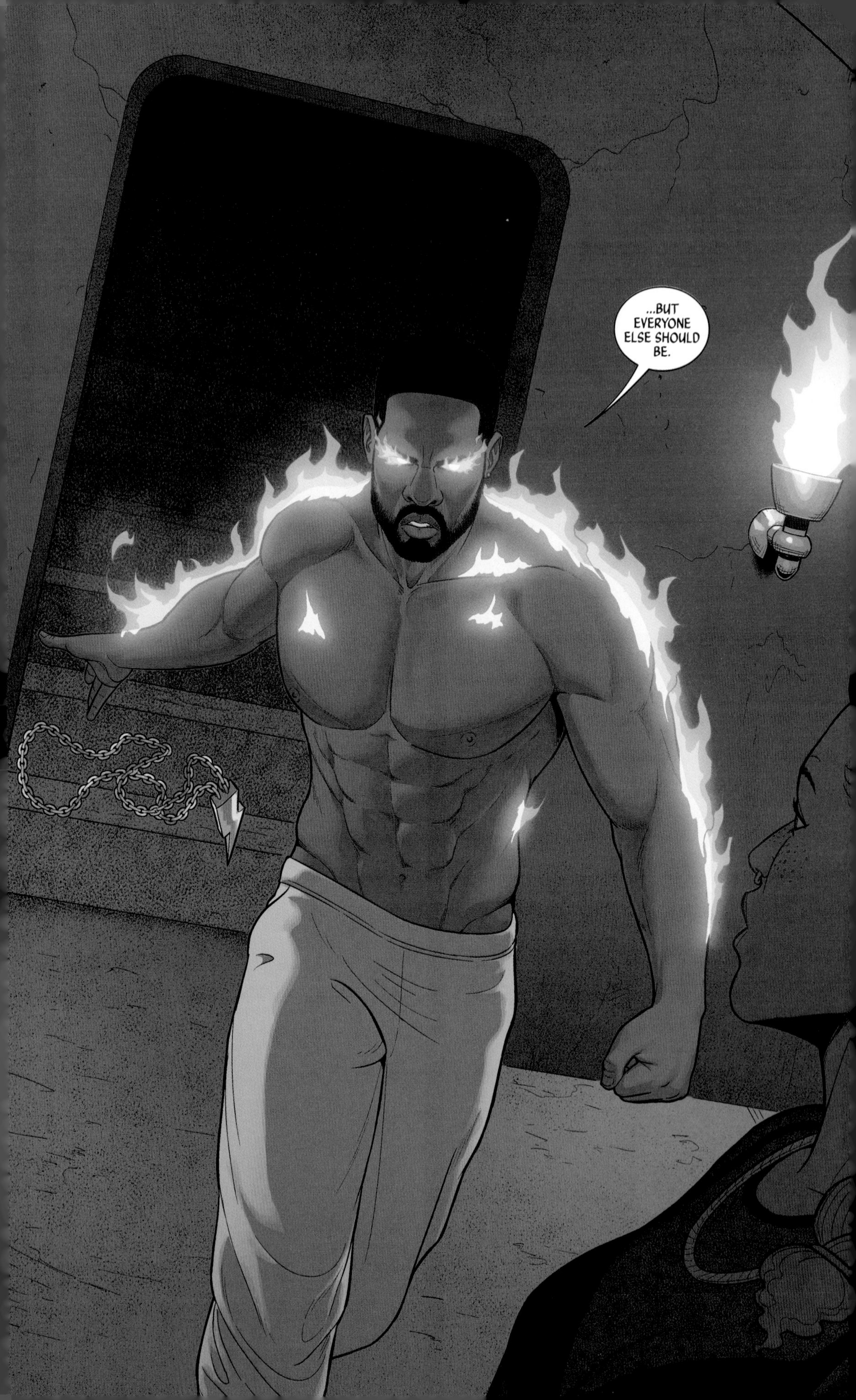
...BUT EVERYONE ELSE SHOULD BE.

THE CURSE
IN MY HANDS

9 MARCH 2015

36

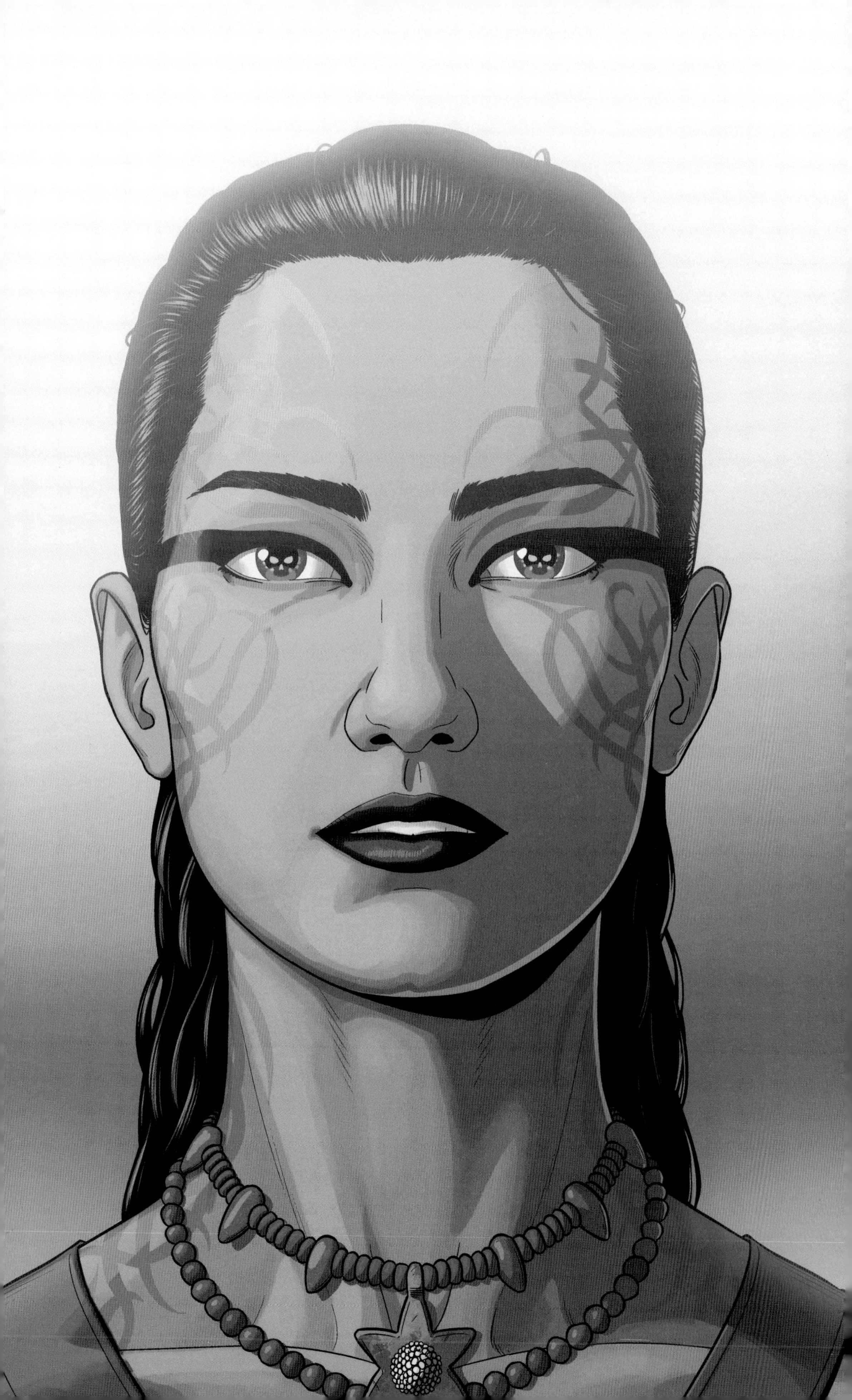

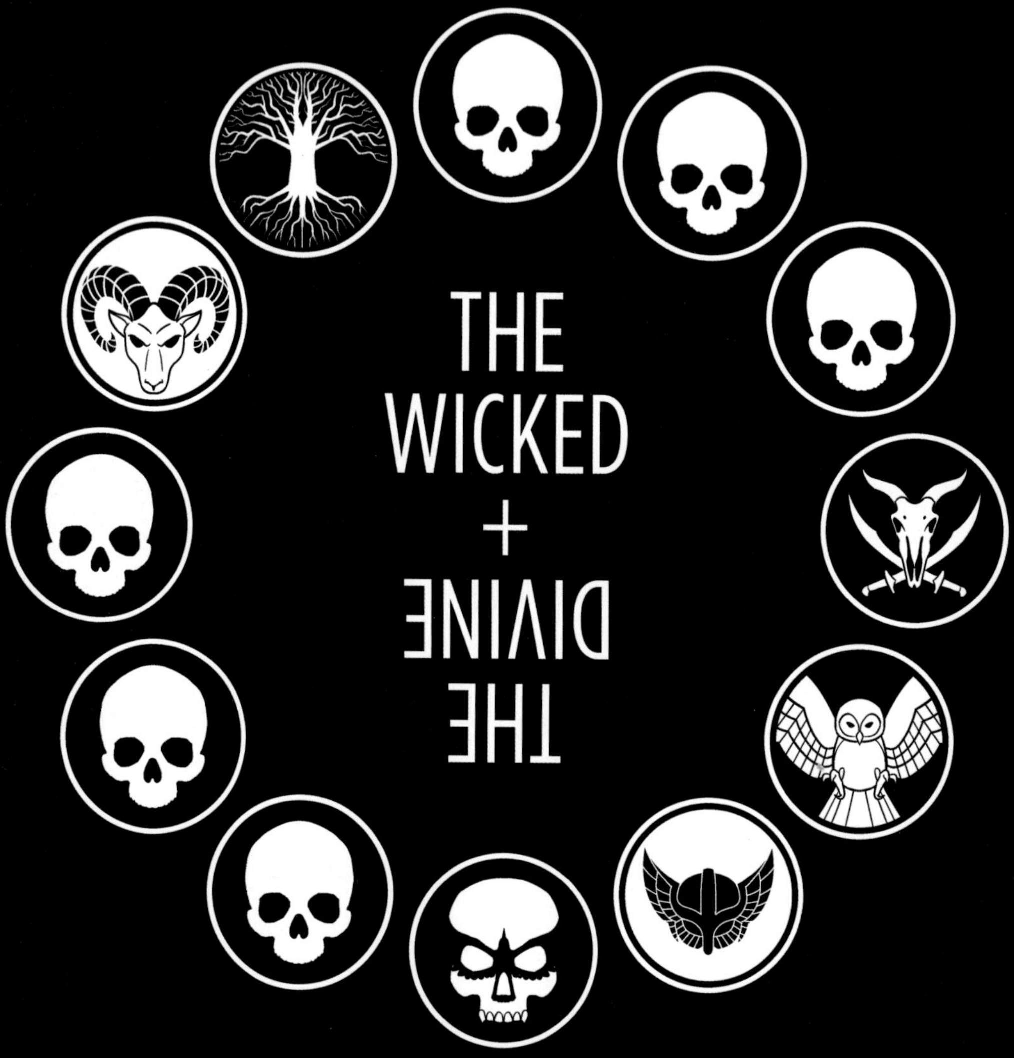
THE
WICKED
+
THE
DIVINE

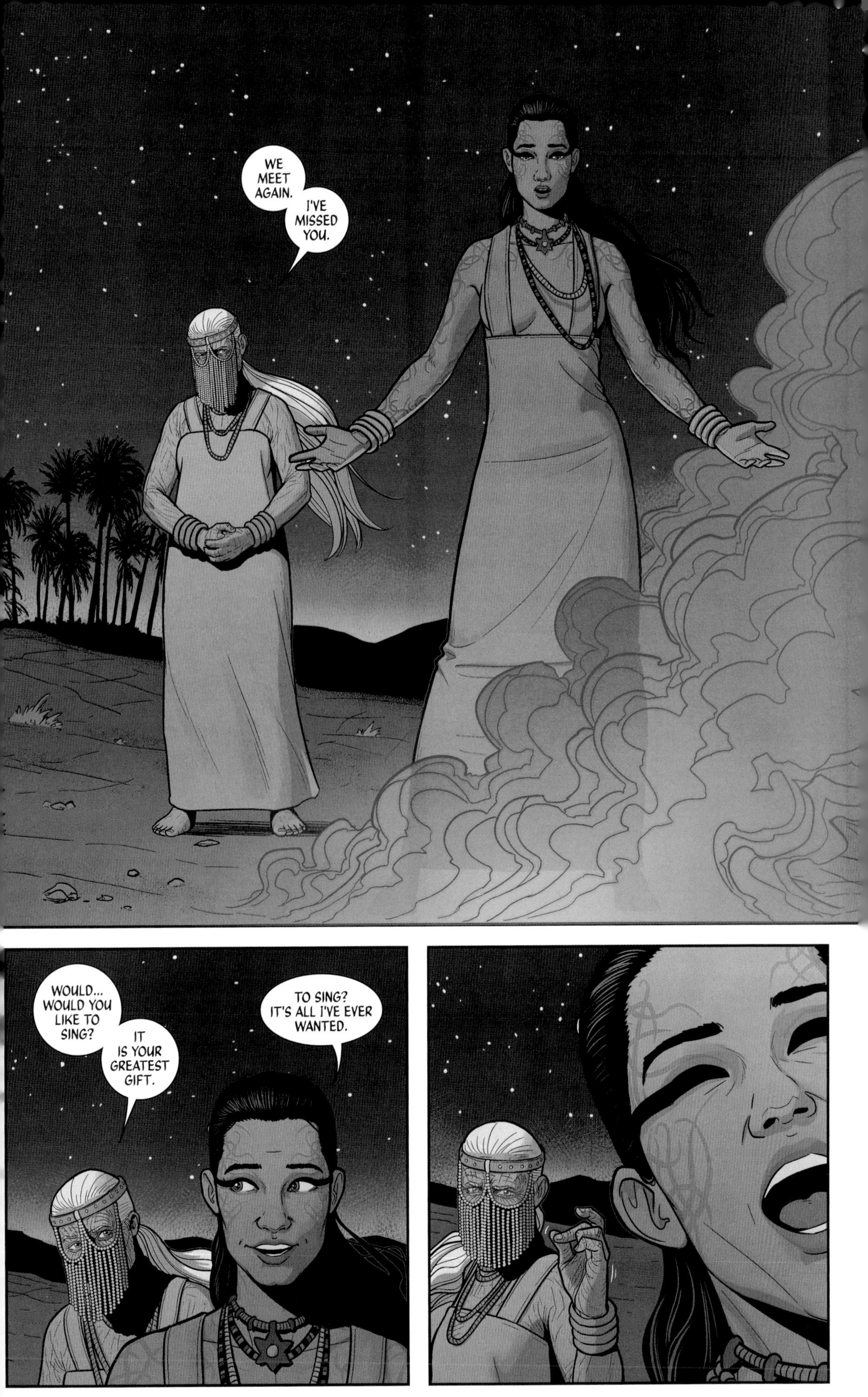
WE MEET AGAIN.
I'VE MISSED YOU.
WOULD... WOULD YOU LIKE TO SING?
IT IS YOUR GREATEST GIFT.
TO SING? IT'S ALL I'VE EVER WANTED.

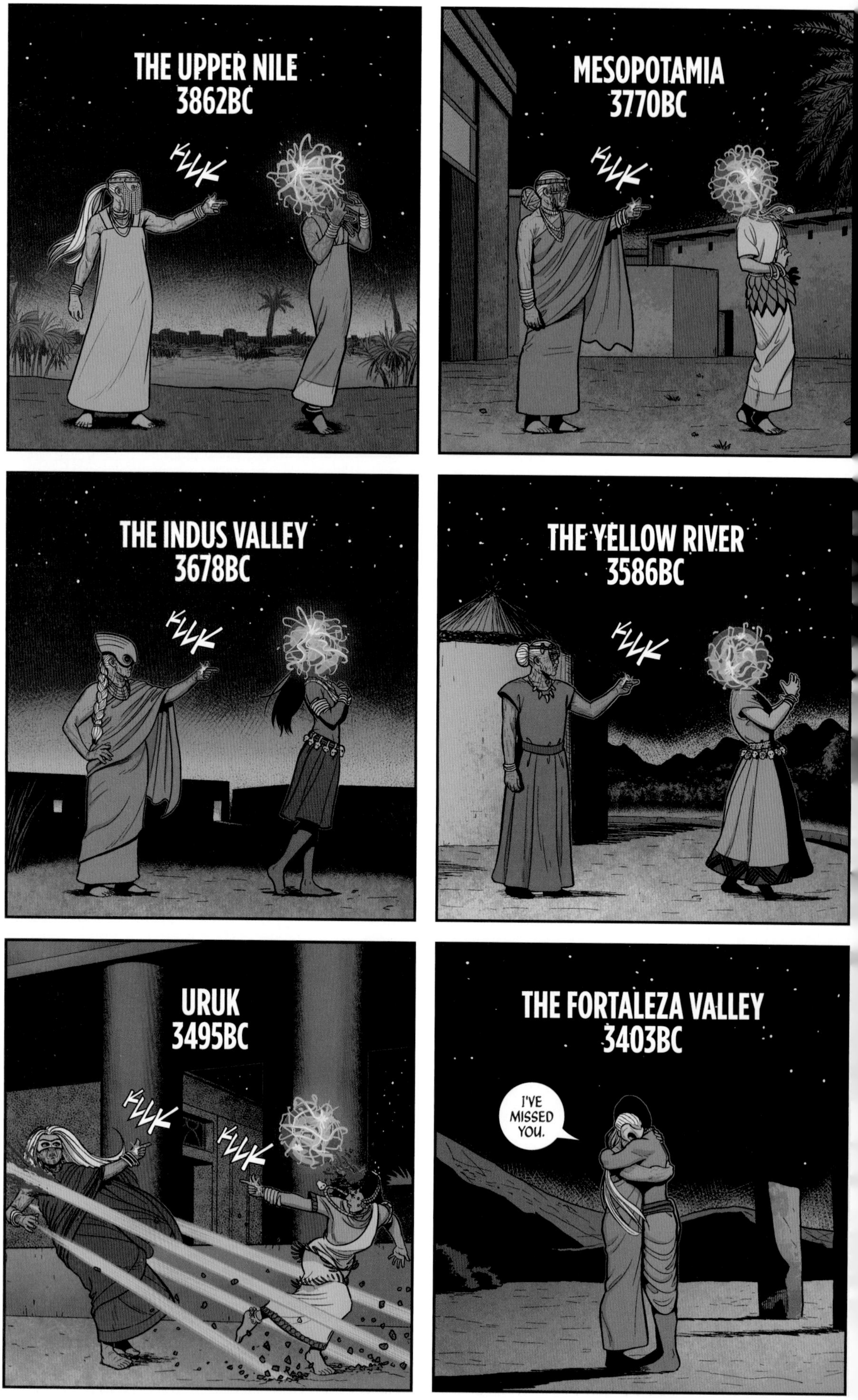
THE UPPER NILE
3862BC
KLLK
MESOPOTAMIA
3770BC
KLLK
THE INDUS VALLEY
3678BC
KLLK
THE YELLOW RIVER
3586BC
KLLK
URUK
3495BC
KLLK
KLLK
THE FORTALEZA VALLEY
3403BC
I'VE MISSED YOU.

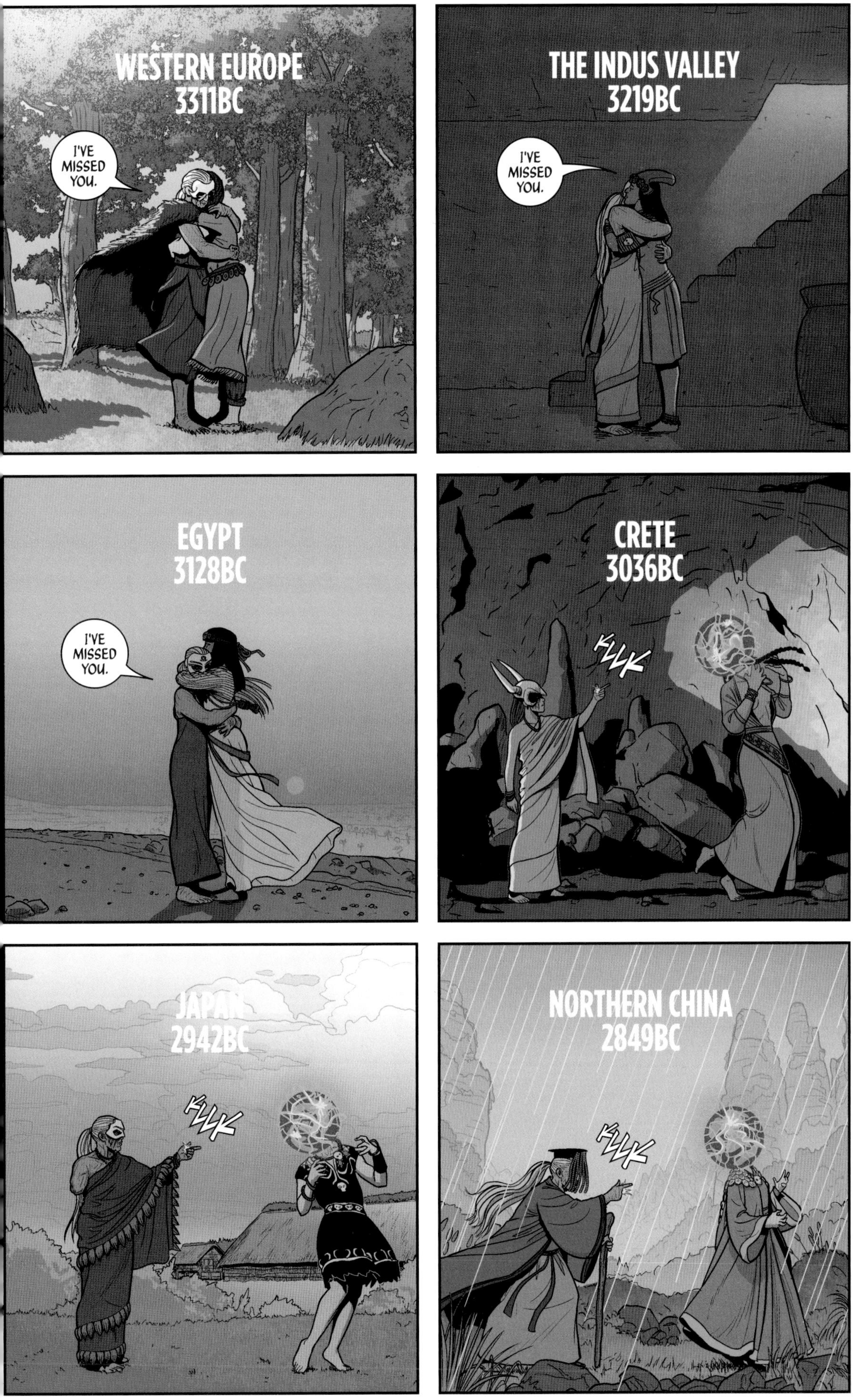
WESTERN EUROPE
3311BC
I'VE MISSED YOU.
THE INDUS VALLEY
3219BC
I'VE MISSED YOU.
EGYPT
3128BC
I'VE MISSED YOU.
CRETE
3036BC
KLLK
JAPAN
2942BC
KLLK
NORTHERN CHINA
2849BC
KLLK

EGYPT 2757BC

KLLK

NORTHERN CHINA 2666BC

KLLK

EGYPT 2574BC

KLLK

KLLK

WRANGEL ISLAND 2483BC

KLLK

HARAPPA 2391BC

I'VE MISSED YOU.

AKKAD 2299BC

KLLK

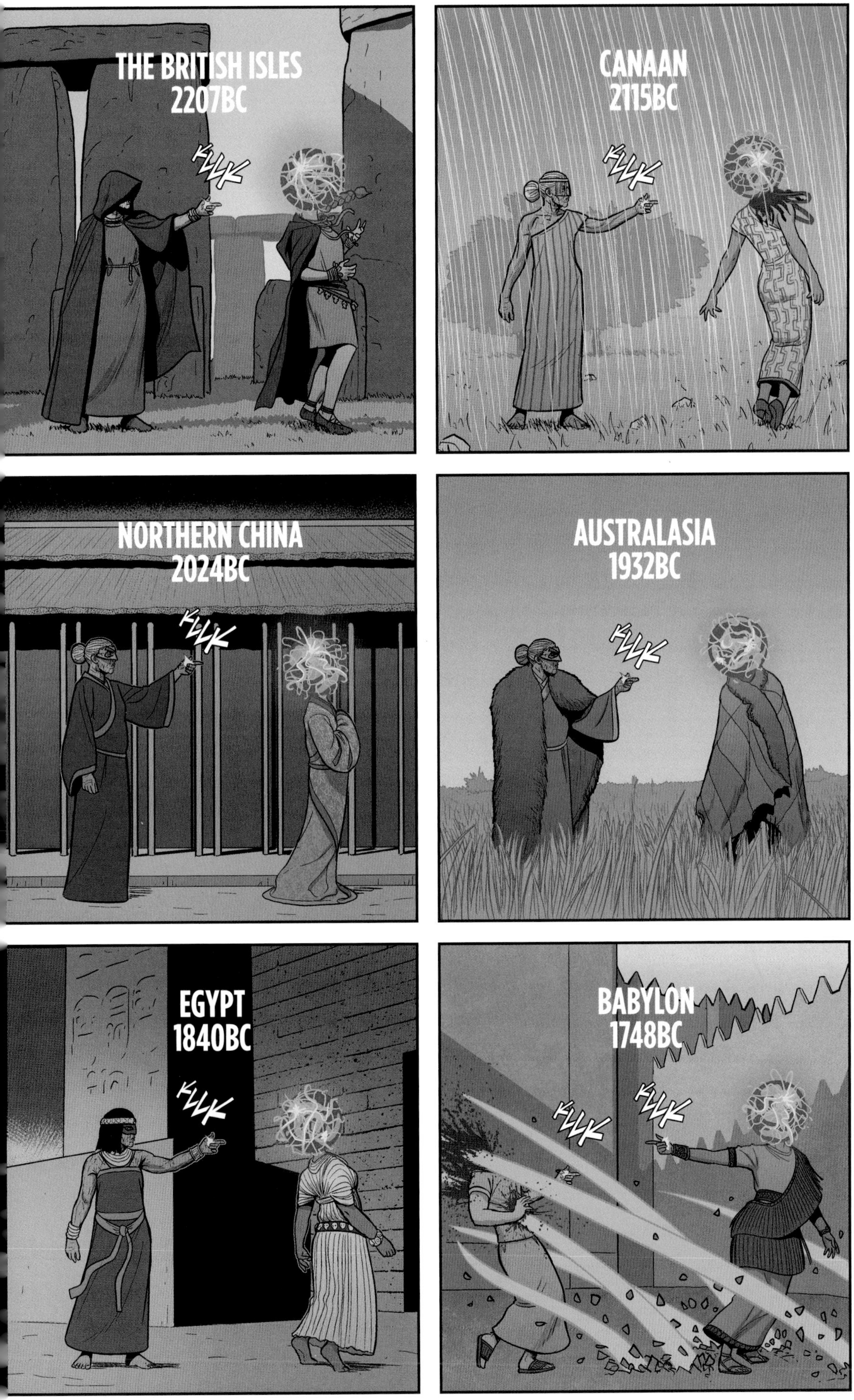
THE BRITISH ISLES
2207BC
KLLK
CANAAN
2115BC
KLLK
NORTHERN CHINA
2024BC
KLLK
AUSTRALASIA
1932BC
KLLK
EGYPT
1840BC
KLLK
BABYLON
1748BC
KLLK
KLLK

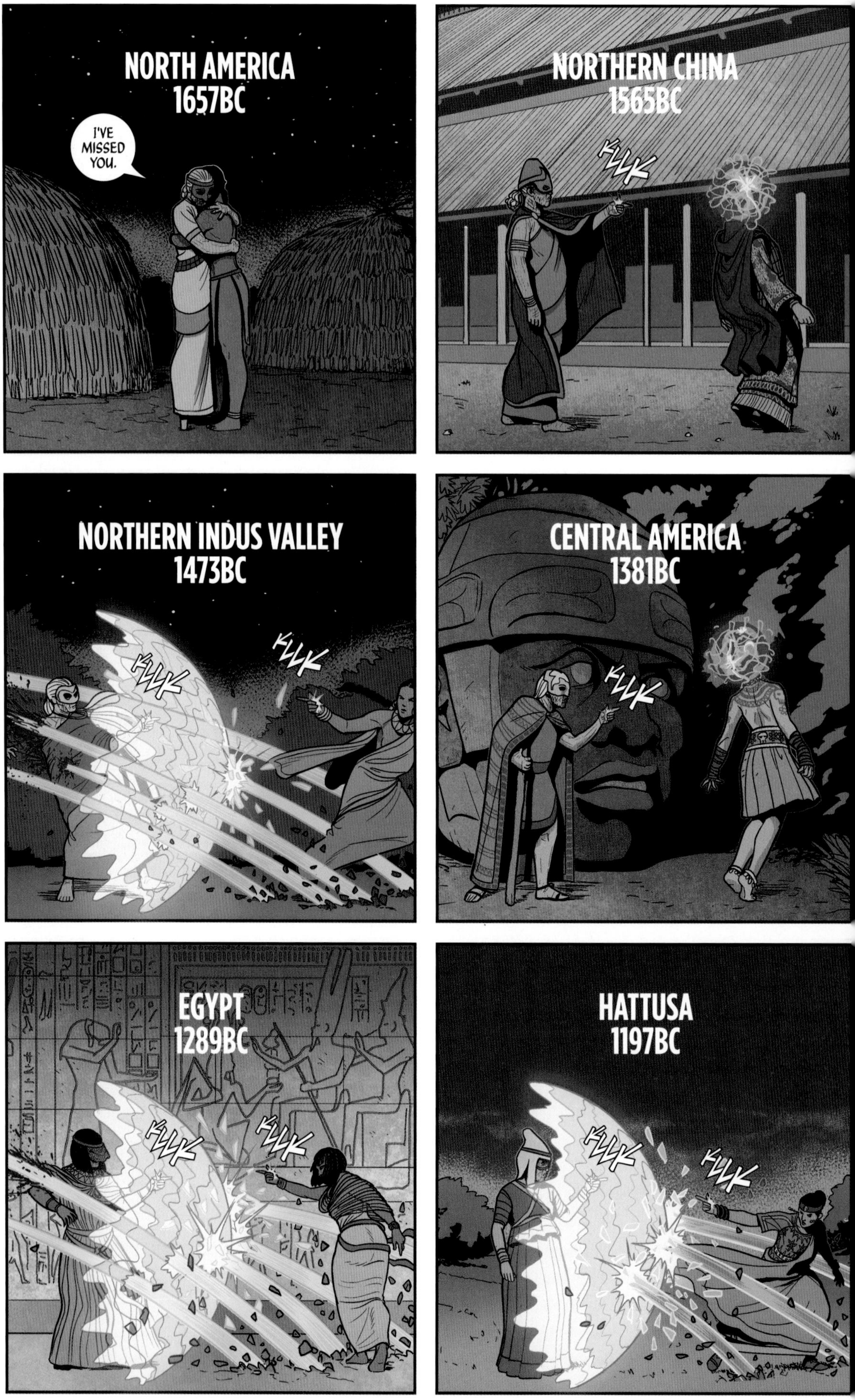
NORTH AMERICA
1657BC
I'VE MISSED YOU.
NORTHERN CHINA
1565BC
KLLK
NORTHERN INDUS VALLEY
1473BC
KLLK
KLLK
CENTRAL AMERICA
1381BC
KLLK
EGYPT
1289BC
KLLK
KLLK
HATTUSA
1197BC
KLLK
KLLK

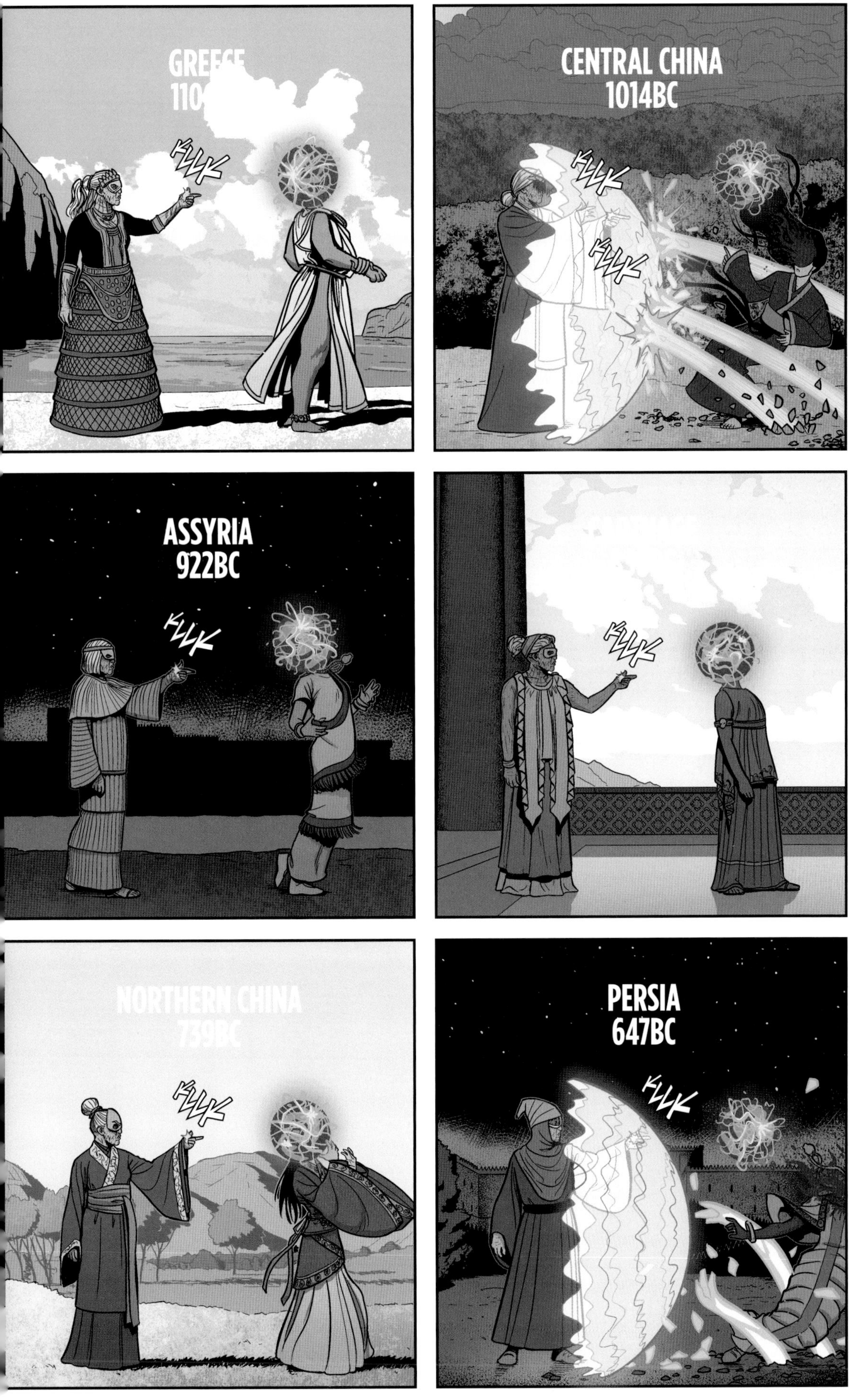

GREECE
110
CENTRAL CHINA
1014BC
ASSYRIA
922BC
NORTHERN CHINA
739BC
PERSIA
647BC

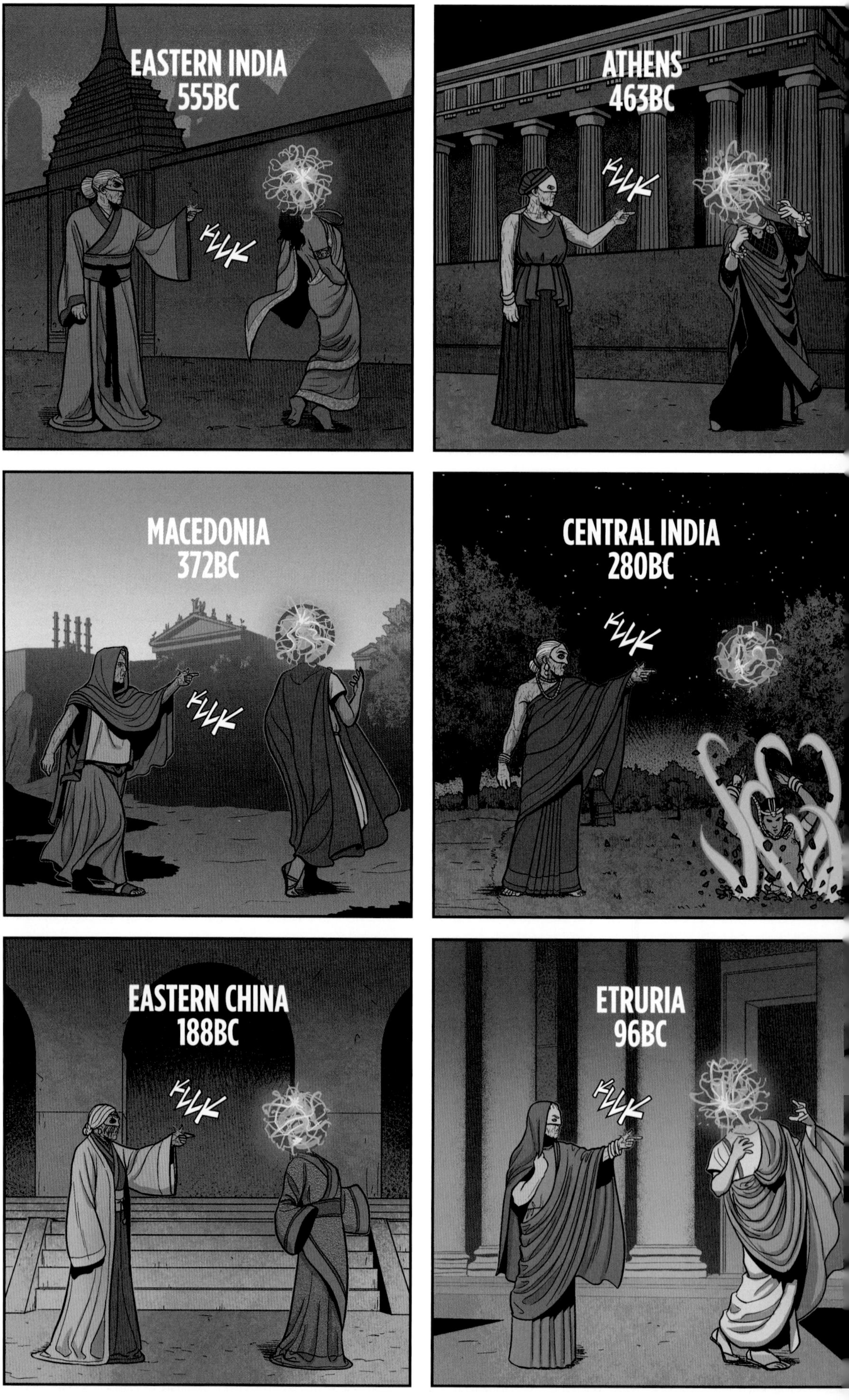
EASTERN INDIA
555BC
ATHENS
463BC
MACEDONIA
372BC
CENTRAL INDIA
280BC
EASTERN CHINA
188BC
ETRURIA
96BC

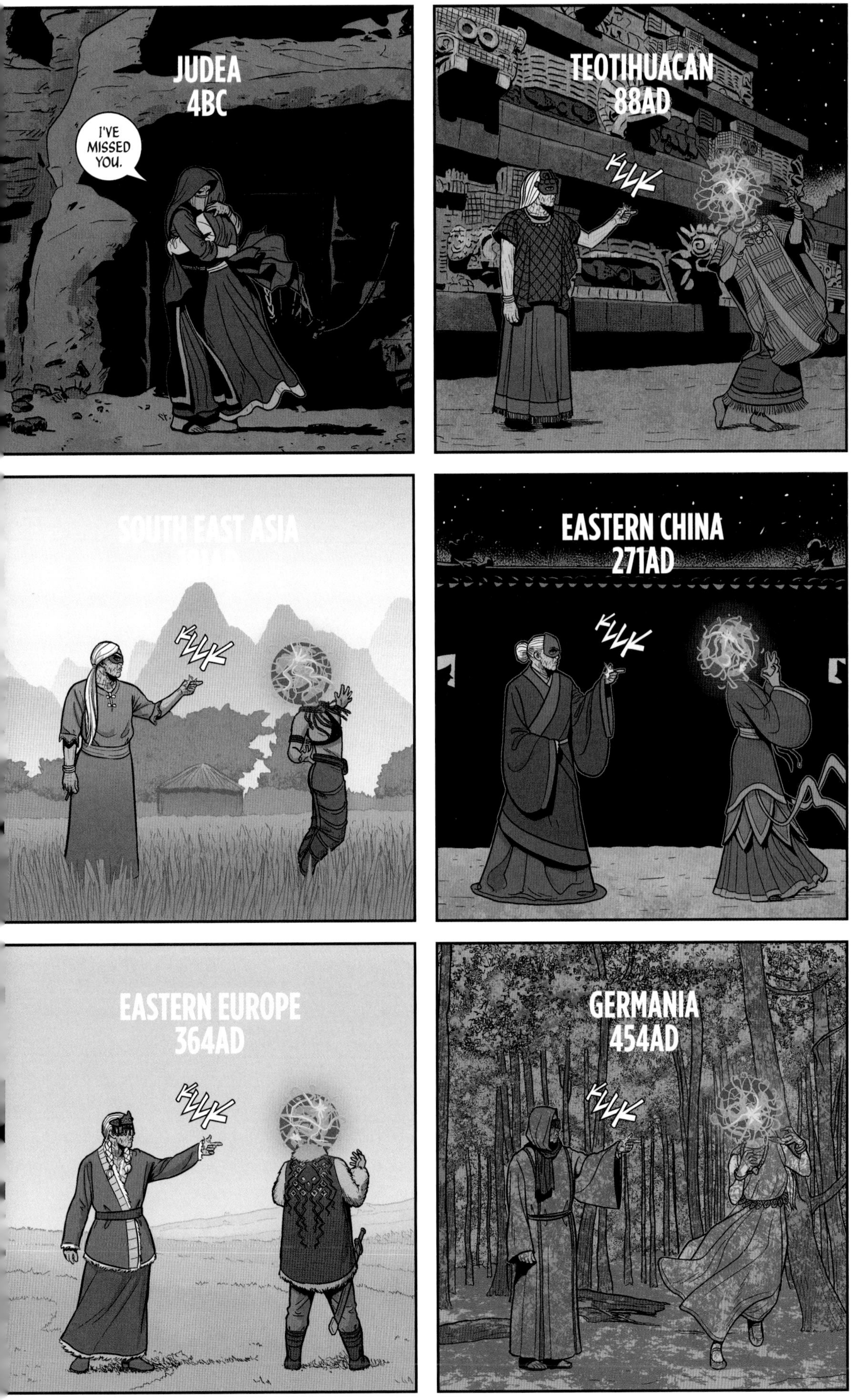
JUDEA
4BC
I'VE MISSED YOU.
TEOTIHUACAN
88AD
KLLK
SOUTH EAST ASIA
KLLK
EASTERN CHINA
271AD
KLLK
EASTERN EUROPE
364AD
KLLK
GERMANIA
454AD
KLLK

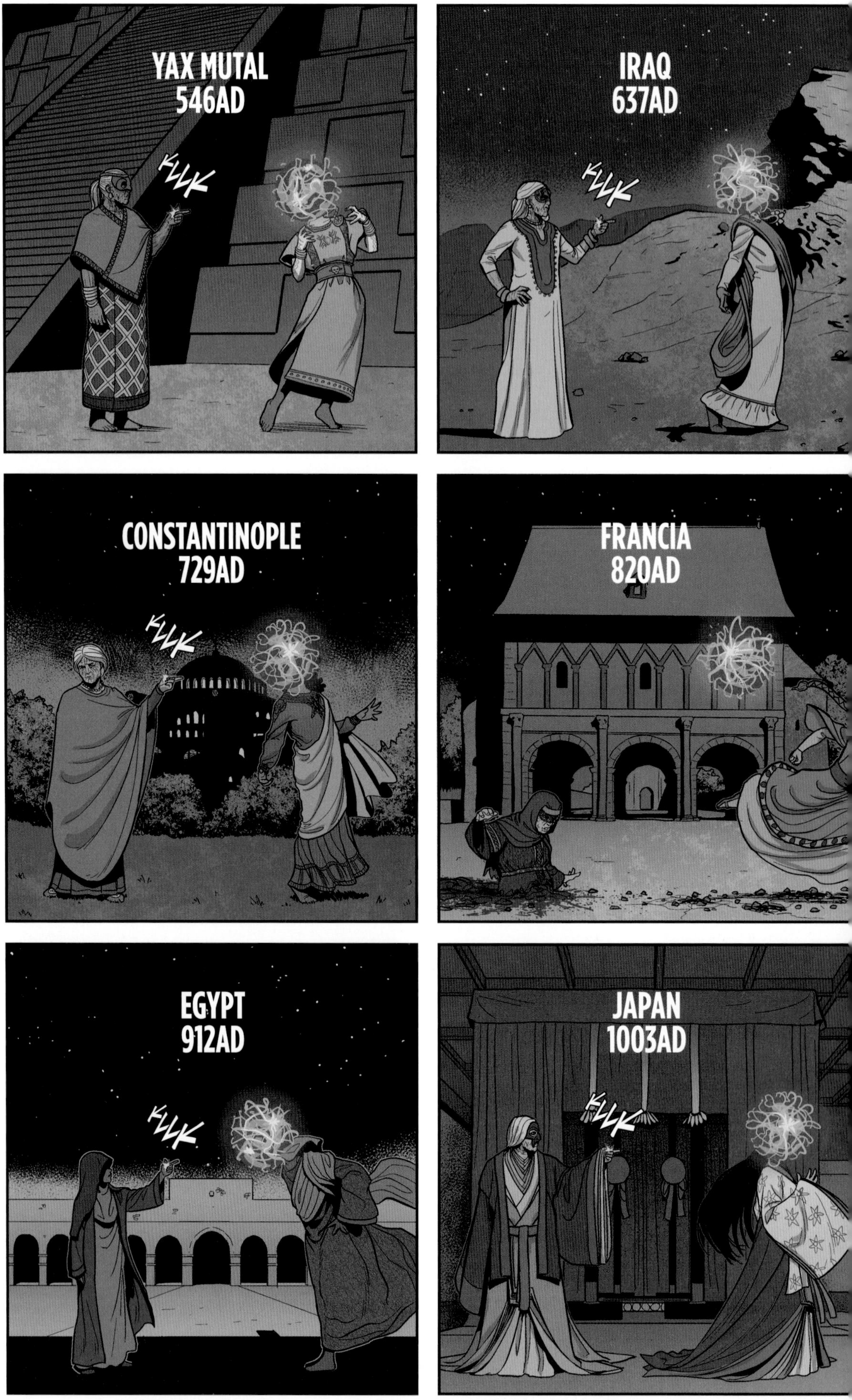
YAX MUTAL
546AD
KLLK
IRAQ
637AD
KLLK
CONSTANTINOPLE
729AD
KLLK
FRANCIA
820AD
EGYPT
912AD
KLLK
JAPAN
1003AD
KLLK

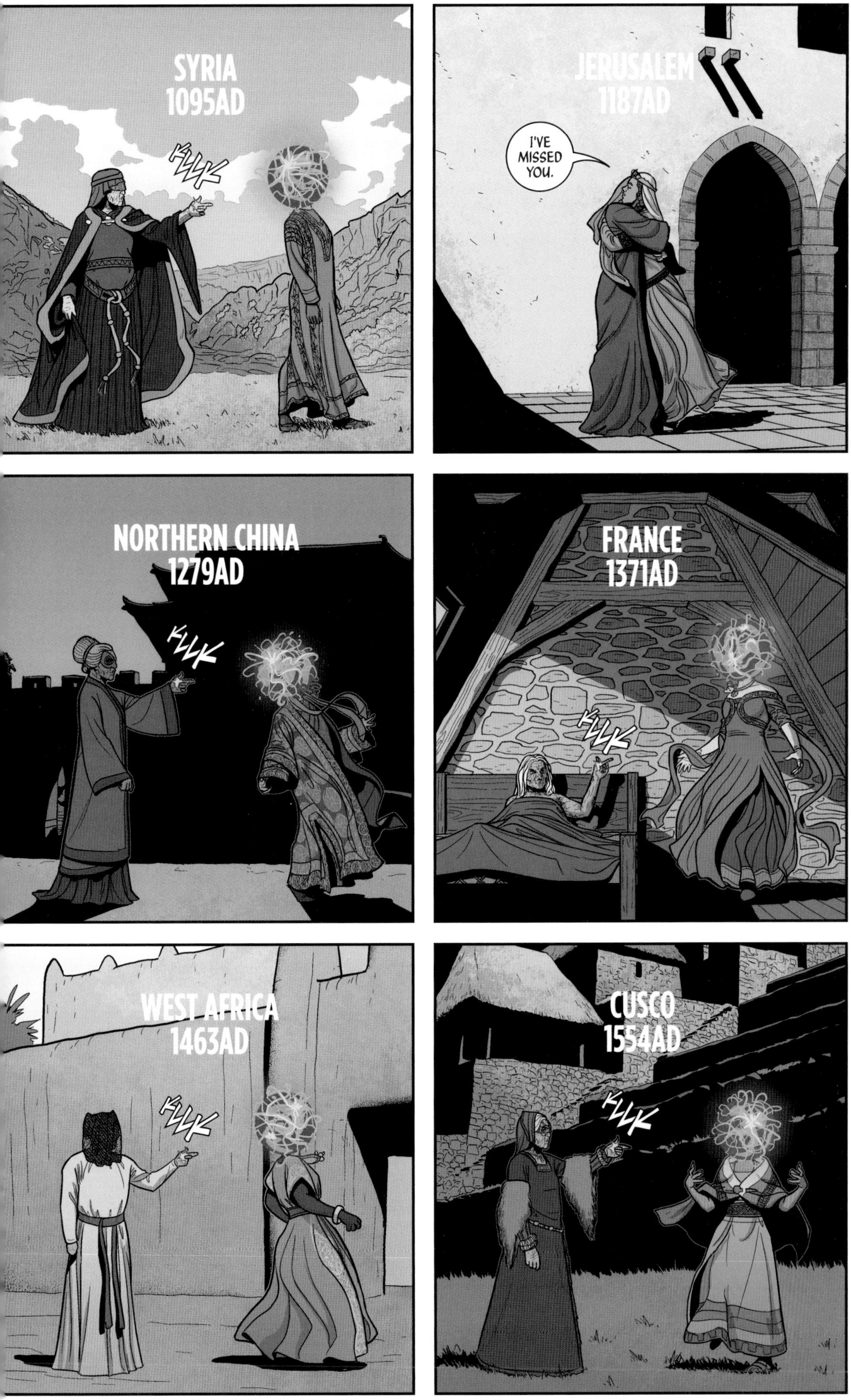
SYRIA
1095AD
KLLK
JERUSALEM
1187AD
I'VE MISSED YOU.
NORTHERN CHINA
1279AD
KLLK
FRANCE
1371AD
KLLK
WEST AFRICA
1463AD
KLLK
CUSCO
1554AD
KLLK

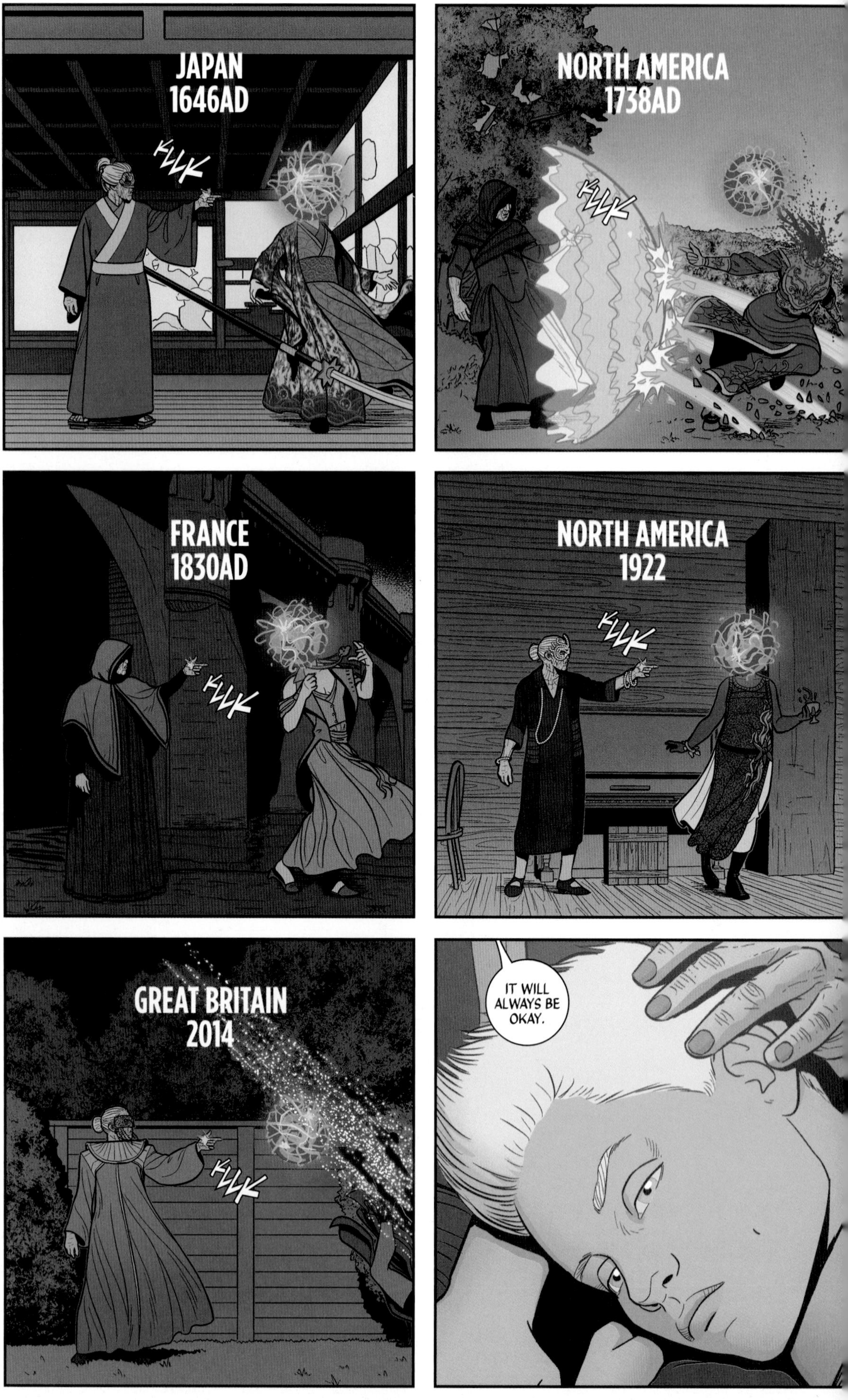
JAPAN
1646AD
KLLK
NORTH AMERICA
1738AD
KLLK
FRANCE
1830AD
KLLK
NORTH AMERICA
1922
KLLK
GREAT BRITAIN
2014
KLLK
IT WILL ALWAYS BE OKAY.

MONSTER

9 MARCH 2015

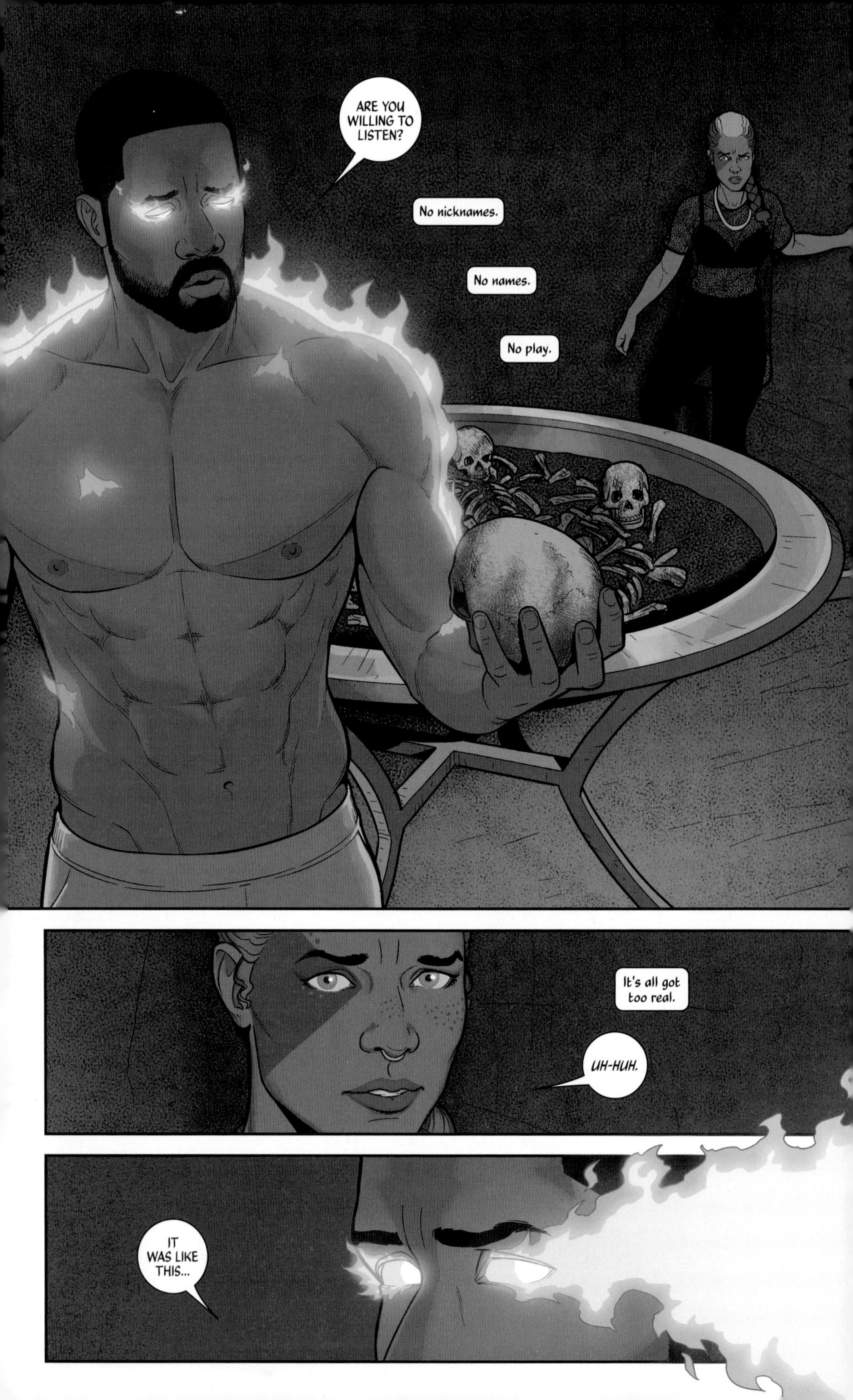
ARE YOU WILLING TO LISTEN?
No nicknames.
No names.
No play.
It's all got too real.
UH-HUH.
IT WAS LIKE THIS...

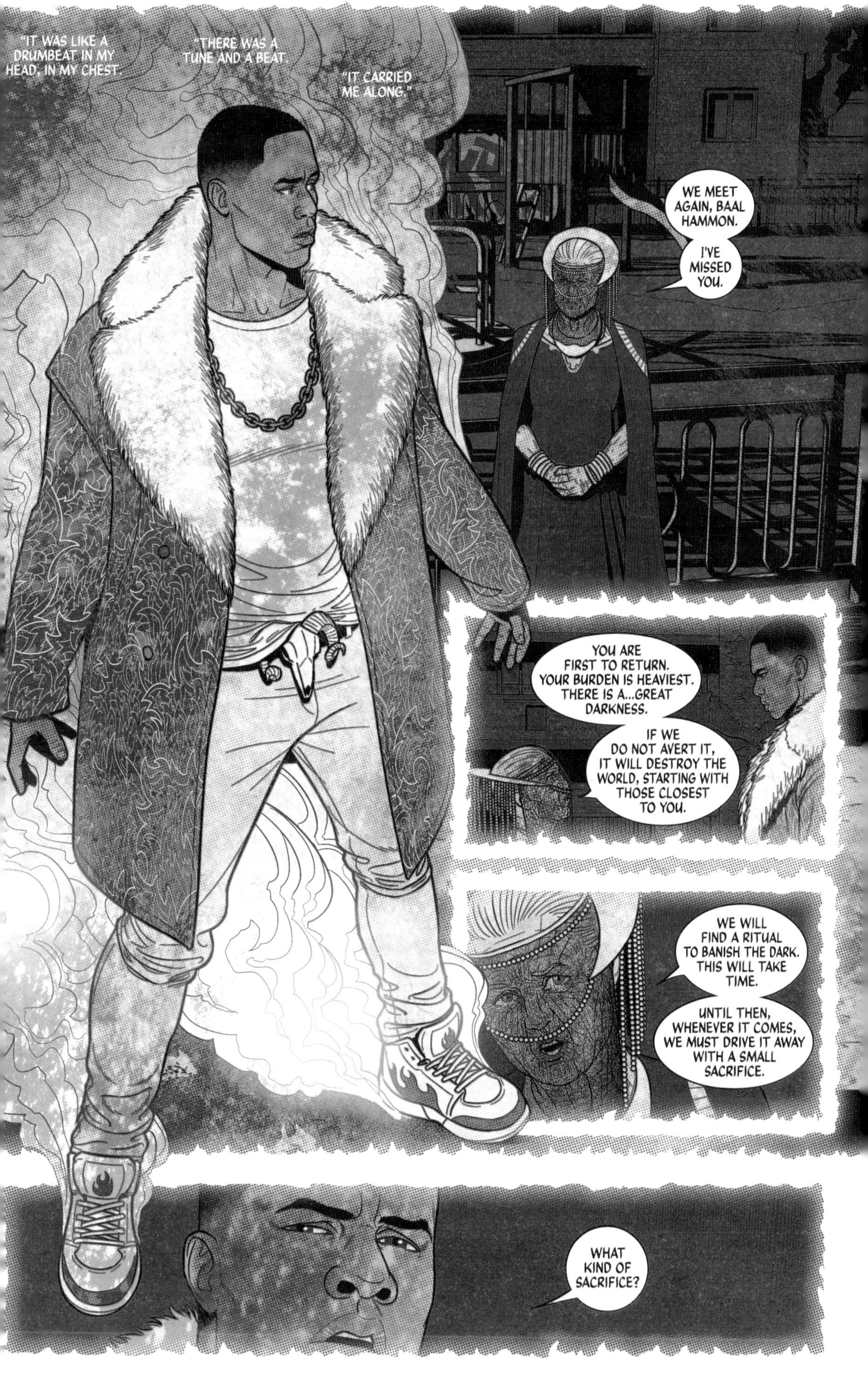
"IT WAS LIKE A DRUMBEAT IN MY HEAD, IN MY CHEST.
"THERE WAS A TUNE AND A BEAT.
"IT CARRIED ME ALONG."
WE MEET AGAIN, BAAL HAMMON.
I'VE MISSED YOU.
YOU ARE FIRST TO RETURN. YOUR BURDEN IS HEAVIEST. THERE IS A...GREAT DARKNESS.
IF WE DO NOT AVERT IT, IT WILL DESTROY THE WORLD, STARTING WITH THOSE CLOSEST TO YOU.
WE WILL FIND A RITUAL TO BANISH THE DARK. THIS WILL TAKE TIME.
UNTIL THEN, WHENEVER IT COMES, WE MUST DRIVE IT AWAY WITH A SMALL SACRIFICE.
WHAT KIND OF SACRIFICE?

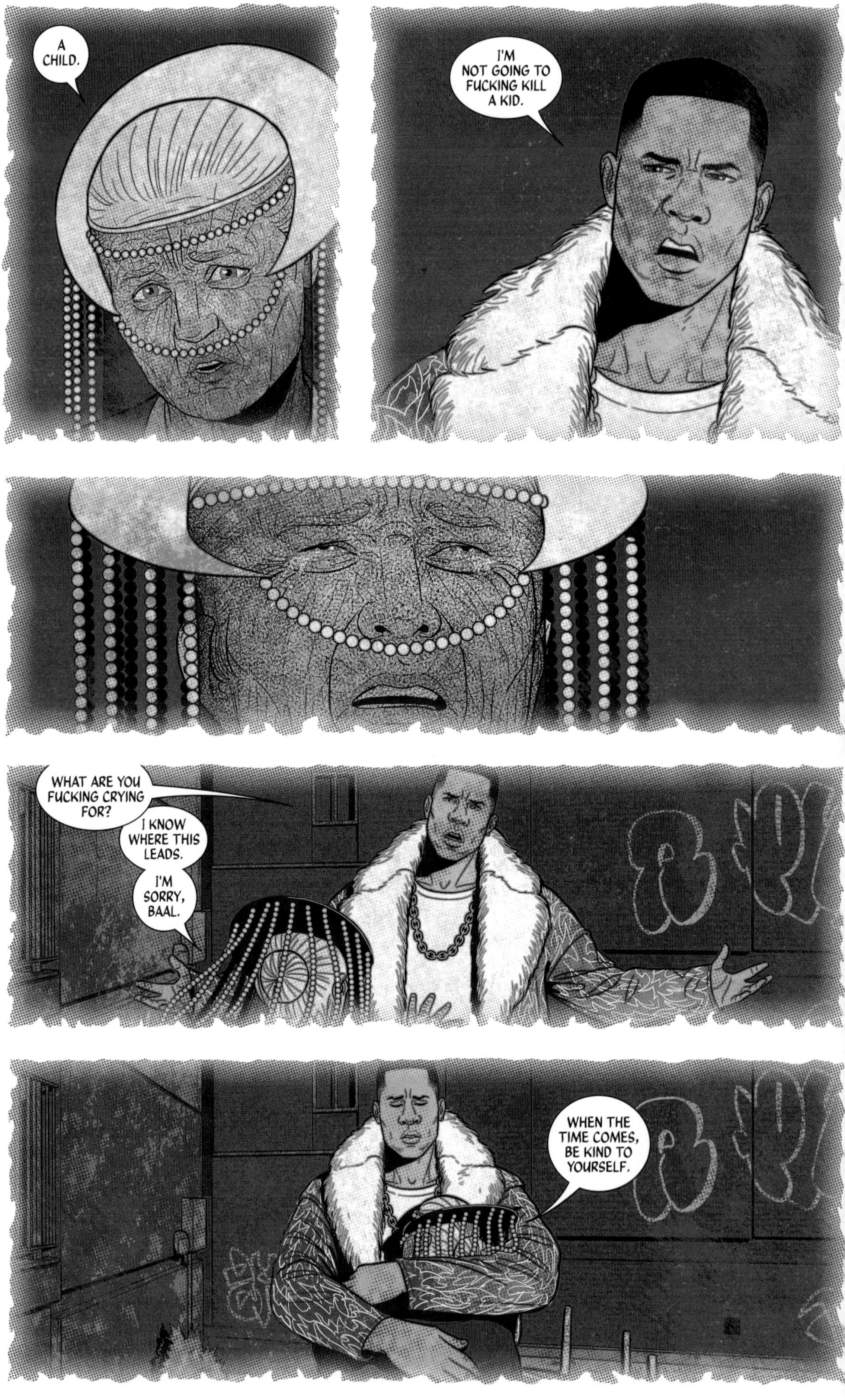
A CHILD.
I'M NOT GOING TO FUCKING KILL A KID.
WHAT ARE YOU FUCKING CRYING FOR?
I KNOW WHERE THIS LEADS.
I'M SORRY, BAAL.
WHEN THE TIME COMES, BE KIND TO YOURSELF.

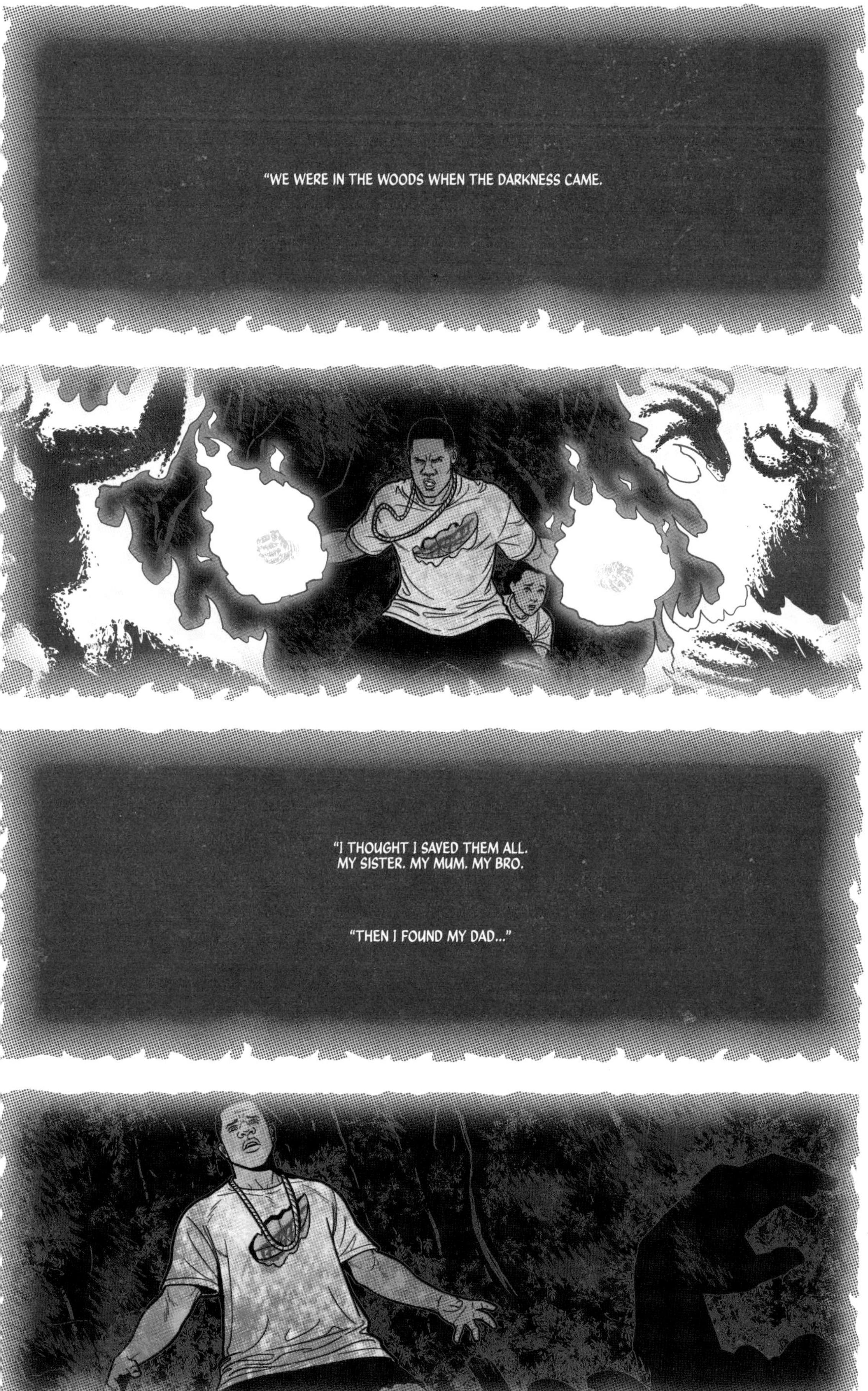
"WE WERE IN THE WOODS WHEN THE DARKNESS CAME.
"I THOUGHT I SAVED THEM ALL. MY SISTER. MY MUM. MY BRO.
"THEN I FOUND MY DAD..."

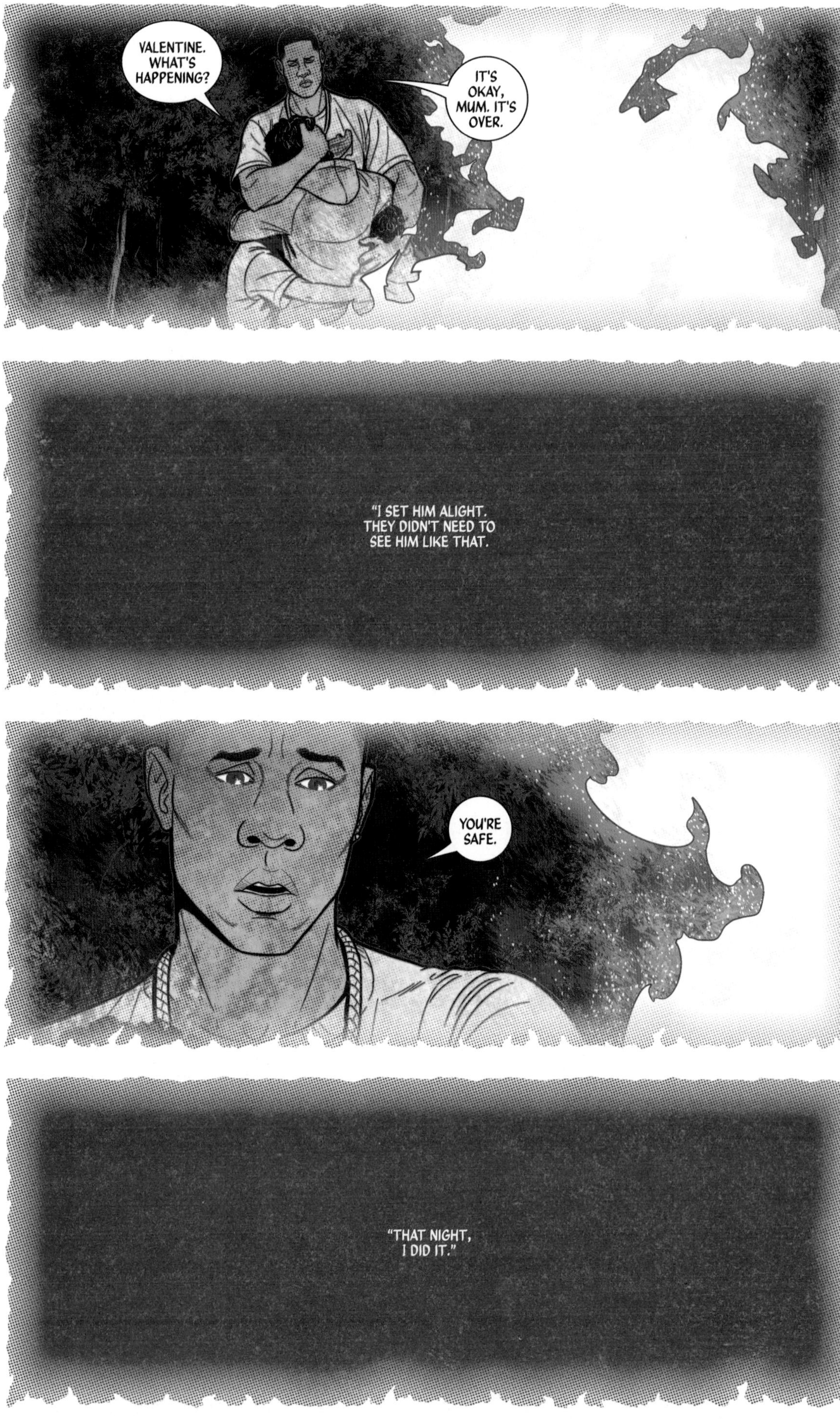
VALENTINE. WHAT'S HAPPENING?
IT'S OKAY, MUM. IT'S OVER.
"I SET HIM ALIGHT. THEY DIDN'T NEED TO SEE HIM LIKE THAT.
YOU'RE SAFE.
"THAT NIGHT, I DID IT."

"IN JANUARY, I
DID IT *AGAIN*.

"MAY,
AGAIN.

"SEPTEMBER,
AGAIN.

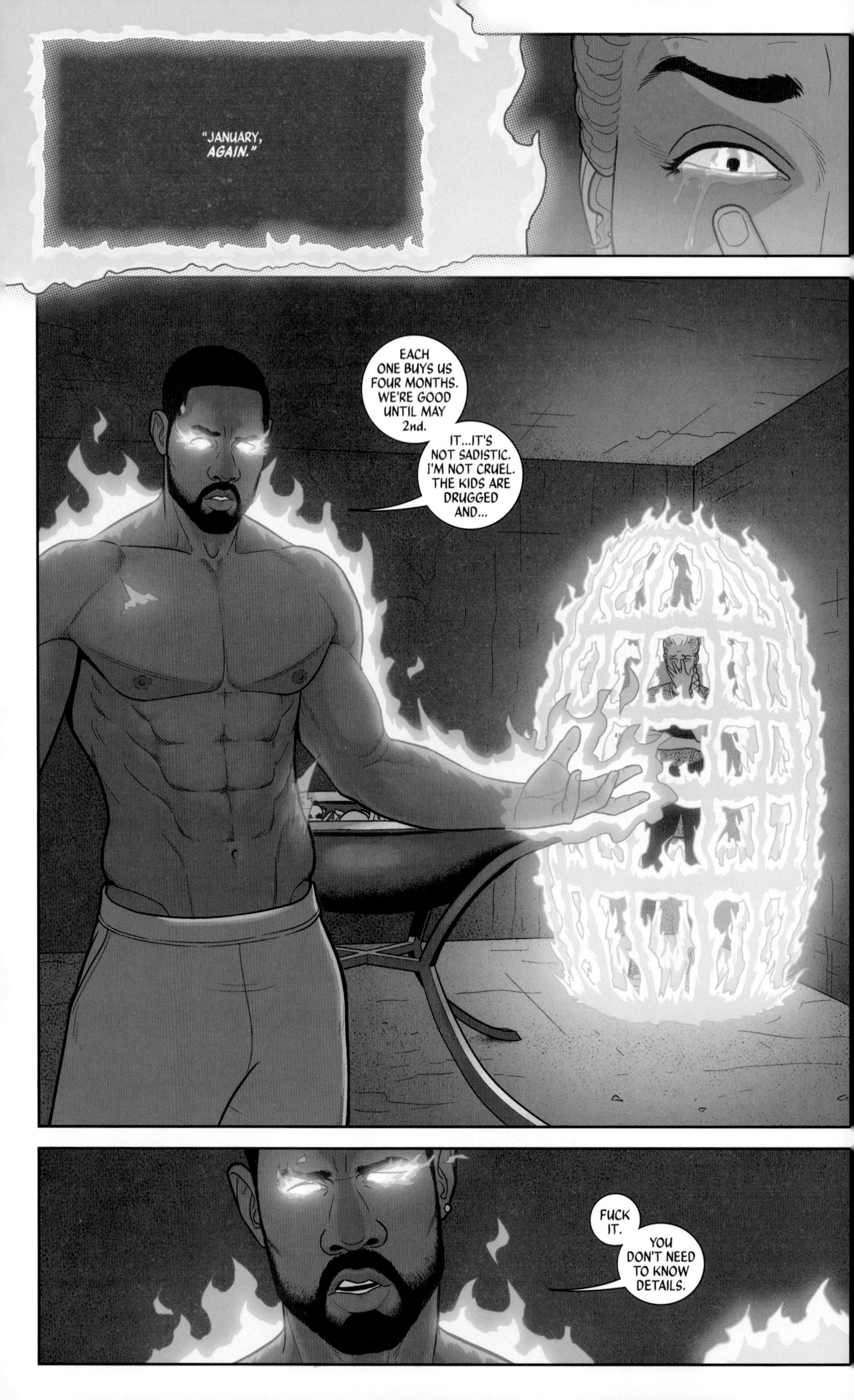
"JANUARY, AGAIN."
EACH ONE BUYS US FOUR MONTHS. WE'RE GOOD UNTIL MAY 2nd.
IT...IT'S NOT SADISTIC. I'M NOT CRUEL. THE KIDS ARE DRUGGED AND...
FUCK IT.
YOU DON'T NEED TO KNOW DETAILS.

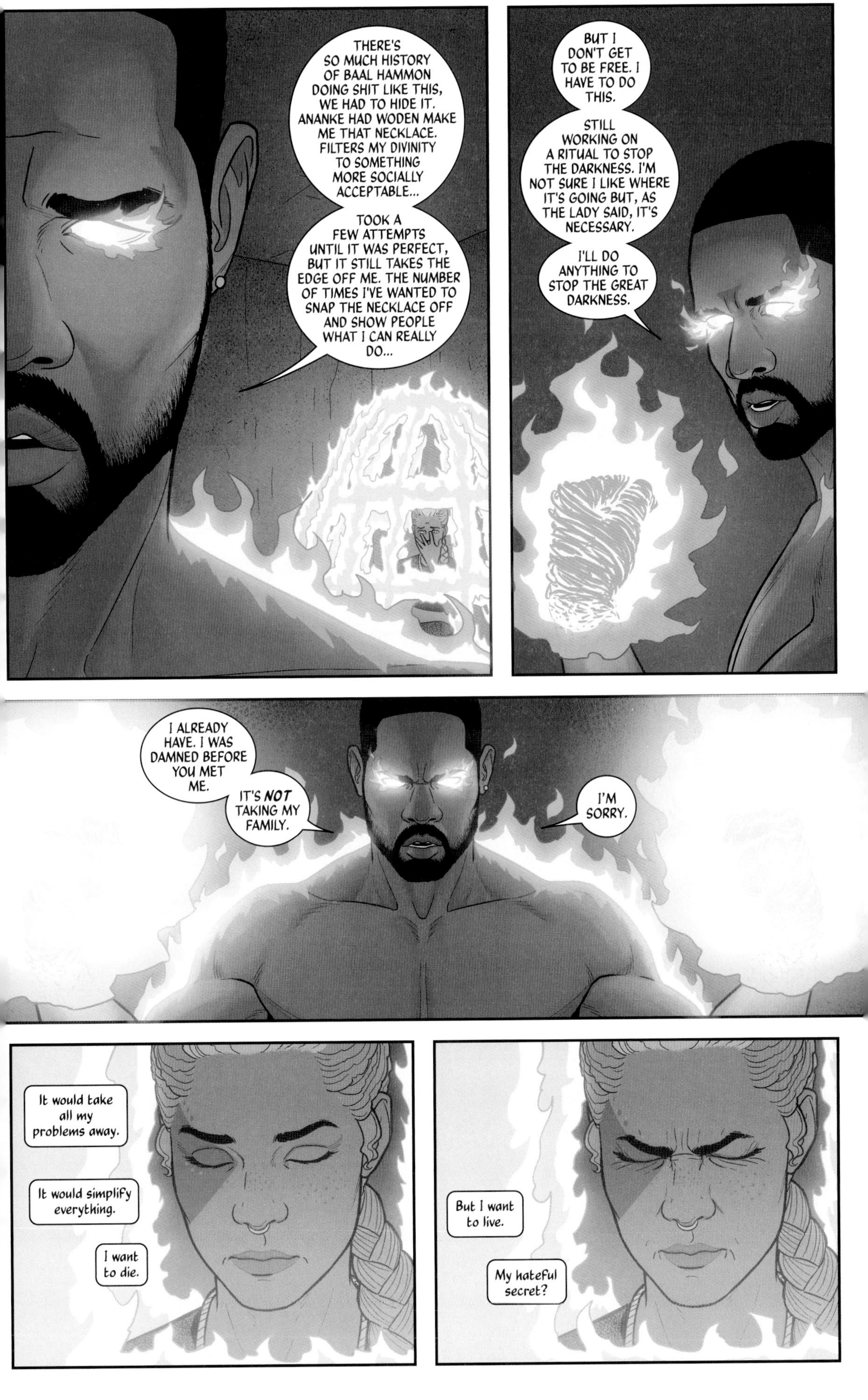
THERE'S SO MUCH HISTORY OF BAAL HAMMON DOING SHIT LIKE THIS, WE HAD TO HIDE IT. ANANKE HAD WODEN MAKE ME THAT NECKLACE. FILTERS MY DIVINITY TO SOMETHING MORE SOCIALLY ACCEPTABLE...
TOOK A FEW ATTEMPTS UNTIL IT WAS PERFECT, BUT IT STILL TAKES THE EDGE OFF ME. THE NUMBER OF TIMES I'VE WANTED TO SNAP THE NECKLACE OFF AND SHOW PEOPLE WHAT I CAN REALLY DO...
BUT I DON'T GET TO BE FREE. I HAVE TO DO THIS.
STILL WORKING ON A RITUAL TO STOP THE DARKNESS. I'M NOT SURE I LIKE WHERE IT'S GOING BUT, AS THE LADY SAID, IT'S NECESSARY.
I'LL DO ANYTHING TO STOP THE GREAT DARKNESS.
I ALREADY HAVE. I WAS DAMNED BEFORE YOU MET ME.
IT'S ***NOT*** TAKING MY FAMILY.
I'M SORRY.
It would take all my problems away.
It would simplify everything.
I want to die.
But I want to live.
My hateful secret?

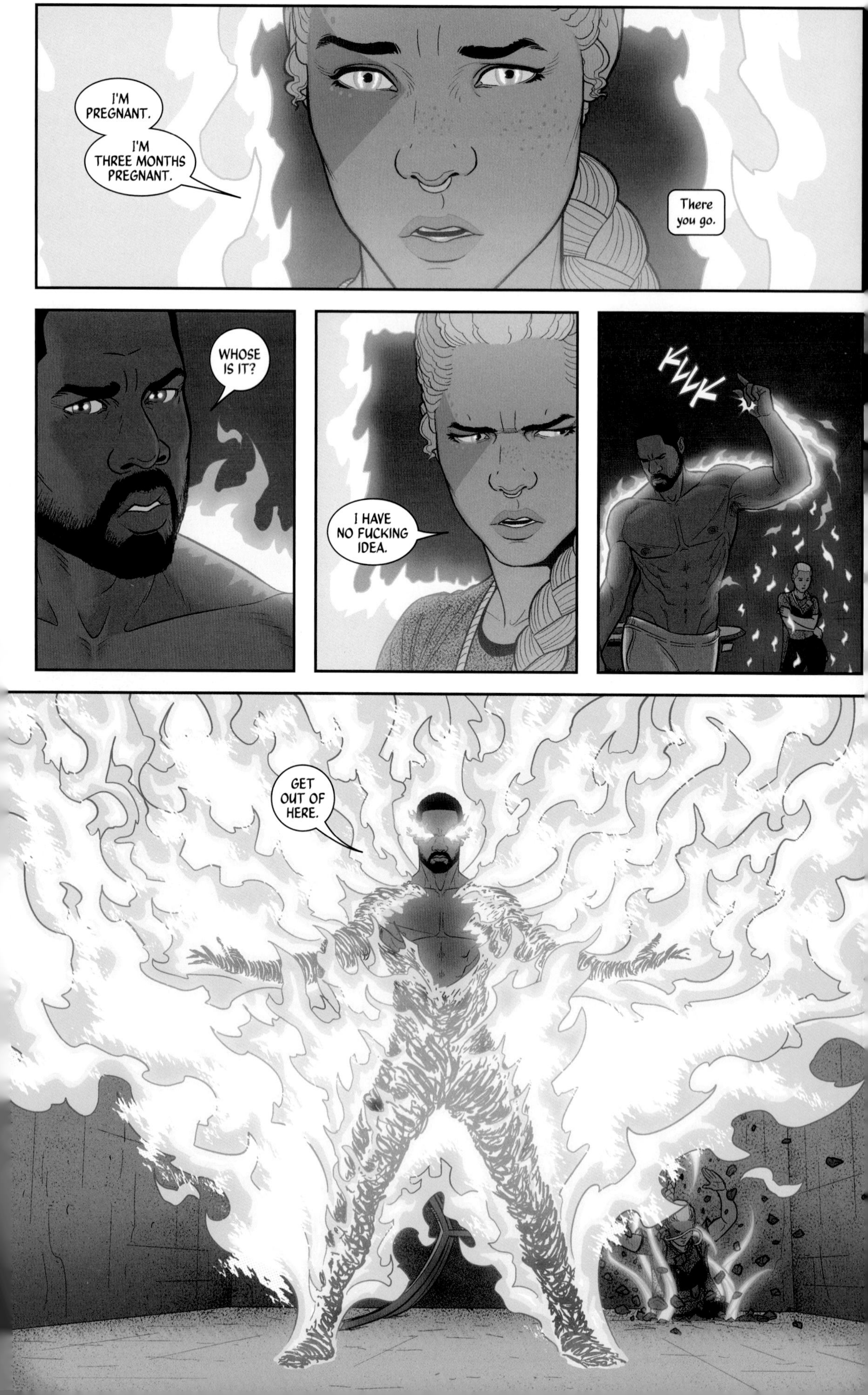
I'M PREGNANT.
I'M THREE MONTHS PREGNANT.
There you go.
WHOSE IS IT?
I HAVE NO FUCKING IDEA.
KLLK
GET OUT OF HERE.

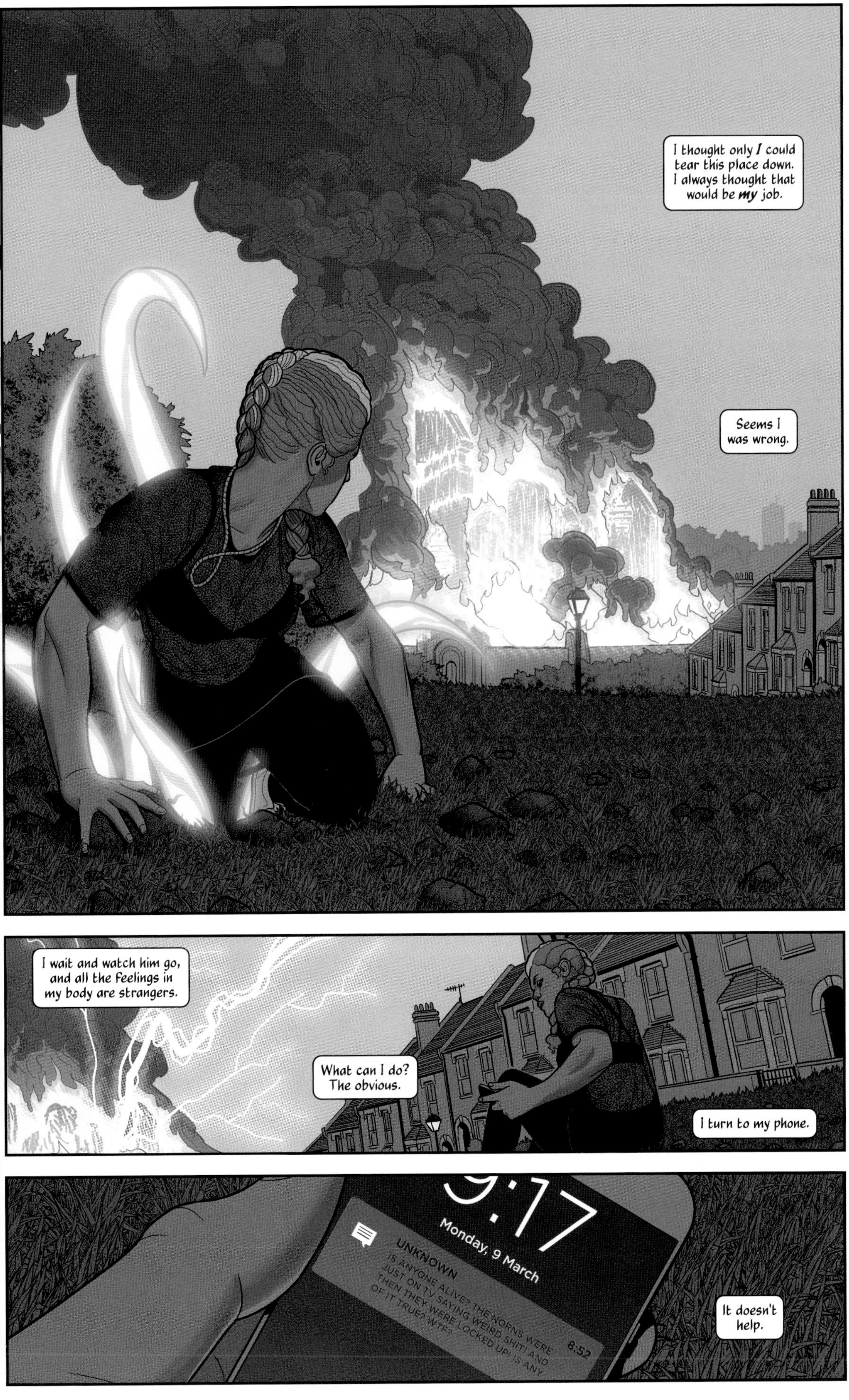

I thought only *I* could tear this place down. I always thought that would be ***my*** job.
Seems I was wrong.
I wait and watch him go, and all the feelings in my body are strangers.
What can I do? The obvious.
I turn to my phone.
9:17
Monday, 9 March
UNKNOWN
8:52
IS ANYONE ALIVE? THE NORNS WERE JUST ON TV SAYING WEIRD SHIT! AND THEN THEY WERE LOCKED UP! IS ANY OF IT TRUE? WTF?
It doesn't help.

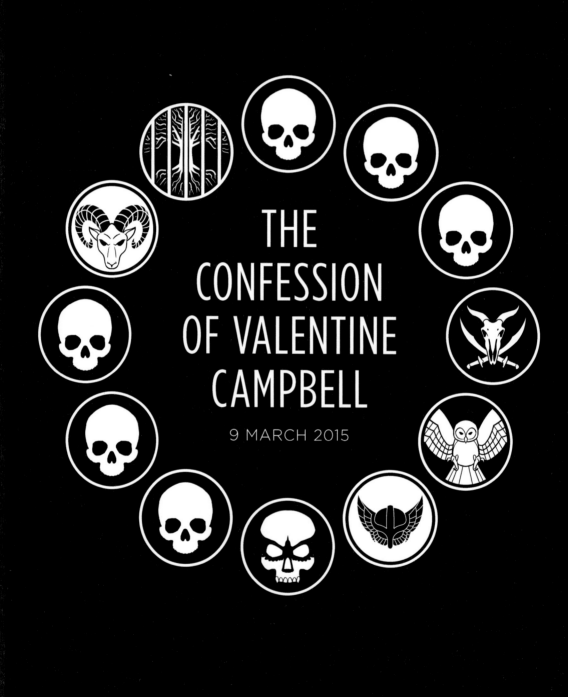

THE
CONFESSION
OF VALENTINE
CAMPBELL

9 MARCH 2015

THE
WICKED
+
THE
DIVINE

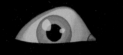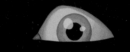

THE
WICKED
+
THE DIVINE

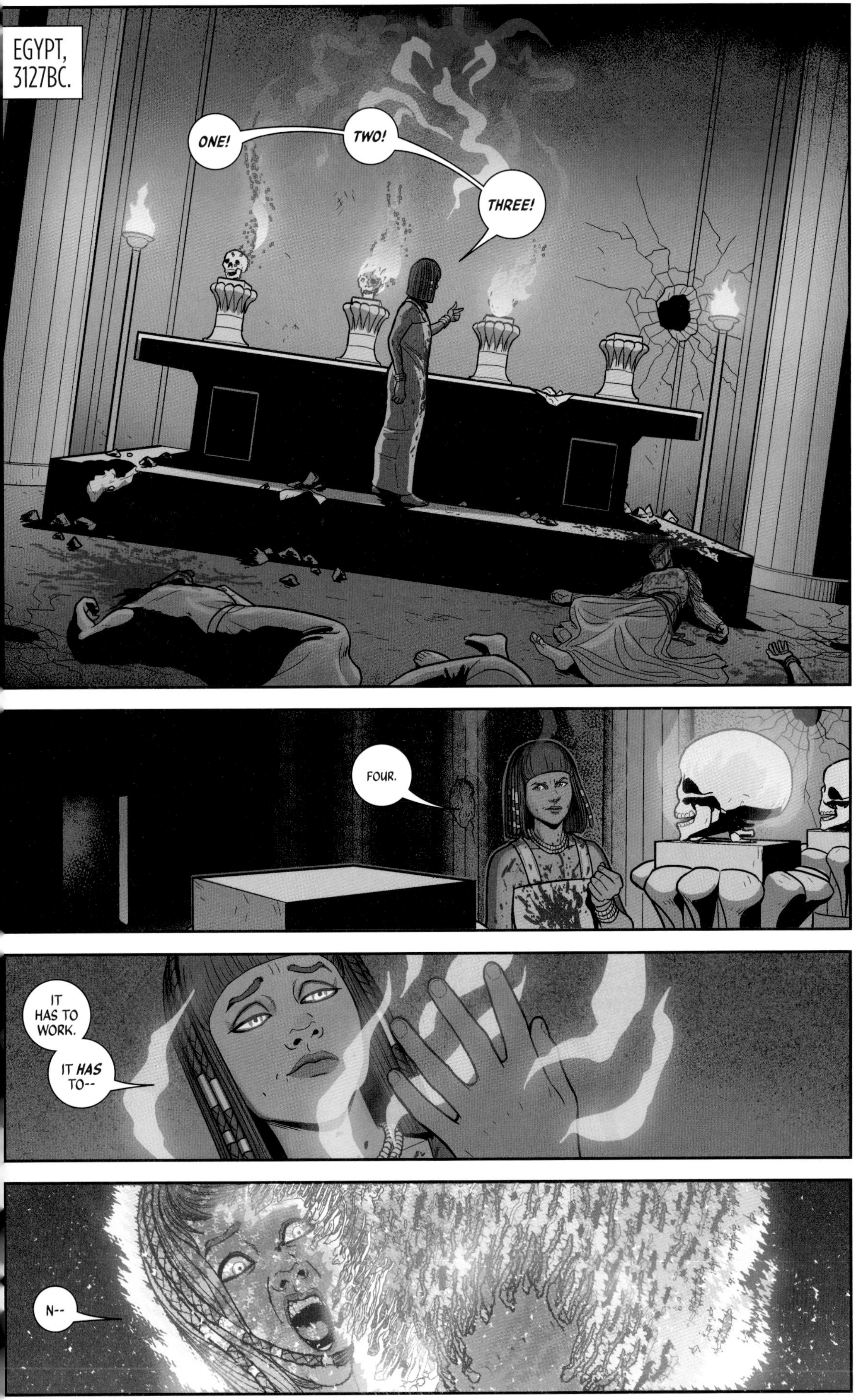
EGYPT, 3127BC.
ONE!
TWO!
THREE!
FOUR.
IT HAS TO WORK.
IT HAS TO--
N--

3126BC	**3125BC**	**3124BC**
3123BC	**3122BC**	**3121BC**
3120BC	**3119BC**	**3118BC**

3117BC	3116BC	3115BC
3114BC	3113BC	3112BC
3111BC	3110BC	3109BC

3108BC	3107BC	3106BC
3105BC	3104BC	3103BC
3102BC	3101BC	3100BC

3099BC

3098BC

3097BC

3096BC

3095BC

3094BC

3093BC

3092BC

3091BC

3090BC	3089BC	3088BC
3087BC	3086BC	3085BC
3084BC	3083BC	3082BC

3081BC

3080BC

3079BC

3078BC

3077BC

3076BC

3075BC

3074BC

3073BC

3072BC	3071BC	3070BC
3069BC	3068BC	3067BC
3066BC	3065BC	3064BC

3063BC	3062BC	3061BC

3060BC	3059BC	3058BC

3057BC	3056BC	3055BC

3054BC	3053BC	3052BC

3051BC	3050BC	3049BC

3048BC	3047BC	3046BC

3045BC	3044BC	3043BC
3042BC	3041BC	3040BC
3039BC	3038BC	3037BC

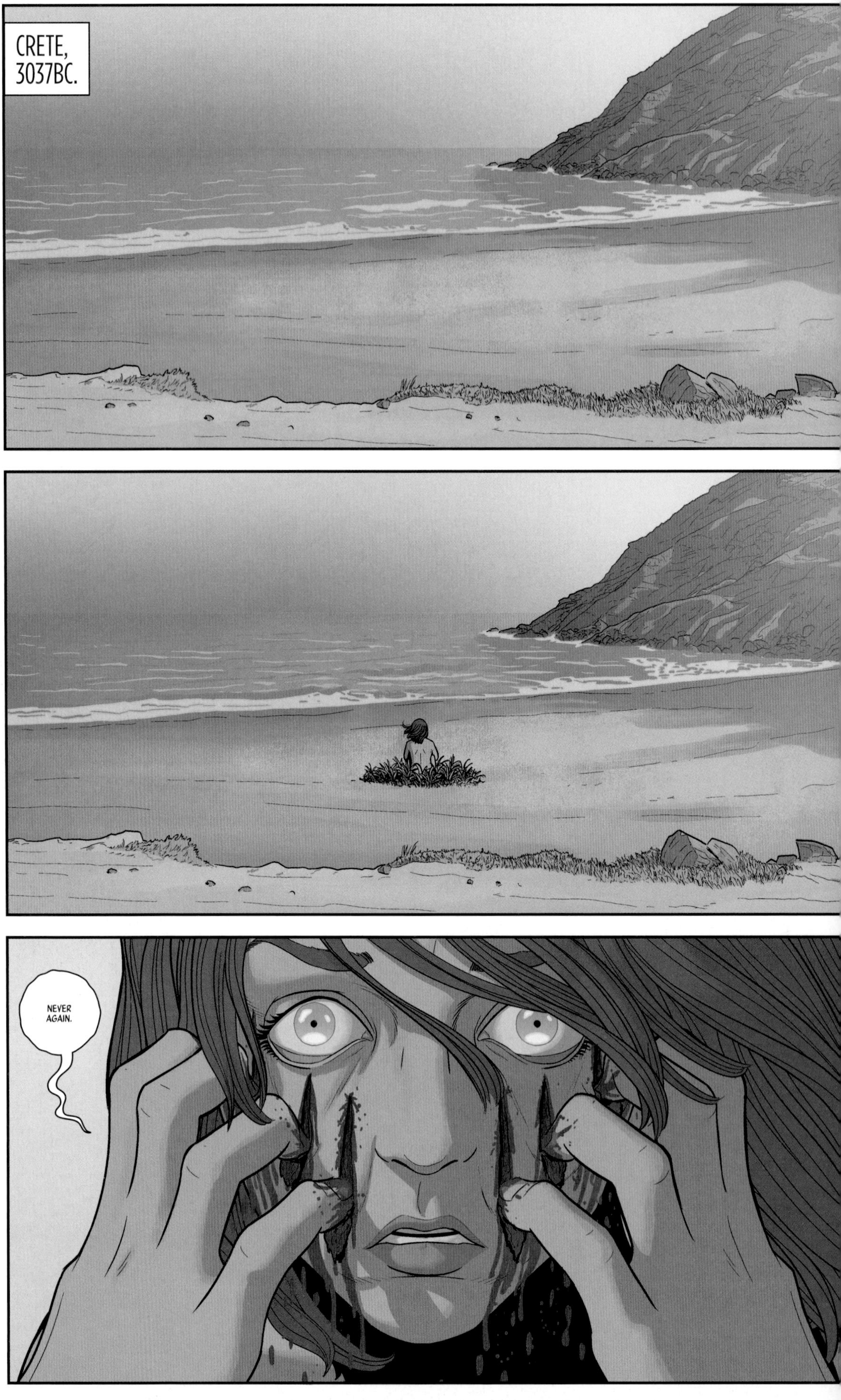
CRETE,
3037BC.
NEVER AGAIN.

NOTHING TO
BE SCARED OF

9 MARCH 2015

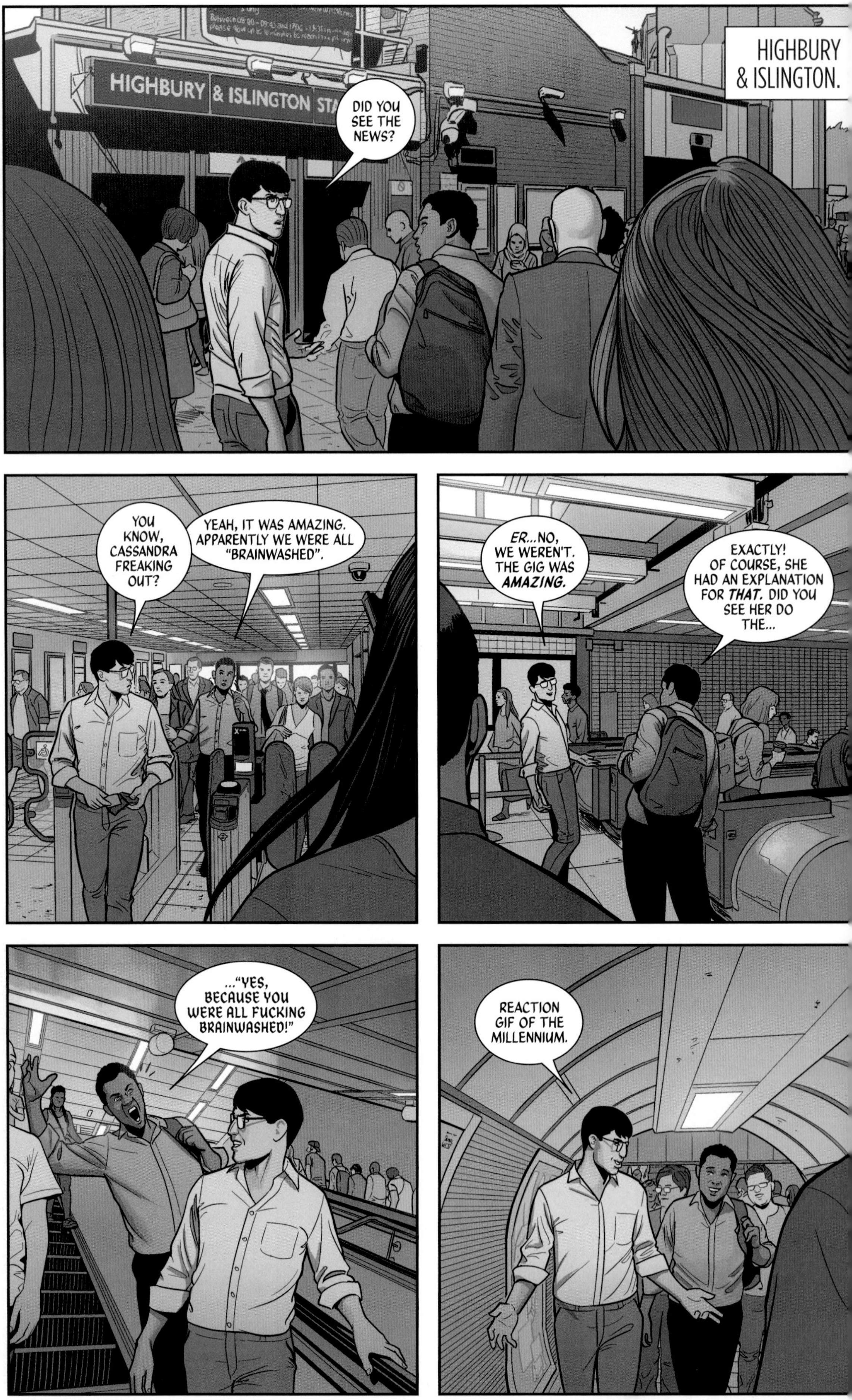
HIGHBURY & ISLINGTON.
HIGHBURY & ISLINGTON STA
DID YOU SEE THE NEWS?
YOU KNOW, CASSANDRA FREAKING OUT?
YEAH, IT WAS AMAZING. APPARENTLY WE WERE ALL "BRAINWASHED".
ER...NO, WE WEREN'T. THE GIG WAS AMAZING.
EXACTLY! OF COURSE, SHE HAD AN EXPLANATION FOR THAT. DID YOU SEE HER DO THE...
..."YES, BECAUSE YOU WERE ALL FUCKING BRAINWASHED!"
REACTION GIF OF THE MILLENNIUM.

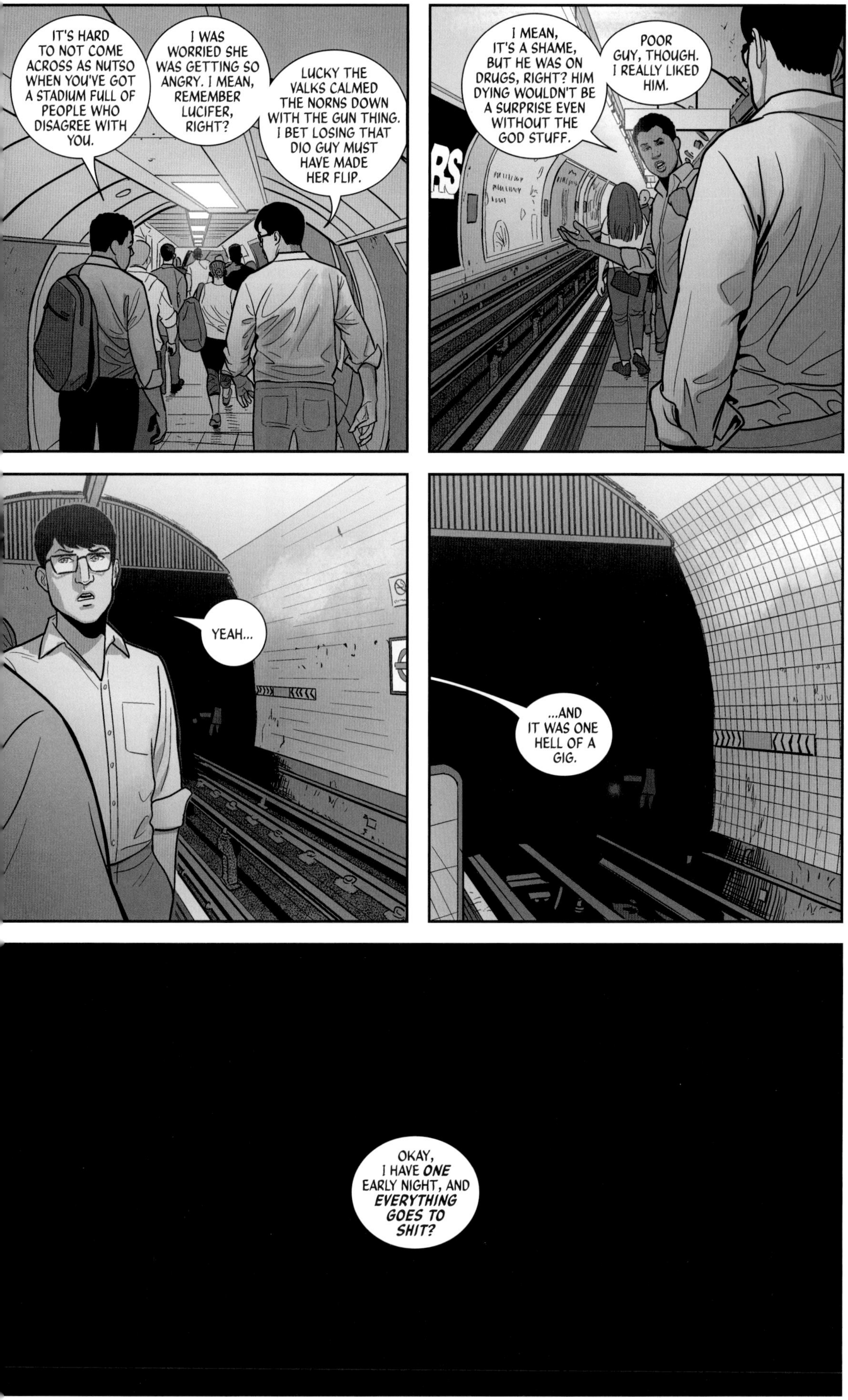
IT'S HARD TO NOT COME ACROSS AS NUTSO WHEN YOU'VE GOT A STADIUM FULL OF PEOPLE WHO DISAGREE WITH YOU.
I WAS WORRIED SHE WAS GETTING SO ANGRY. I MEAN, REMEMBER LUCIFER, RIGHT?
LUCKY THE VALKS CALMED THE NORNS DOWN WITH THE GUN THING. I BET LOSING THAT DIO GUY MUST HAVE MADE HER FLIP.
I MEAN, IT'S A SHAME, BUT HE WAS ON DRUGS, RIGHT? HIM DYING WOULDN'T BE A SURPRISE EVEN WITHOUT THE GOD STUFF.
POOR GUY, THOUGH. I REALLY LIKED HIM.
YEAH...
...AND IT WAS ONE HELL OF A GIG.
OKAY, I HAVE *ONE* EARLY NIGHT, AND *EVERYTHING GOES TO SHIT?*

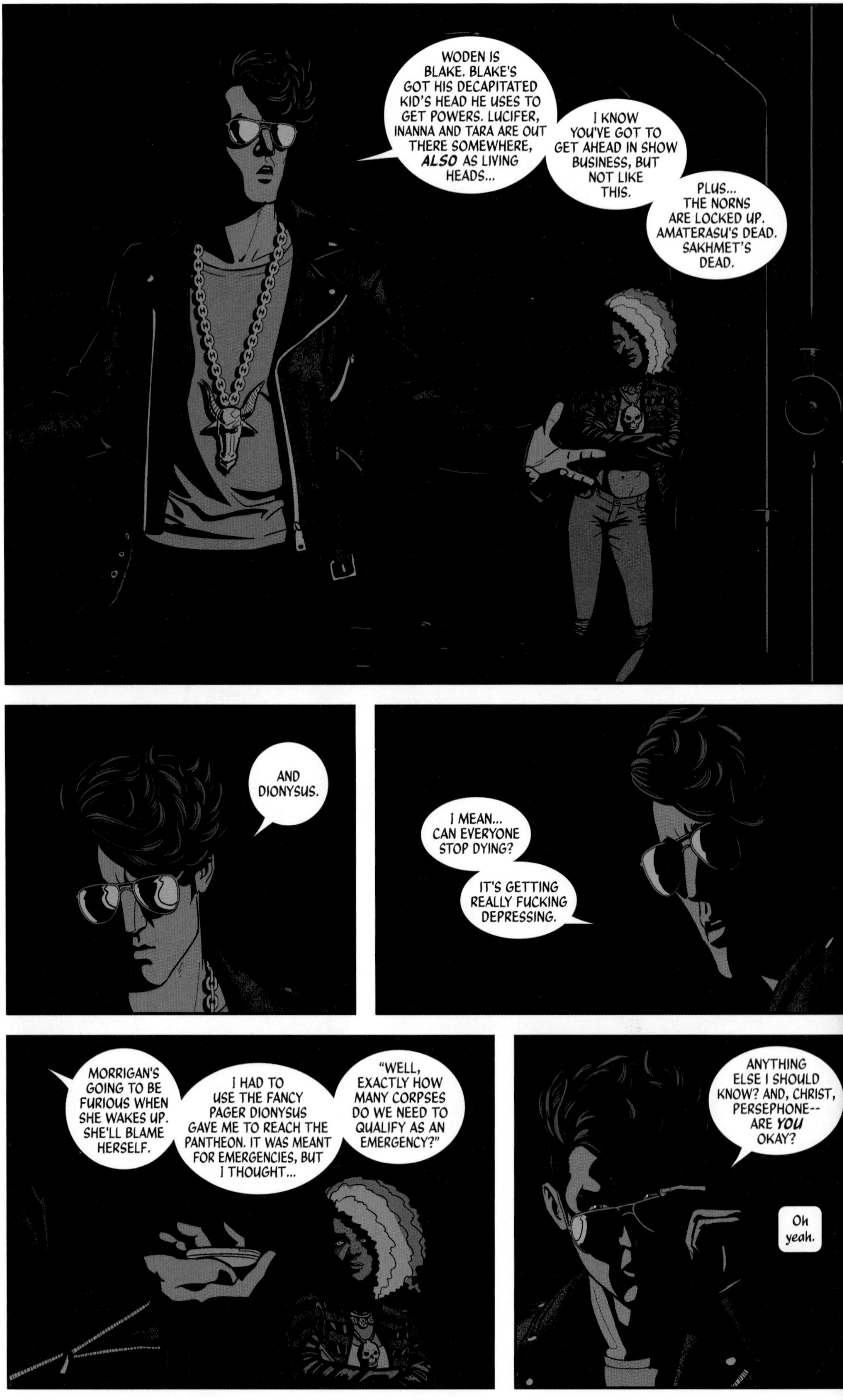
WODEN IS BLAKE. BLAKE'S GOT HIS DECAPITATED KID'S HEAD HE USES TO GET POWERS. LUCIFER, INANNA AND TARA ARE OUT THERE SOMEWHERE, ALSO AS LIVING HEADS...
I KNOW YOU'VE GOT TO GET AHEAD IN SHOW BUSINESS, BUT NOT LIKE THIS.
PLUS... THE NORNS ARE LOCKED UP. AMATERASU'S DEAD. SAKHMET'S DEAD.
AND DIONYSUS.
I MEAN... CAN EVERYONE STOP DYING?
IT'S GETTING REALLY FUCKING DEPRESSING.
MORRIGAN'S GOING TO BE FURIOUS WHEN SHE WAKES UP. SHE'LL BLAME HERSELF.
I HAD TO USE THE FANCY PAGER DIONYSUS GAVE ME TO REACH THE PANTHEON. IT WAS MEANT FOR EMERGENCIES, BUT I THOUGHT...
"WELL, EXACTLY HOW MANY CORPSES DO WE NEED TO QUALIFY AS AN EMERGENCY?"
ANYTHING ELSE I SHOULD KNOW? AND, CHRIST, PERSEPHONE-- ARE YOU OKAY?
Oh yeah.

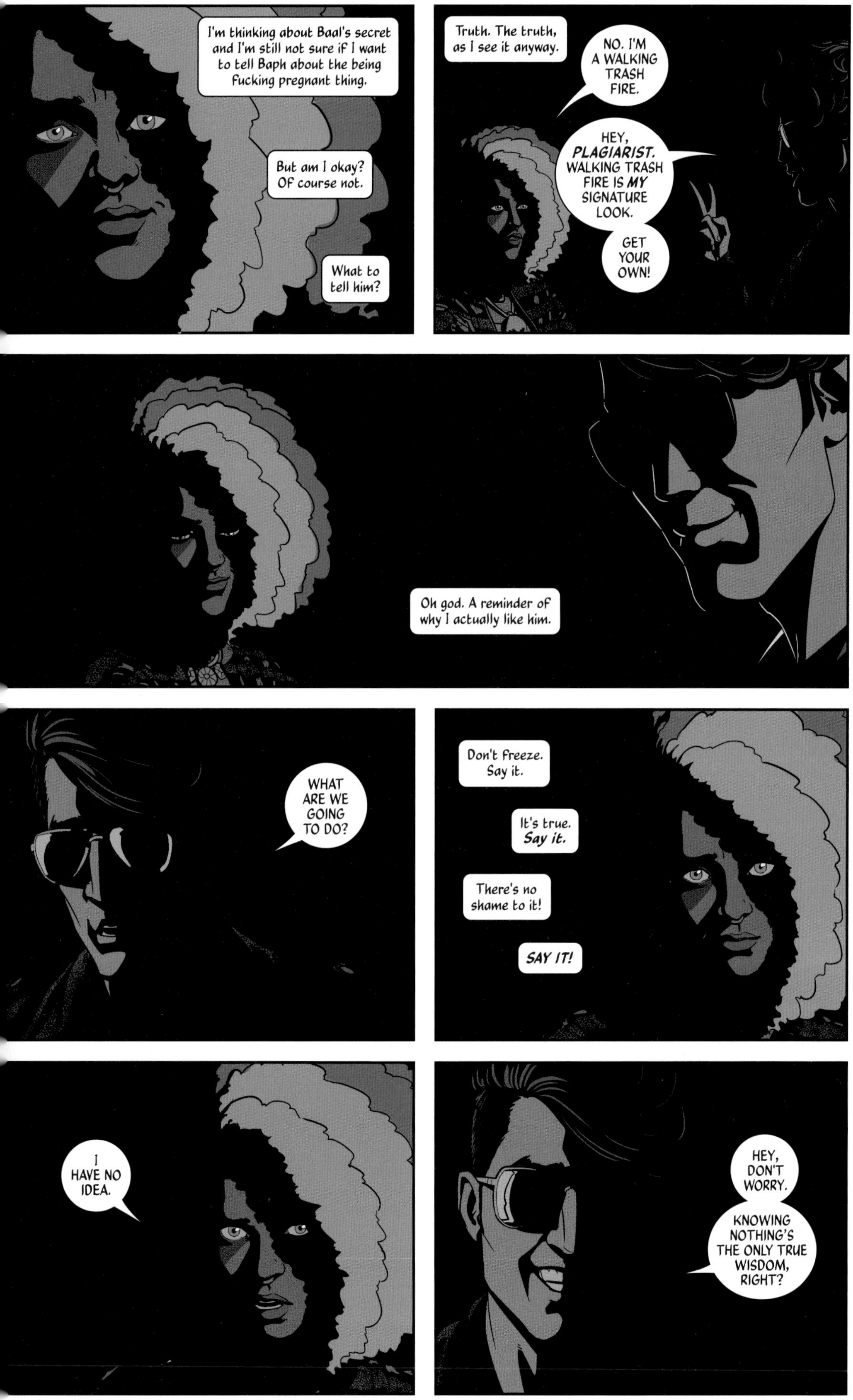
I'm thinking about Baal's secret and I'm still not sure if I want to tell Baph about the being fucking pregnant thing.
But am I okay? Of course not.
What to tell him?
Truth. The truth, as I see it anyway.
NO. I'M A WALKING TRASH FIRE.
HEY, *PLAGIARIST.* WALKING TRASH FIRE IS *MY* SIGNATURE LOOK.
GET YOUR OWN!
Oh god. A reminder of why I actually like him.
WHAT ARE WE GOING TO DO?
Don't freeze. Say it.
It's true. *Say it.*
There's no shame to it!
SAY IT!
I HAVE NO IDEA.
HEY, DON'T WORRY.
KNOWING NOTHING'S THE ONLY TRUE WISDOM, RIGHT?

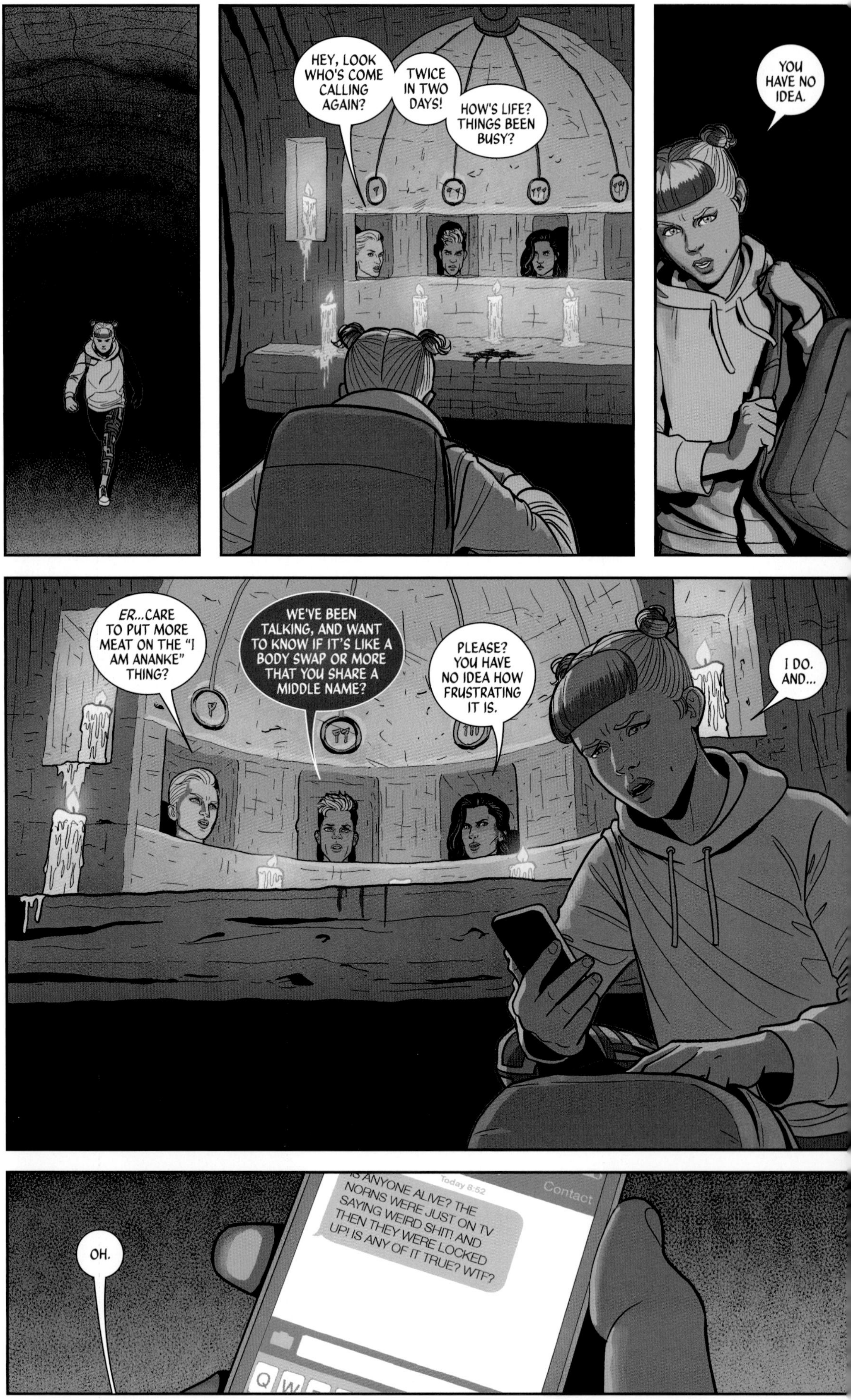
HEY, LOOK WHO'S COME CALLING AGAIN?
TWICE IN TWO DAYS!
HOW'S LIFE? THINGS BEEN BUSY?
YOU HAVE NO IDEA.
ER...CARE TO PUT MORE MEAT ON THE "I AM ANANKE" THING?
WE'VE BEEN TALKING, AND WANT TO KNOW IF IT'S LIKE A BODY SWAP OR MORE THAT YOU SHARE A MIDDLE NAME?
PLEASE? YOU HAVE NO IDEA HOW FRUSTRATING IT IS.
I DO. AND...
Today 8:52
Contact
IS ANYONE ALIVE? THE NORNS WERE JUST ON TV SAYING WEIRD SHIT! AND THEN THEY WERE LOCKED UP! IS ANY OF IT TRUE? WTF?
OH.

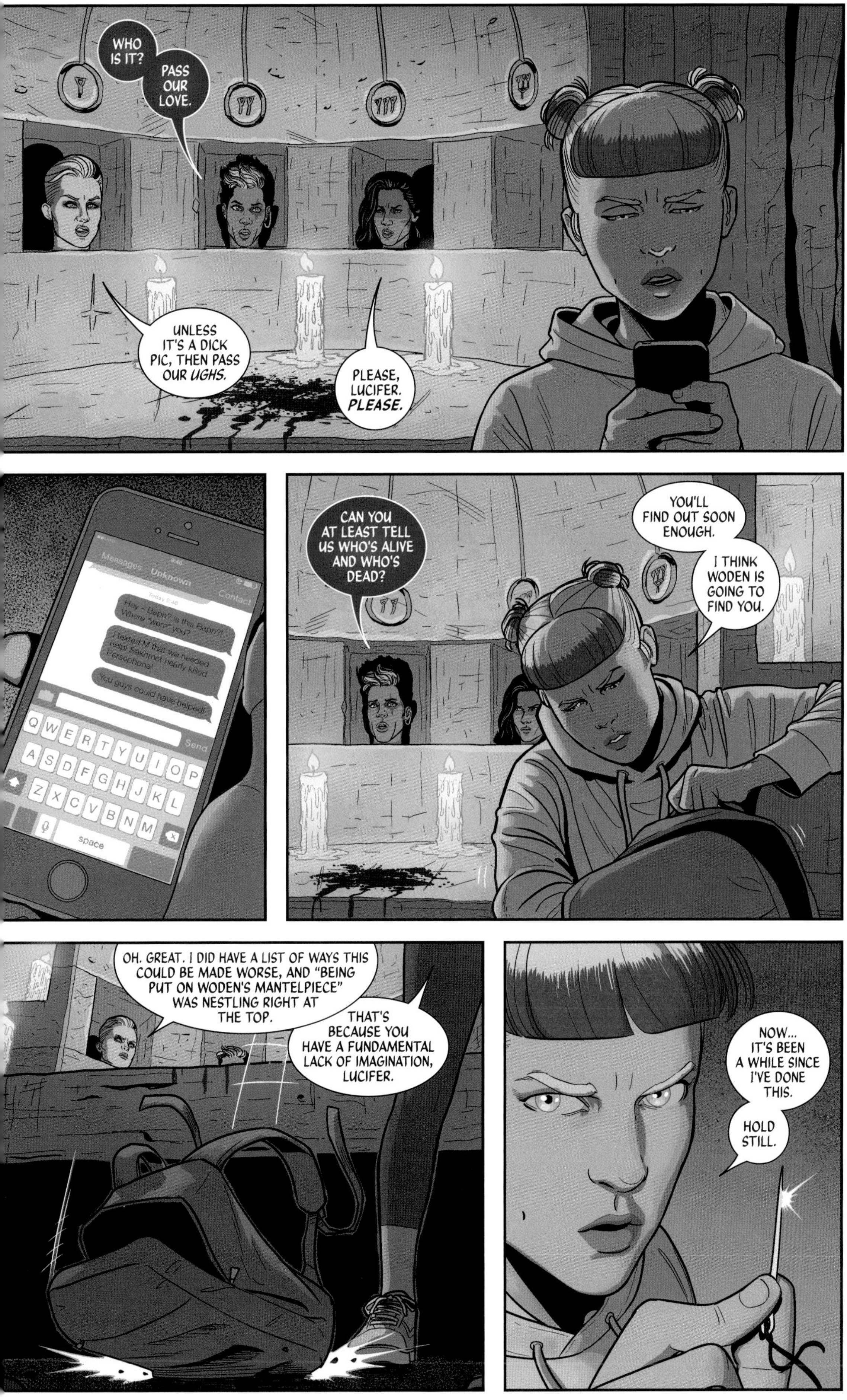
WHO IS IT?
PASS OUR LOVE.
UNLESS IT'S A DICK PIC, THEN PASS OUR *UGHS.*
PLEASE, LUCIFER. ***PLEASE.***
Messages Unknown Contact
Hey – Baph? Is this Baph?! Where *were* you?
I texted M that we needed help! Sakhmet nearly killed Persephone!
You guys could have helped!
CAN YOU AT LEAST TELL US WHO'S ALIVE AND WHO'S DEAD?
YOU'LL FIND OUT SOON ENOUGH.
I THINK WODEN IS GOING TO FIND YOU.
OH. GREAT. I DID HAVE A LIST OF WAYS THIS COULD BE MADE WORSE, AND "BEING PUT ON WODEN'S MANTELPIECE" WAS NESTLING RIGHT AT THE TOP.
THAT'S BECAUSE YOU HAVE A FUNDAMENTAL LACK OF IMAGINATION, LUCIFER.
NOW... IT'S BEEN A WHILE SINCE I'VE DONE THIS.
HOLD STILL.

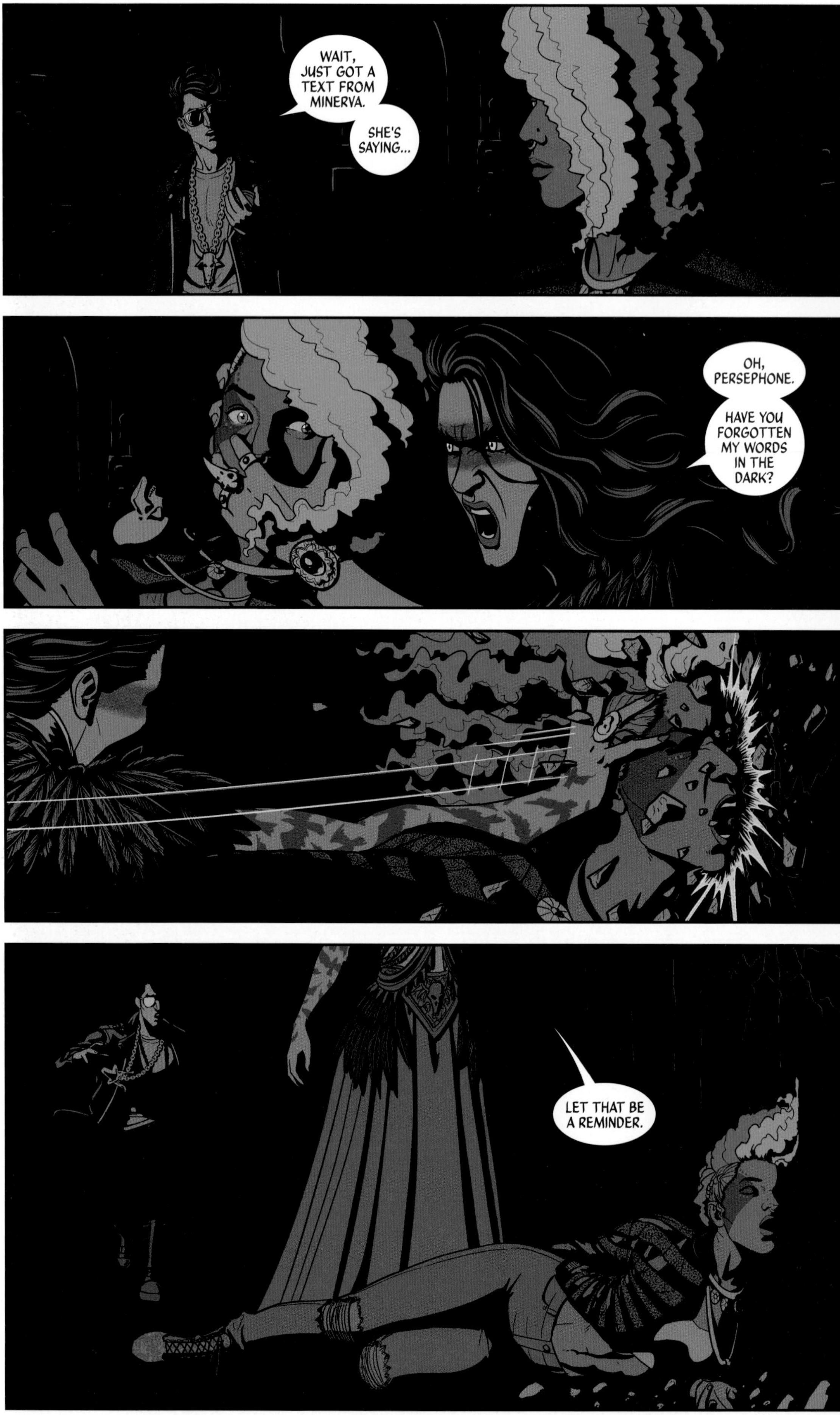
WAIT, JUST GOT A TEXT FROM MINERVA.
SHE'S SAYING...
OH, PERSEPHONE.
HAVE YOU FORGOTTEN MY WORDS IN THE DARK?
LET THAT BE A REMINDER.

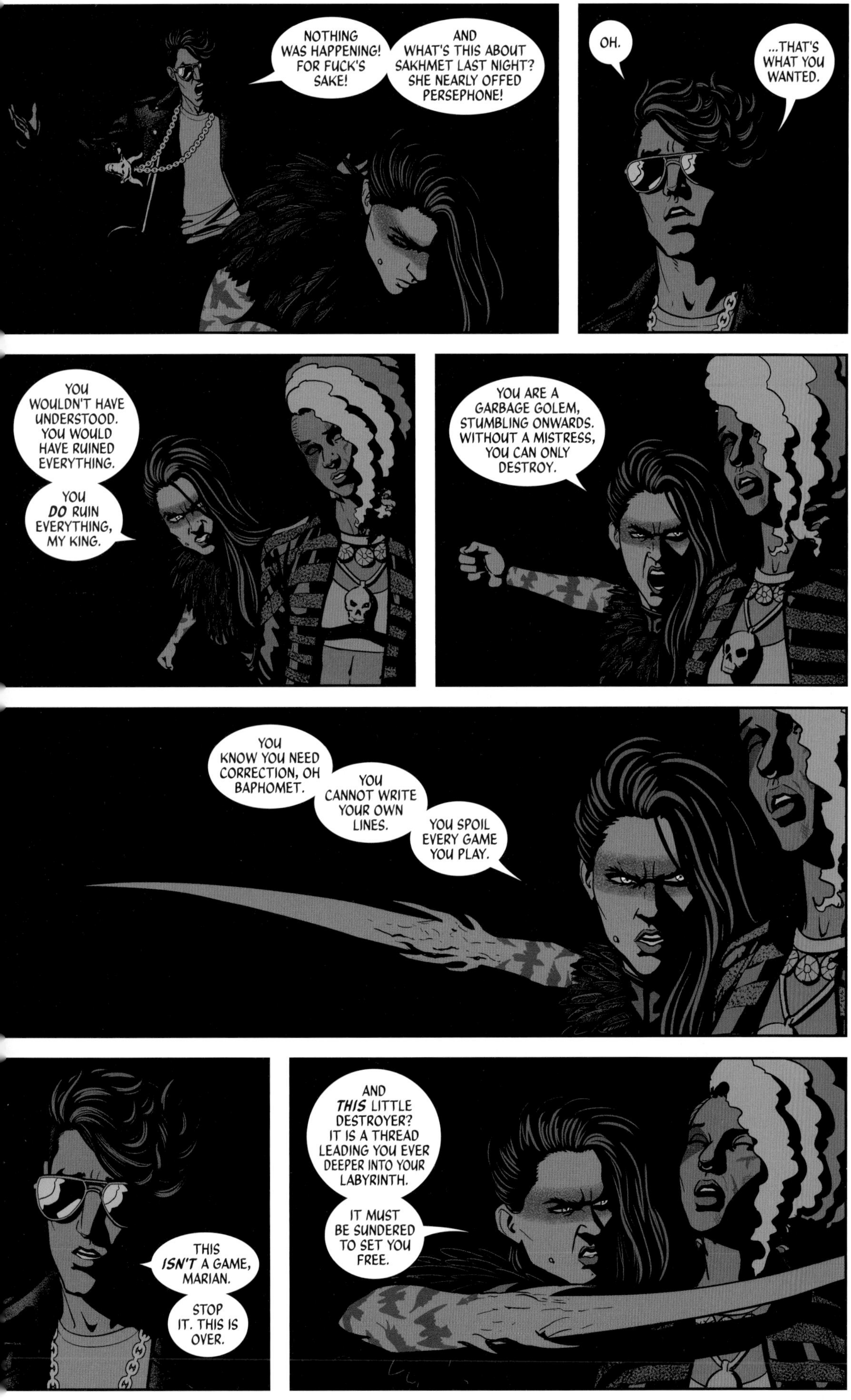
NOTHING WAS HAPPENING! FOR FUCK'S SAKE!
AND WHAT'S THIS ABOUT SAKHMET LAST NIGHT? SHE NEARLY OFFED PERSEPHONE!
OH.
...THAT'S WHAT YOU WANTED.
YOU WOULDN'T HAVE UNDERSTOOD. YOU WOULD HAVE RUINED EVERYTHING.
YOU *DO* RUIN EVERYTHING, MY KING.
YOU ARE A GARBAGE GOLEM, STUMBLING ONWARDS. WITHOUT A MISTRESS, YOU CAN ONLY DESTROY.
YOU KNOW YOU NEED CORRECTION, OH BAPHOMET.
YOU CANNOT WRITE YOUR OWN LINES.
YOU SPOIL EVERY GAME YOU PLAY.
THIS *ISN'T* A GAME, MARIAN.
STOP IT. THIS IS OVER.
AND *THIS* LITTLE DESTROYER? IT IS A THREAD LEADING YOU EVER DEEPER INTO YOUR LABYRINTH.
IT MUST BE SUNDERED TO SET YOU FREE.

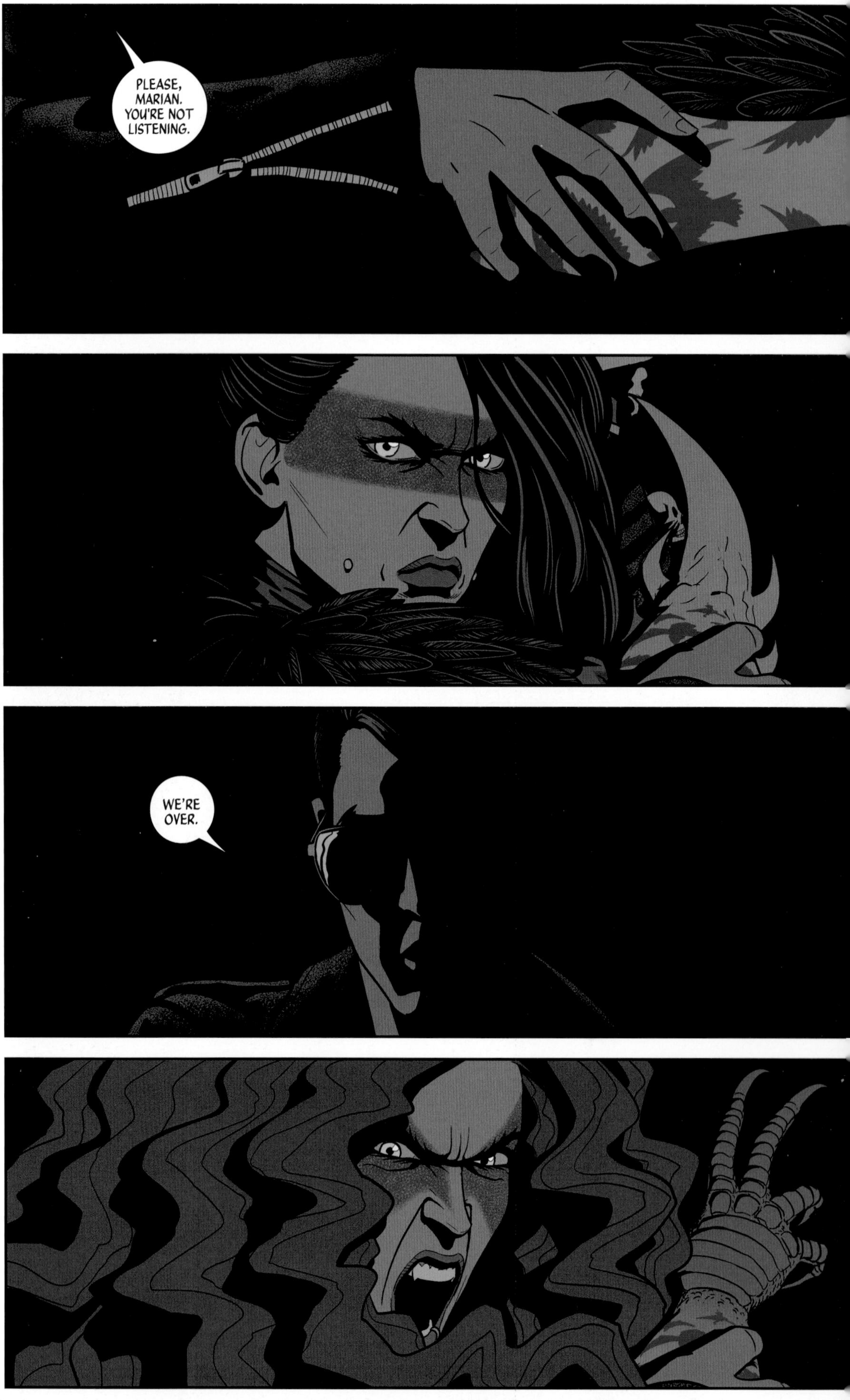
PLEASE, MARIAN. YOU'RE NOT LISTENING.
WE'RE OVER.

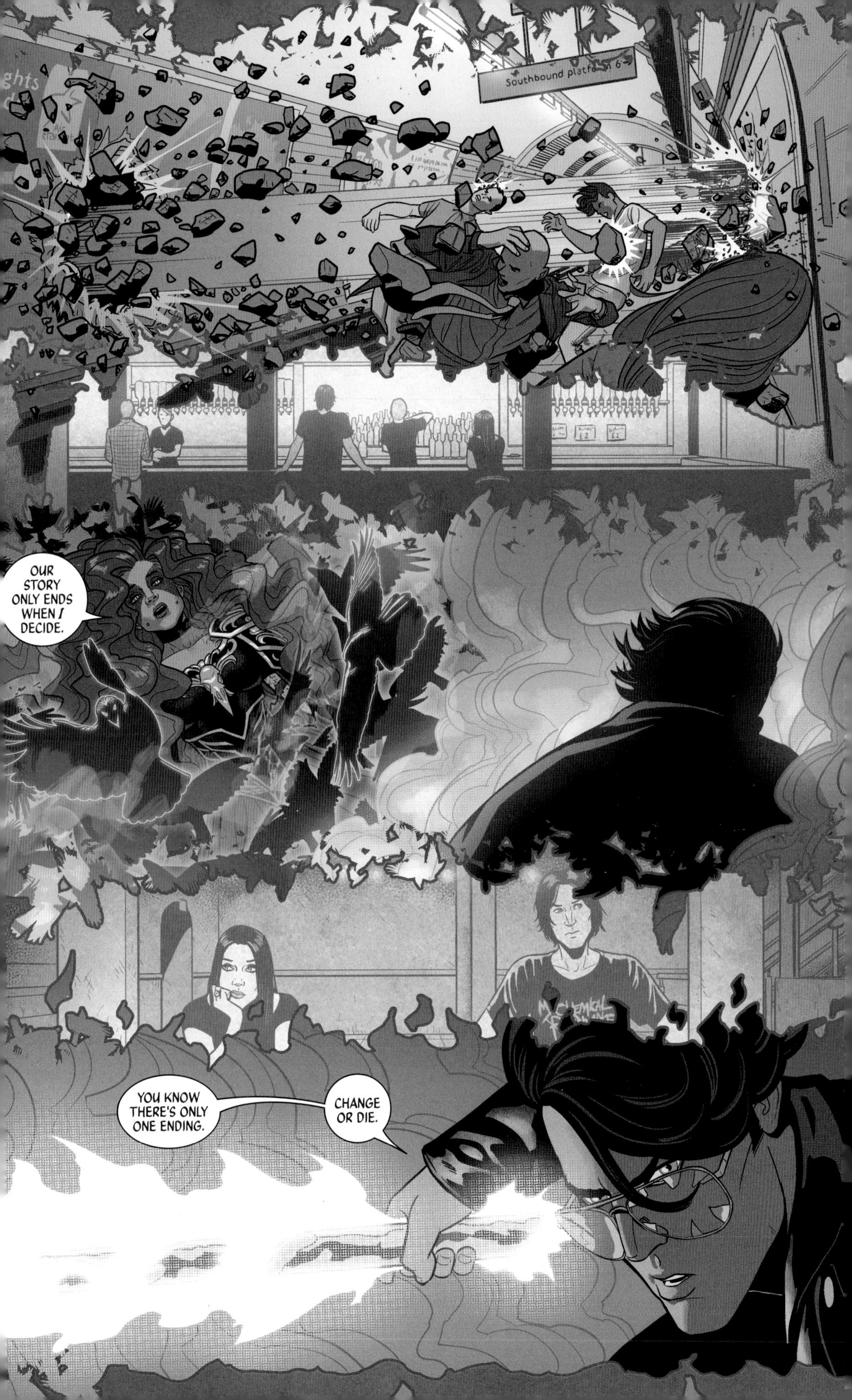
OUR STORY ONLY ENDS WHEN *I* DECIDE.
YOU KNOW THERE'S ONLY ONE ENDING.
CHANGE OR DIE.

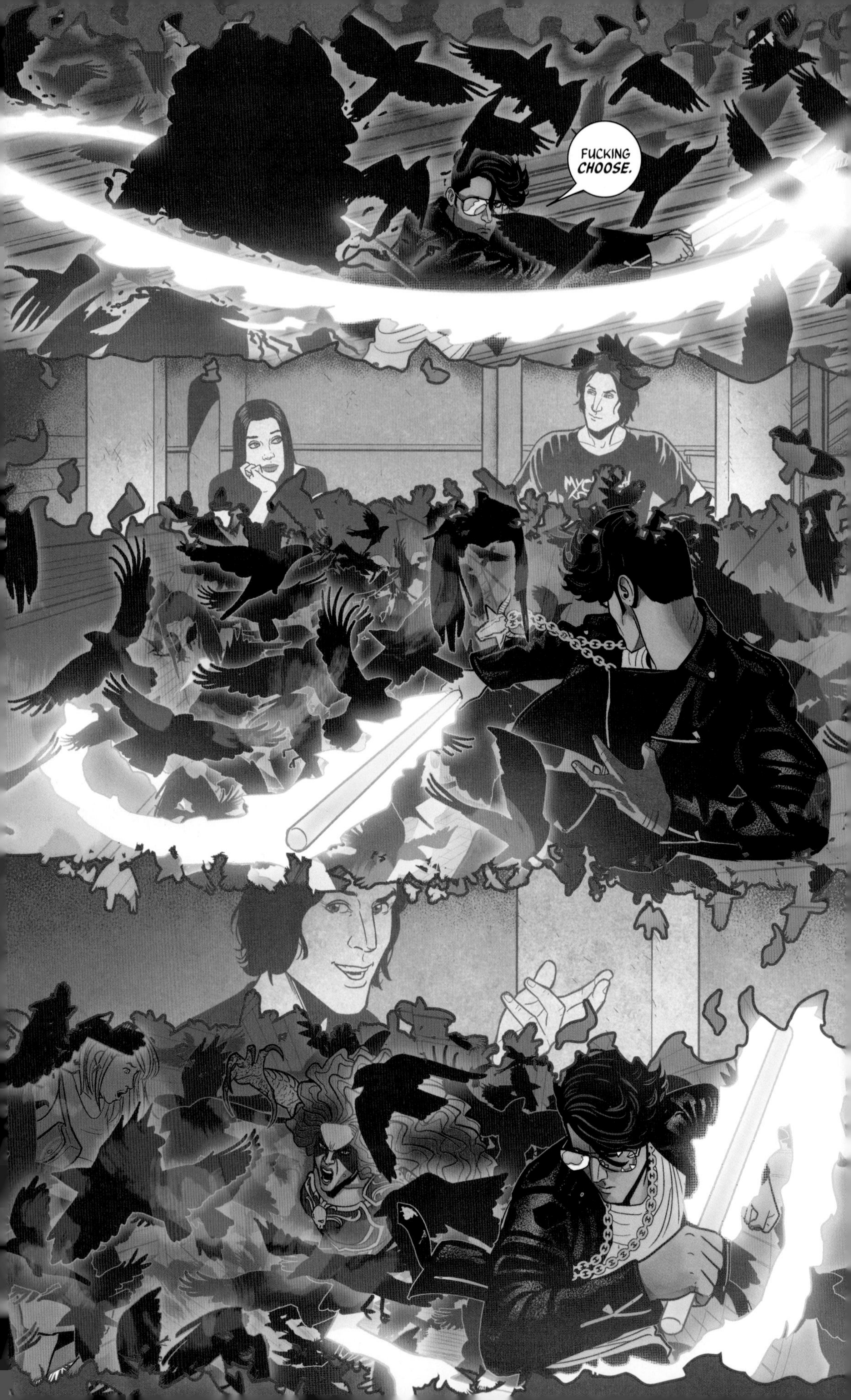
FUCKING CHOOSE.

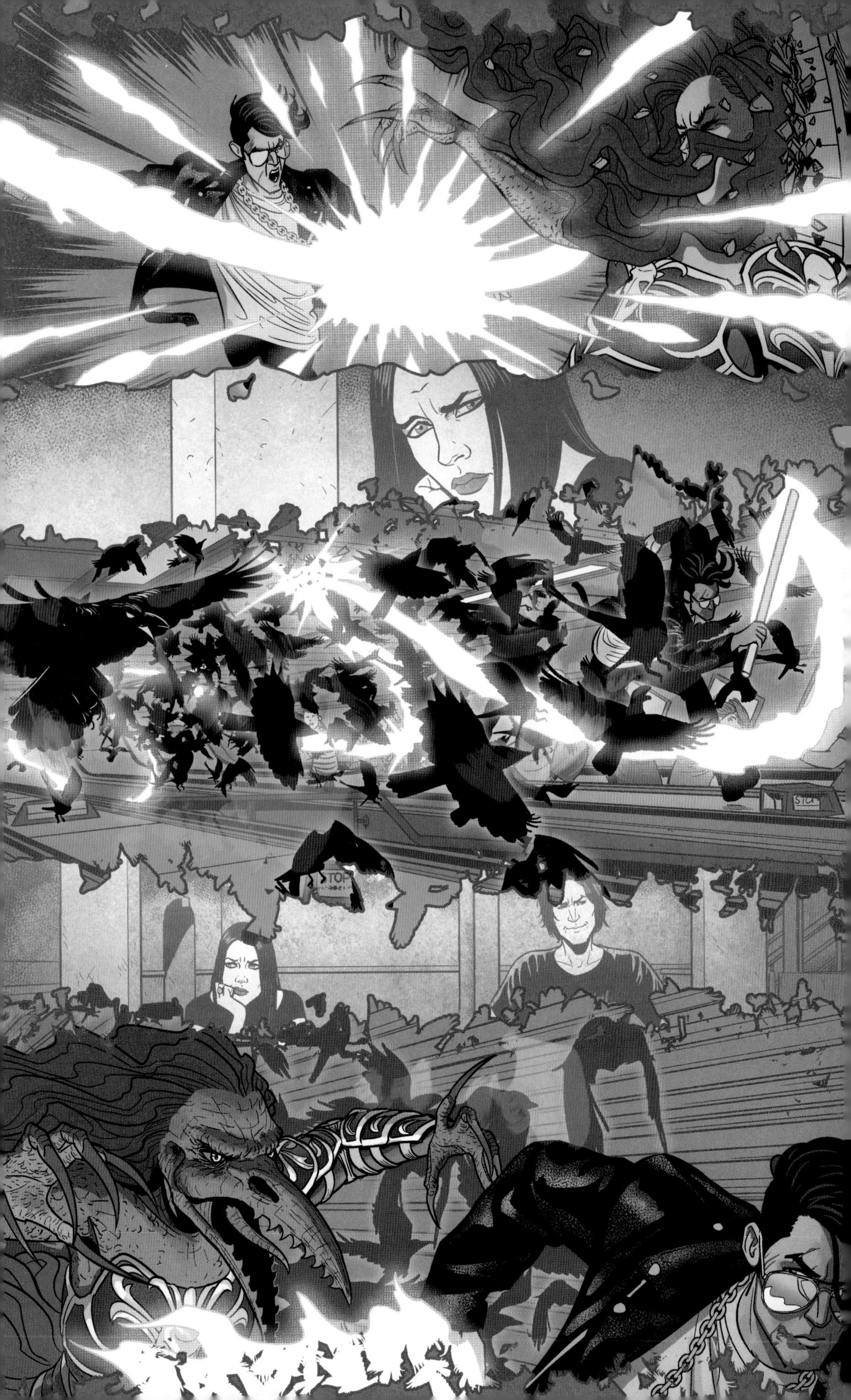

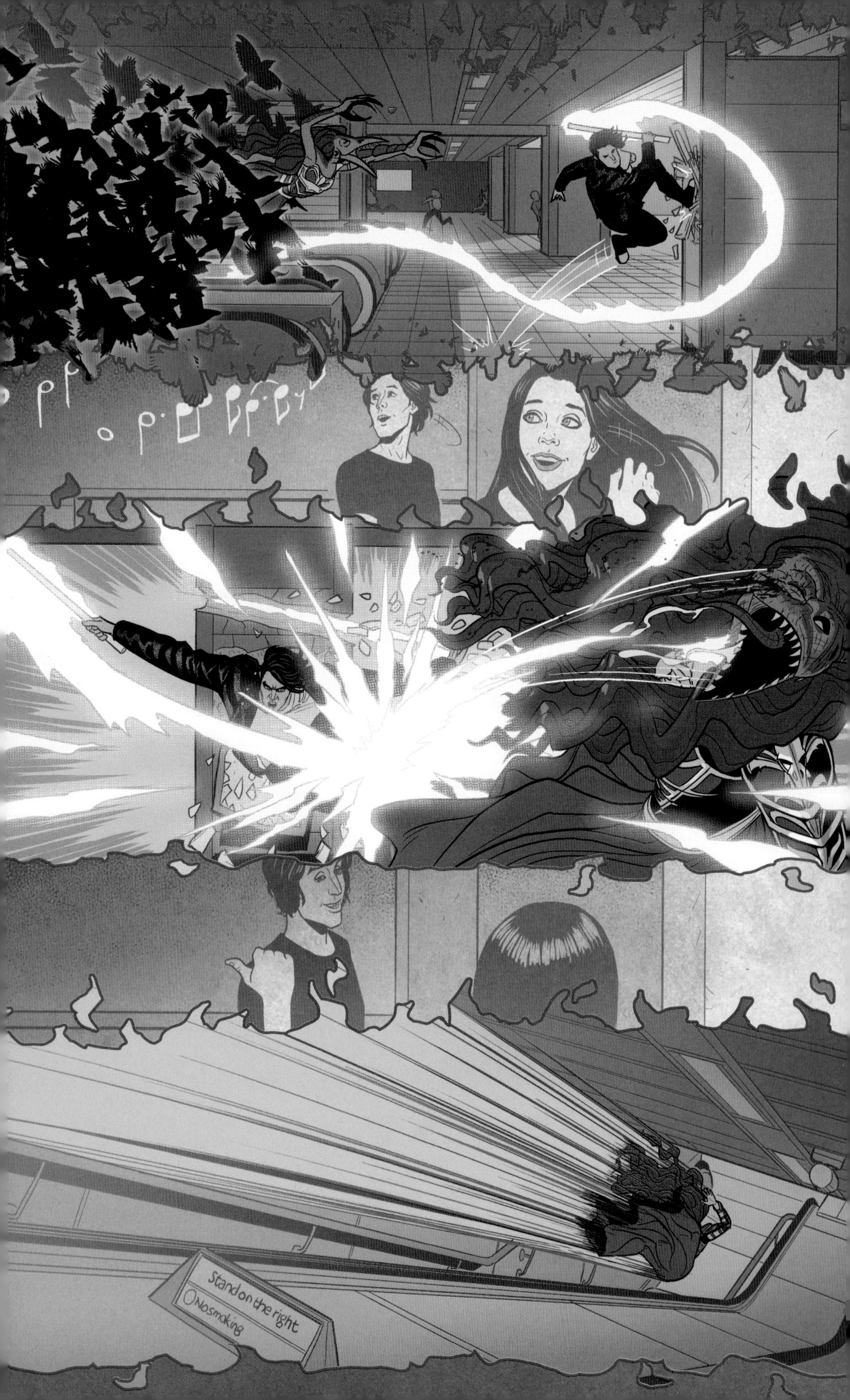
Stand on the right
No smoking

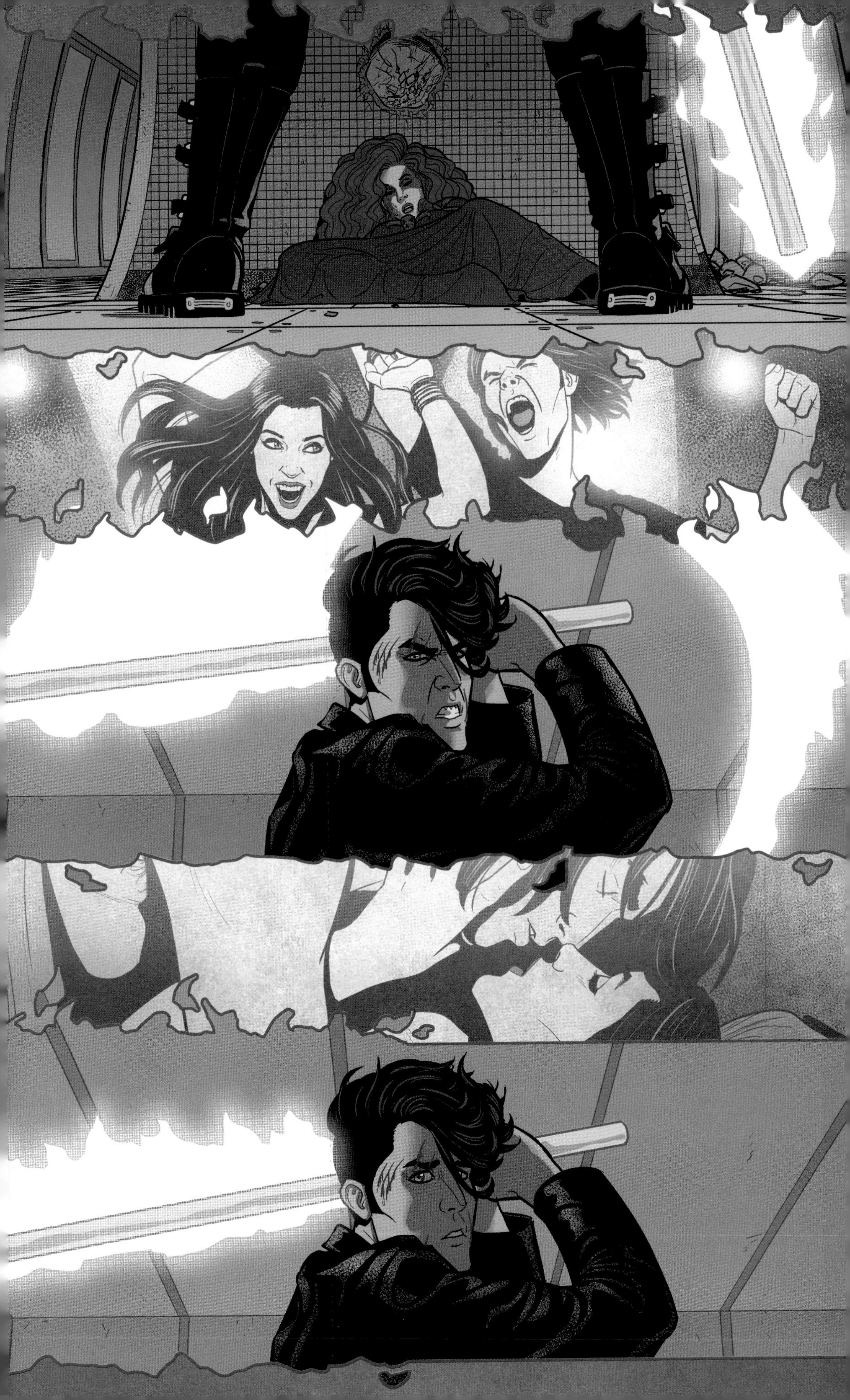

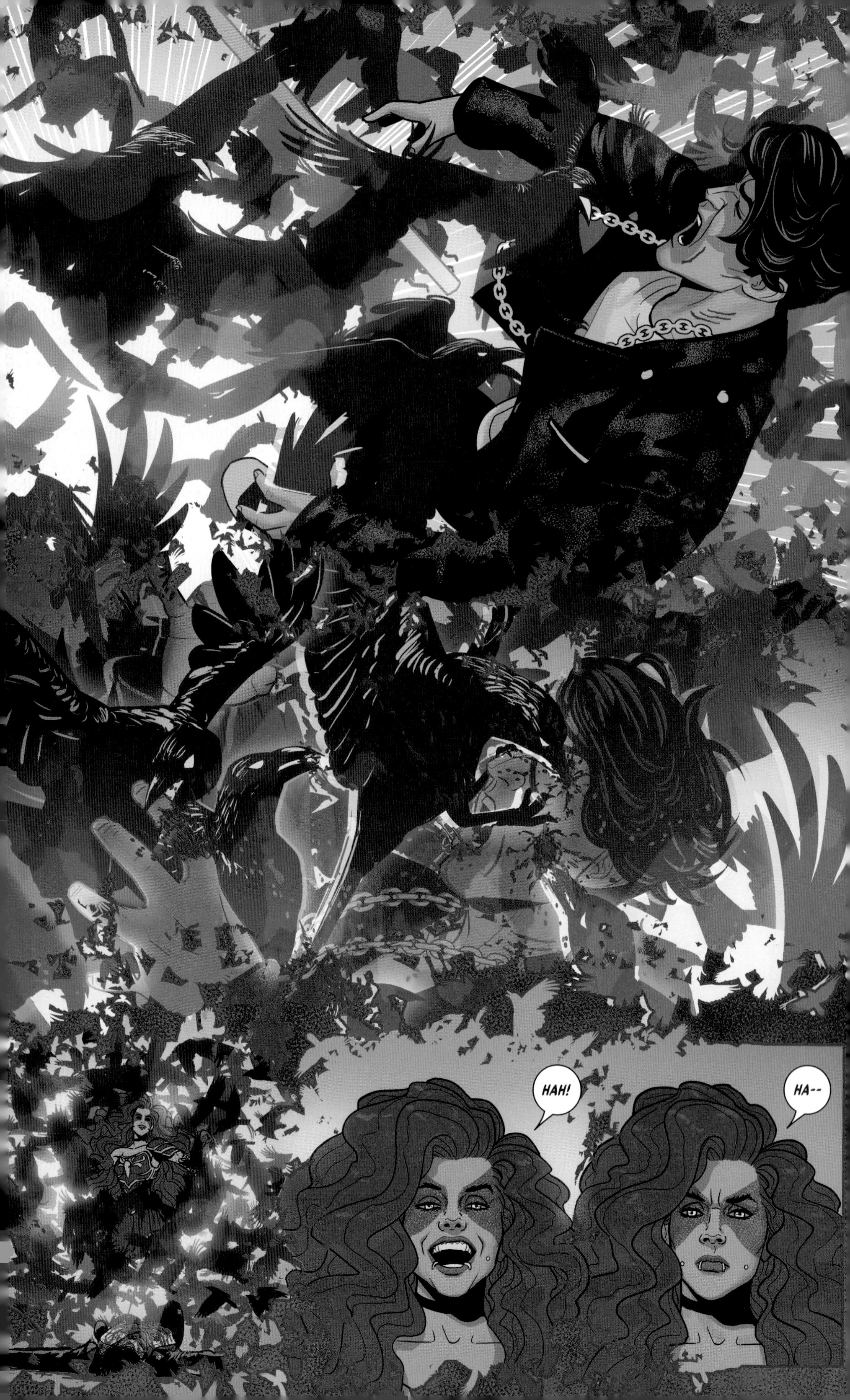
HAH!
HA--

BAPHOMET

9 MARCH 2015

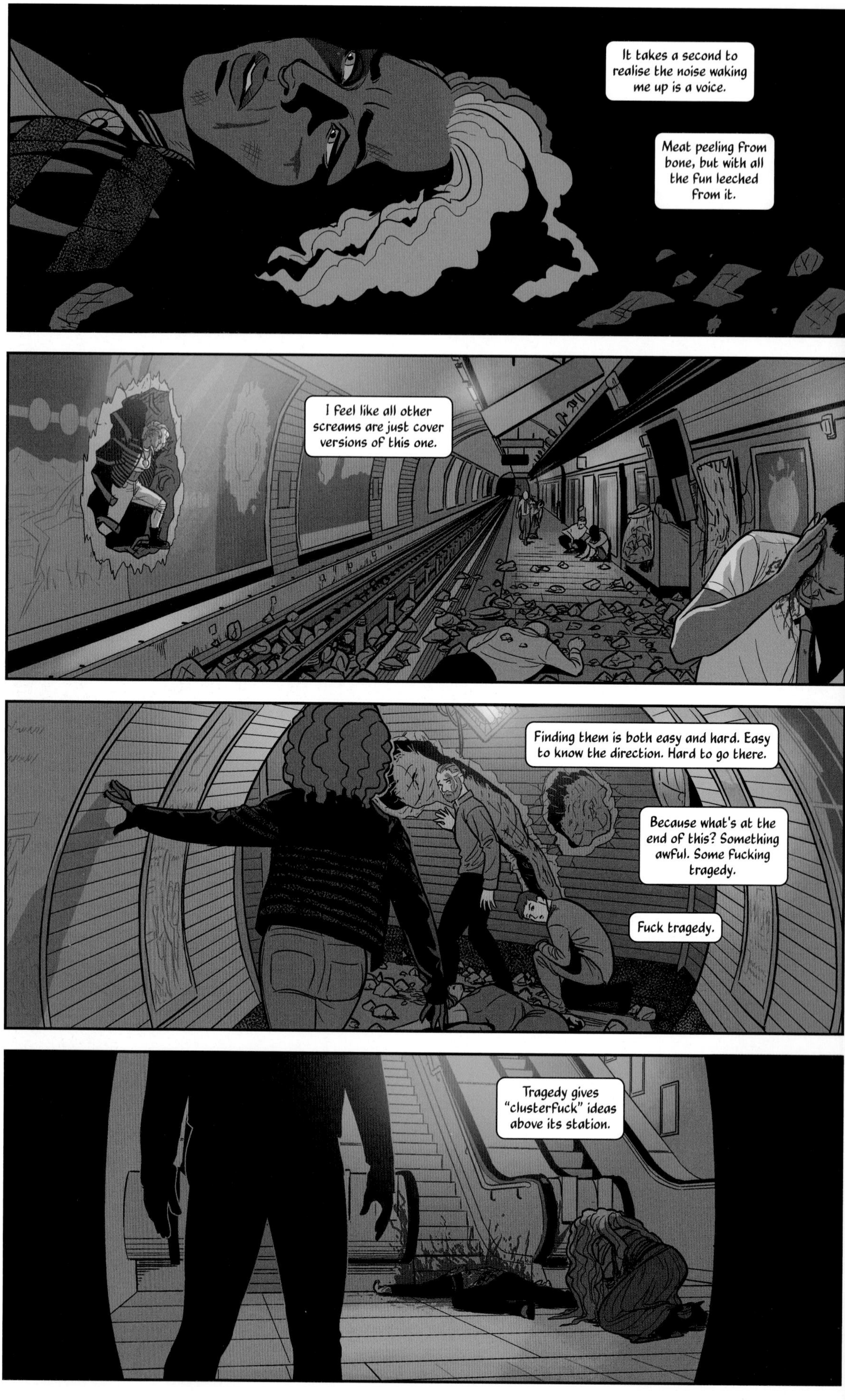
It takes a second to realise the noise waking me up is a voice.
Meat peeling from bone, but with all the fun leeched from it.
I feel like all other screams are just cover versions of this one.
Finding them is both easy and hard. Easy to know the direction. Hard to go there.
Because what's at the end of this? Something awful. Some fucking tragedy.
Fuck tragedy.
Tragedy gives "clusterfuck" ideas above its station.

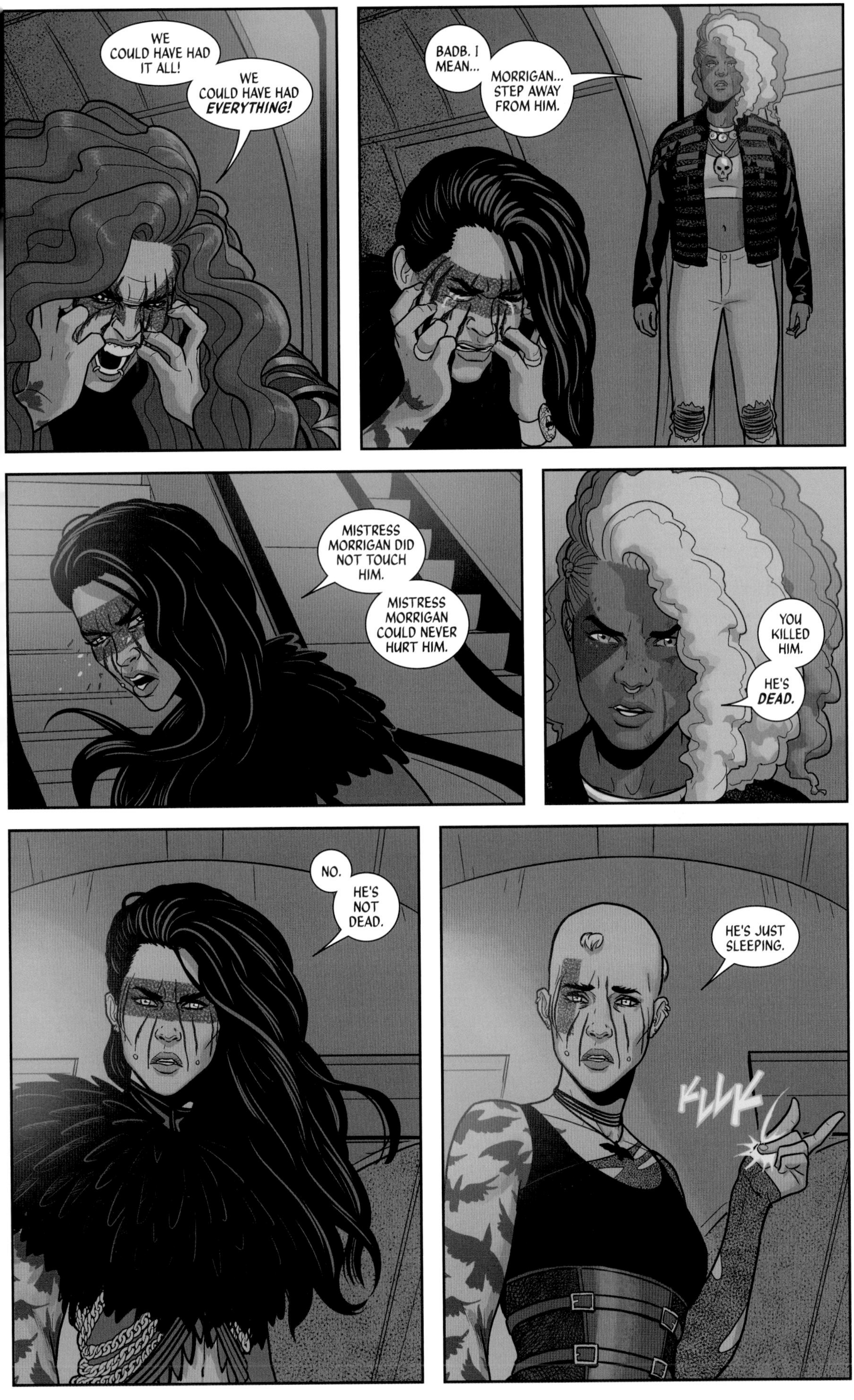
WE COULD HAVE HAD IT ALL!
WE COULD HAVE HAD *EVERYTHING!*
BADB. I MEAN...
MORRIGAN... STEP AWAY FROM HIM.
MISTRESS MORRIGAN DID NOT TOUCH HIM.
MISTRESS MORRIGAN COULD NEVER HURT HIM.
YOU KILLED HIM.
HE'S *DEAD.*
NO.
HE'S NOT DEAD.
HE'S JUST SLEEPING.
KLIK

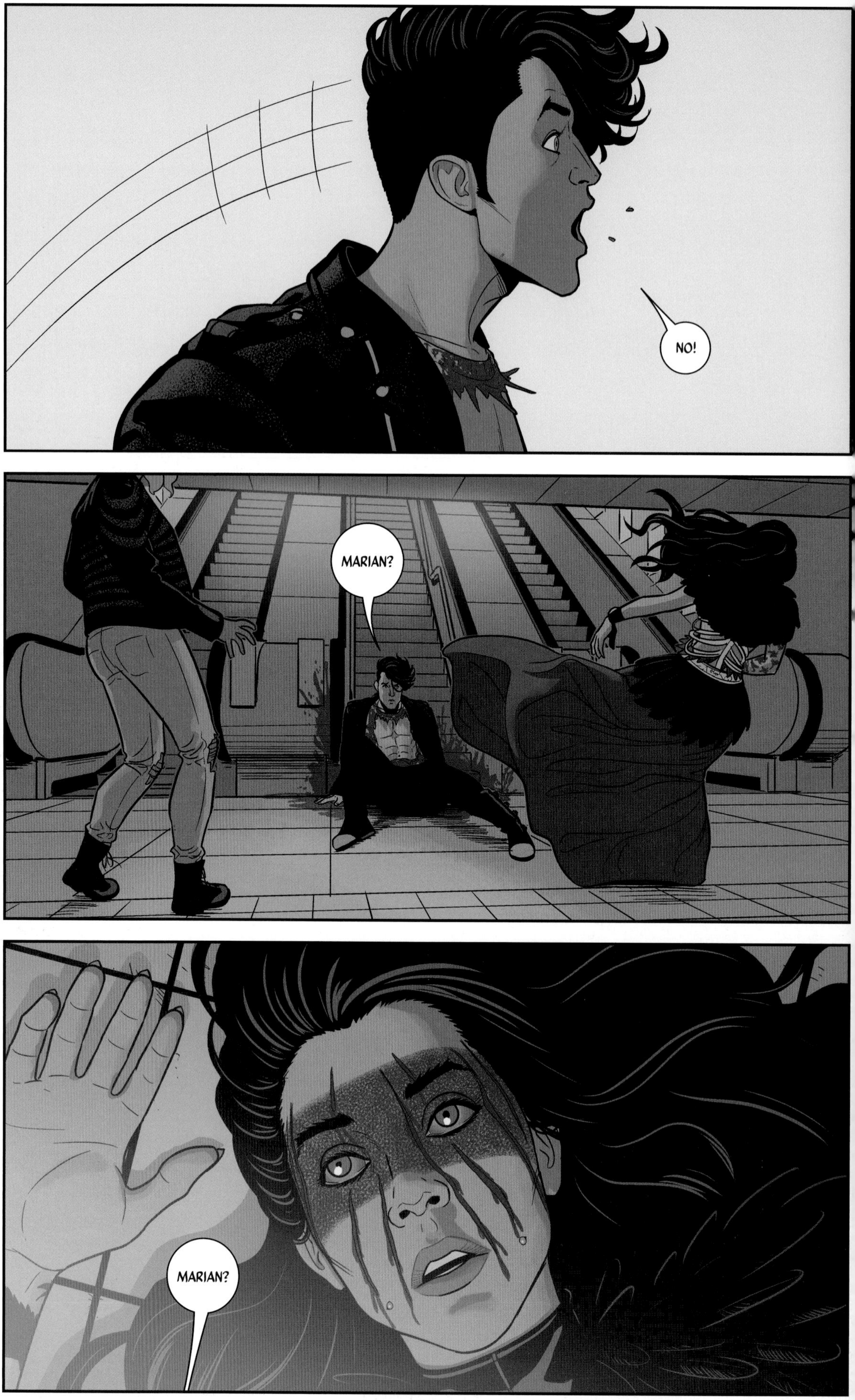
NO!
MARIAN?
MARIAN?

NO OTHER
CHOICE

9 MARCH 2015

38

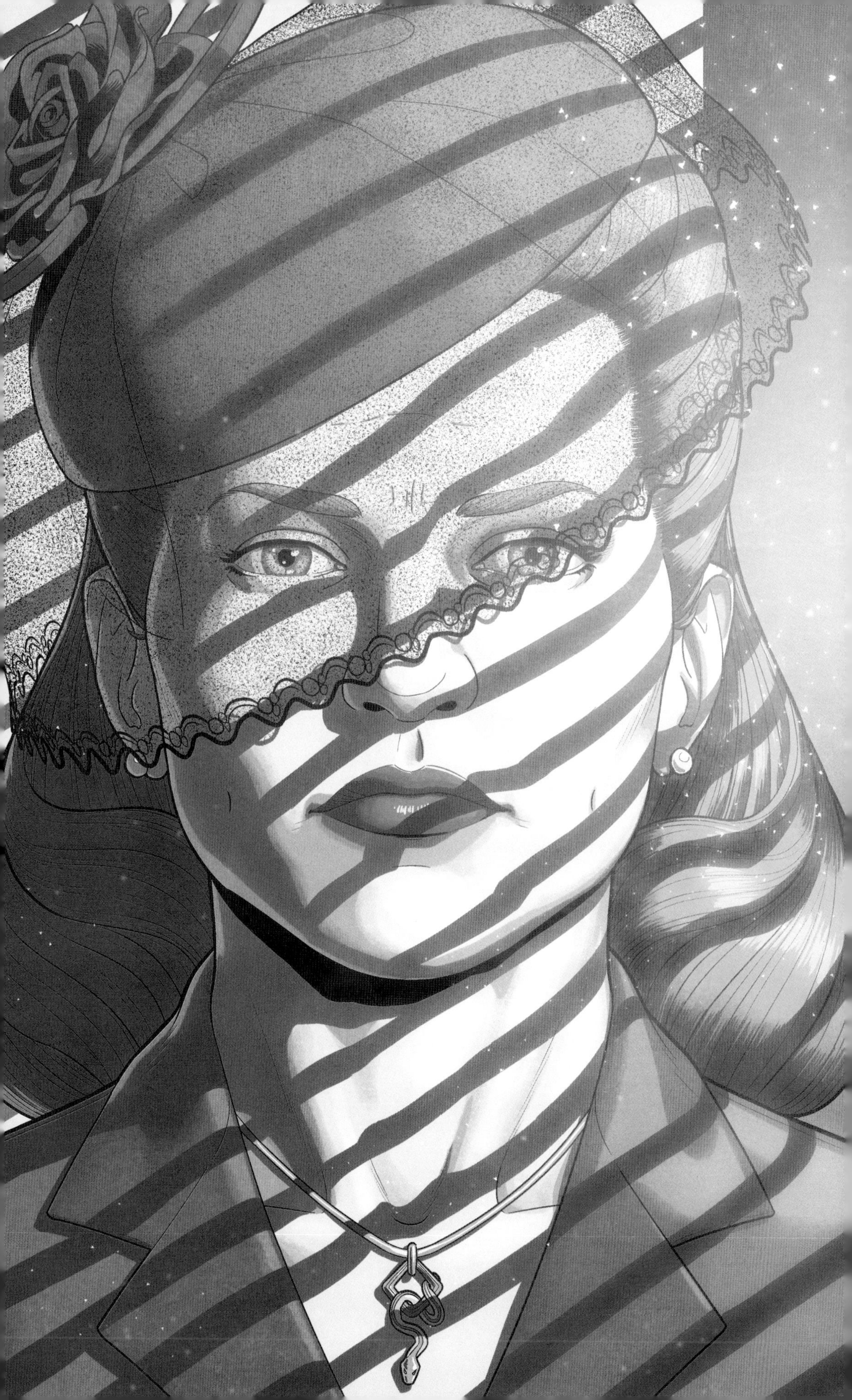

THE
WICKED
+
DIVINE
THE

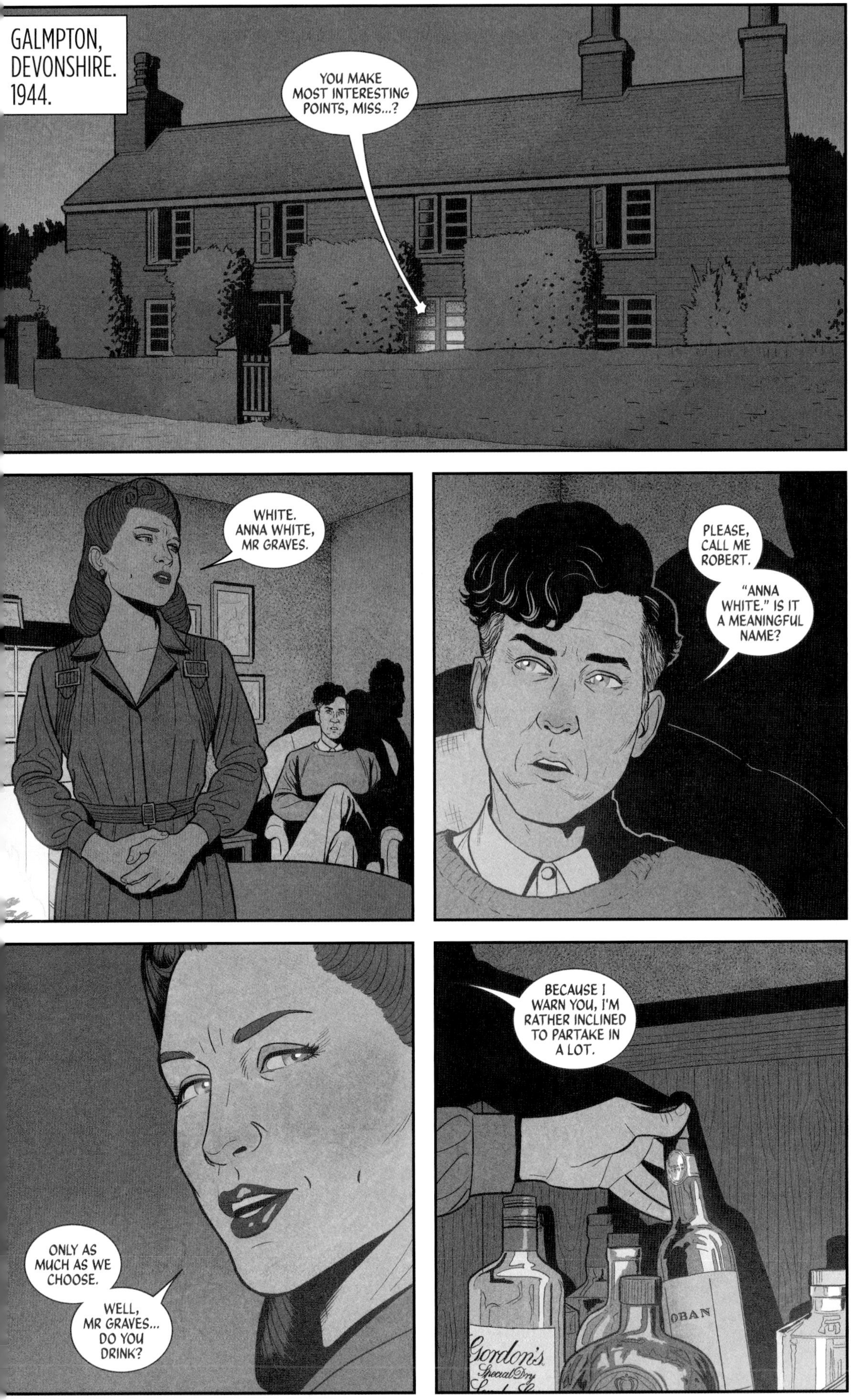
GALMPTON, DEVONSHIRE. 1944.
YOU MAKE MOST INTERESTING POINTS, MISS...?
WHITE. ANNA WHITE, MR GRAVES.
PLEASE, CALL ME ROBERT.
"ANNA WHITE." IS IT A MEANINGFUL NAME?
ONLY AS MUCH AS WE CHOOSE.
WELL, MR GRAVES... DO YOU DRINK?
BECAUSE I WARN YOU, I'M RATHER INCLINED TO PARTAKE IN A LOT.
Gordon's Special Dry
OBAN

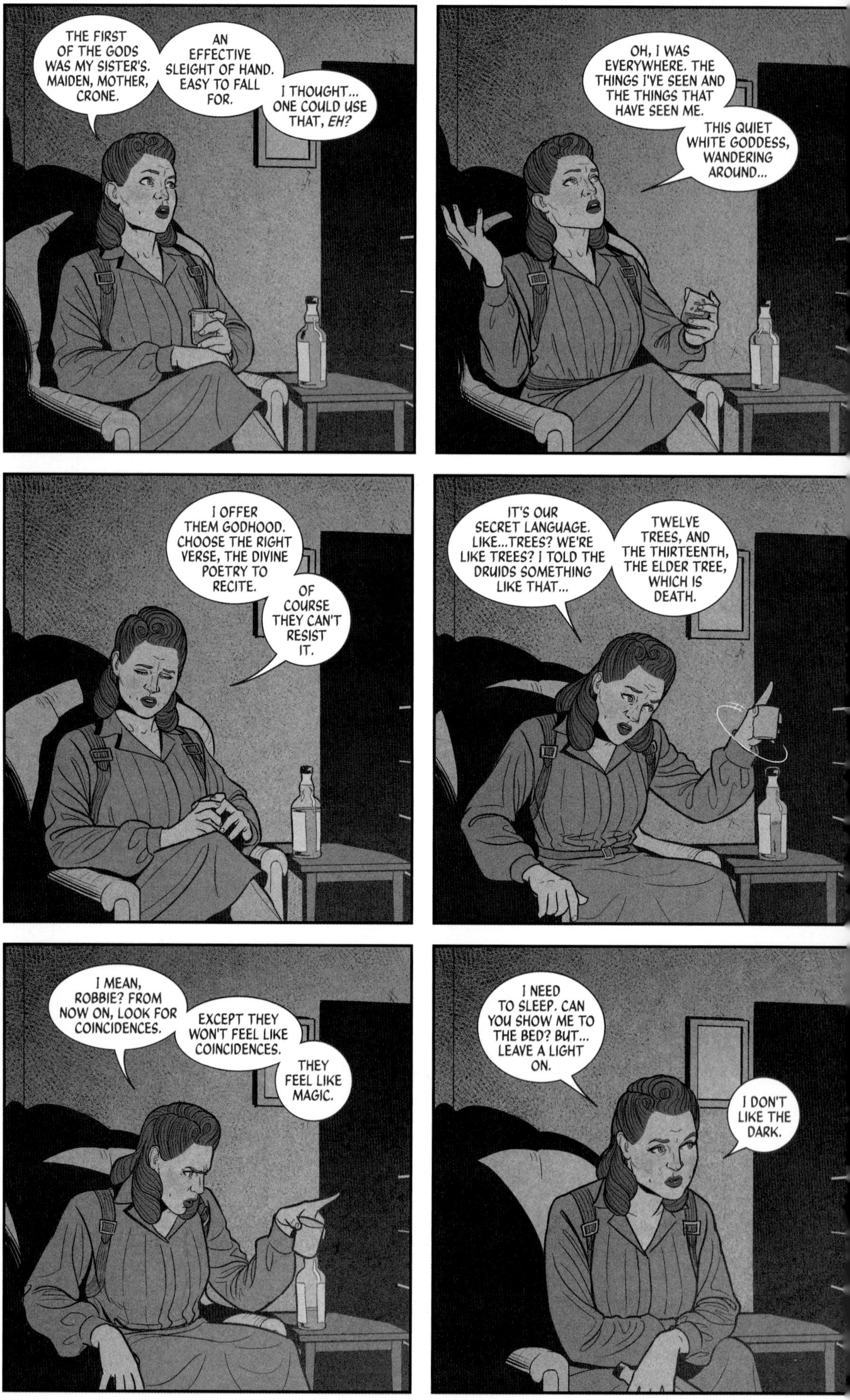
THE FIRST OF THE GODS WAS MY SISTER'S. MAIDEN, MOTHER, CRONE.
AN EFFECTIVE SLEIGHT OF HAND. EASY TO FALL FOR.
I THOUGHT... ONE COULD USE THAT, *EH?*
OH, I WAS EVERYWHERE. THE THINGS I'VE SEEN AND THE THINGS THAT HAVE SEEN ME.
THIS QUIET WHITE GODDESS, WANDERING AROUND...
I OFFER THEM GODHOOD. CHOOSE THE RIGHT VERSE, THE DIVINE POETRY TO RECITE.
OF COURSE THEY CAN'T RESIST IT.
IT'S OUR SECRET LANGUAGE. LIKE...TREES? WE'RE LIKE TREES? I TOLD THE DRUIDS SOMETHING LIKE THAT...
TWELVE TREES, AND THE THIRTEENTH, THE ELDER TREE, WHICH IS DEATH.
I MEAN, ROBBIE? FROM NOW ON, LOOK FOR COINCIDENCES.
EXCEPT THEY WON'T FEEL LIKE COINCIDENCES.
THEY FEEL LIKE MAGIC.
I NEED TO SLEEP. CAN YOU SHOW ME TO THE BED? BUT... LEAVE A LIGHT ON.
I DON'T LIKE THE DARK.

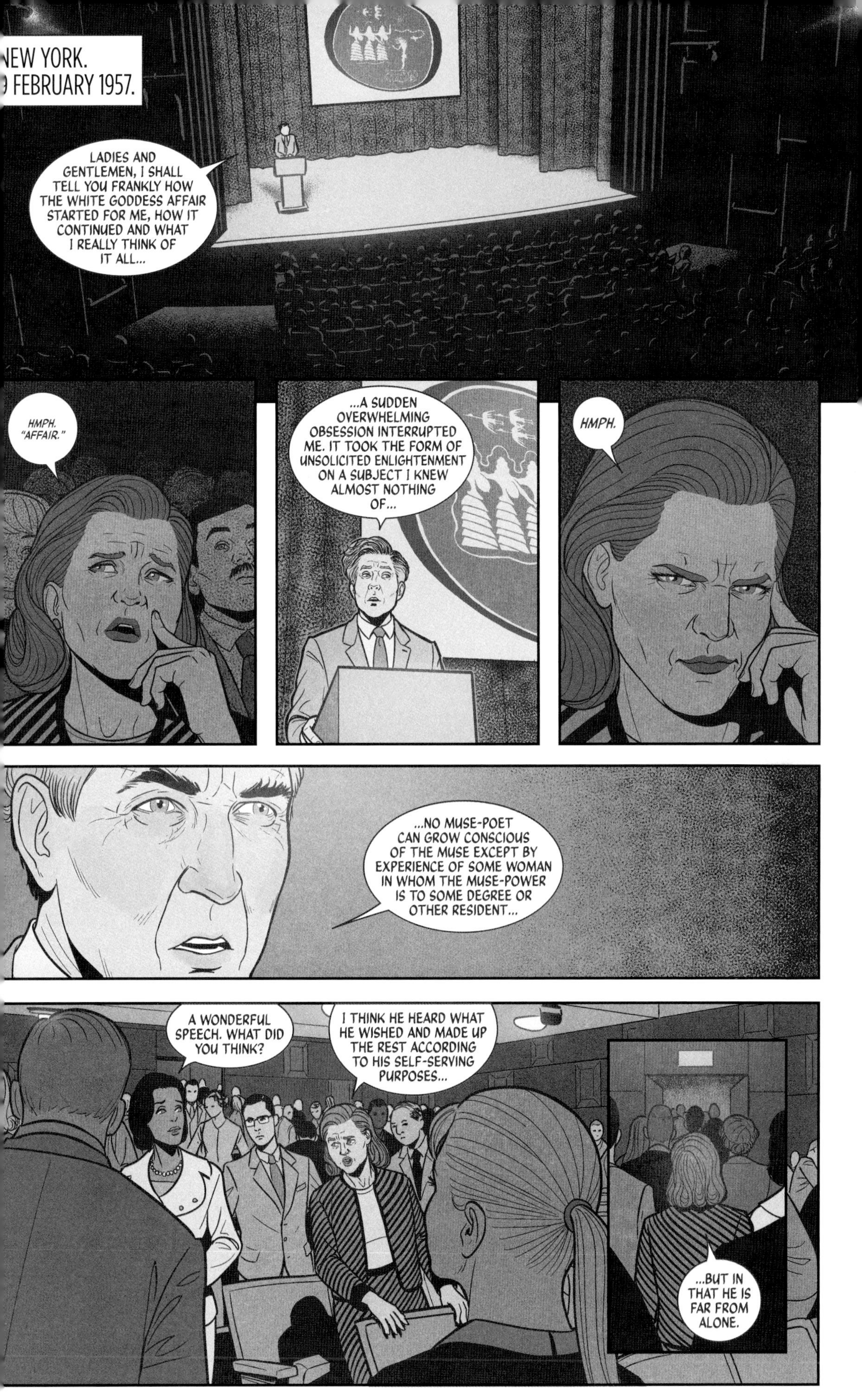
NEW YORK.
9 FEBRUARY 1957.
LADIES AND GENTLEMEN, I SHALL TELL YOU FRANKLY HOW THE WHITE GODDESS AFFAIR STARTED FOR ME, HOW IT CONTINUED AND WHAT I REALLY THINK OF IT ALL...
HMPH. "AFFAIR."
...A SUDDEN OVERWHELMING OBSESSION INTERRUPTED ME. IT TOOK THE FORM OF UNSOLICITED ENLIGHTENMENT ON A SUBJECT I KNEW ALMOST NOTHING OF...
HMPH.
...NO MUSE-POET CAN GROW CONSCIOUS OF THE MUSE EXCEPT BY EXPERIENCE OF SOME WOMAN IN WHOM THE MUSE-POWER IS TO SOME DEGREE OR OTHER RESIDENT...
A WONDERFUL SPEECH. WHAT DID YOU THINK?
I THINK HE HEARD WHAT HE WISHED AND MADE UP THE REST ACCORDING TO HIS SELF-SERVING PURPOSES...
...BUT IN THAT HE IS FAR FROM ALONE.

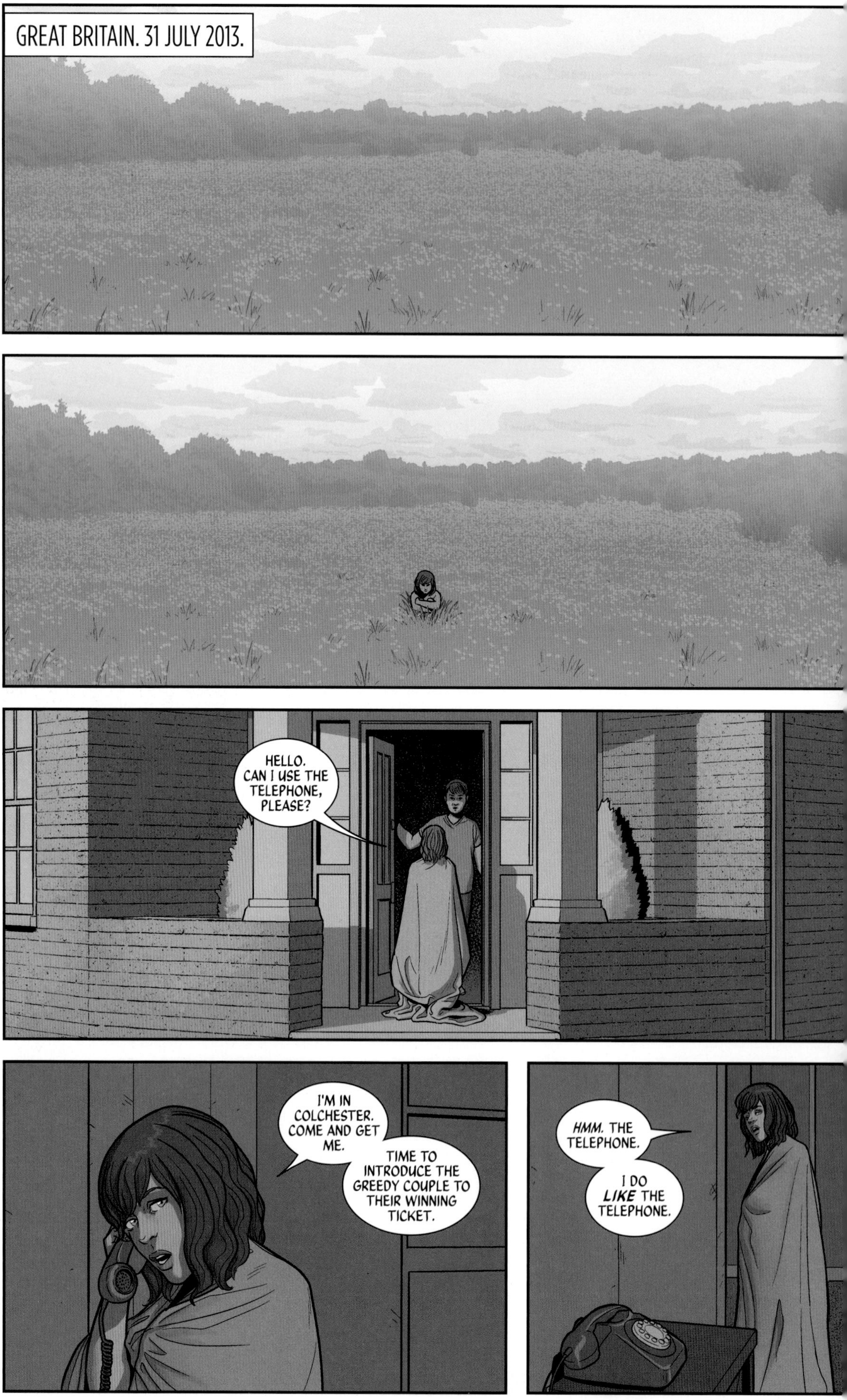
GREAT BRITAIN. 31 JULY 2013.
HELLO. CAN I USE THE TELEPHONE, PLEASE?
I'M IN COLCHESTER. COME AND GET ME.
TIME TO INTRODUCE THE GREEDY COUPLE TO THEIR WINNING TICKET.
HMM. THE TELEPHONE.
I DO LIKE THE TELEPHONE.

VALHALLA.
24 SEPTEMBER
2014.

STOP! THERE'RE NO CAMERAS HERE. WE CAN TALK.

THERE IS INSUFFICIENT TIME TO CHAT. I'VE WRITTEN A LETTER. IT'LL TELEPORT TO THE CAVE. IT SAYS EVERYTHING I NEED TO SAY.

I'M SURE...BUT I'M UNCONVINCED THIS IS THE WISEST COURSE.

YES, BUT WE ARE FAR FROM THE NARROW PATH. THE CHILDREN ARE TOO SUSPICIOUS. WE MUST MOVE THAT AWAY FROM YOU. CARVING YOU UP ON A MEANINGLESS YET OH-SO-IMPRESSIVE ALTAR SHOULD DO THE TRICK.

YES, BUT... REMEMBER: ARMS, CHEST. NOTHING TOO EXPOSED.

IF THERE'S STILL PHOTOGRAPHY IN THE 22nd CENTURY IT'D MAKE IT TOO EASY TO DRAW A LINK BETWEEN ME NOW AND THEN.

WITH ANY LUCK THERE WON'T BE.

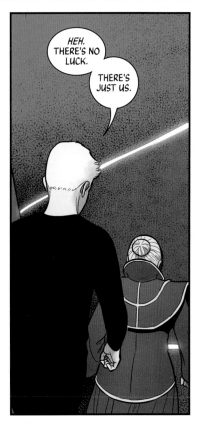

HEH. THERE'S NO LUCK.

THERE'S JUST US.

AMBITION
MAKES YOU
PRETTY.
ALSO, UGLY

9 MARCH 2015

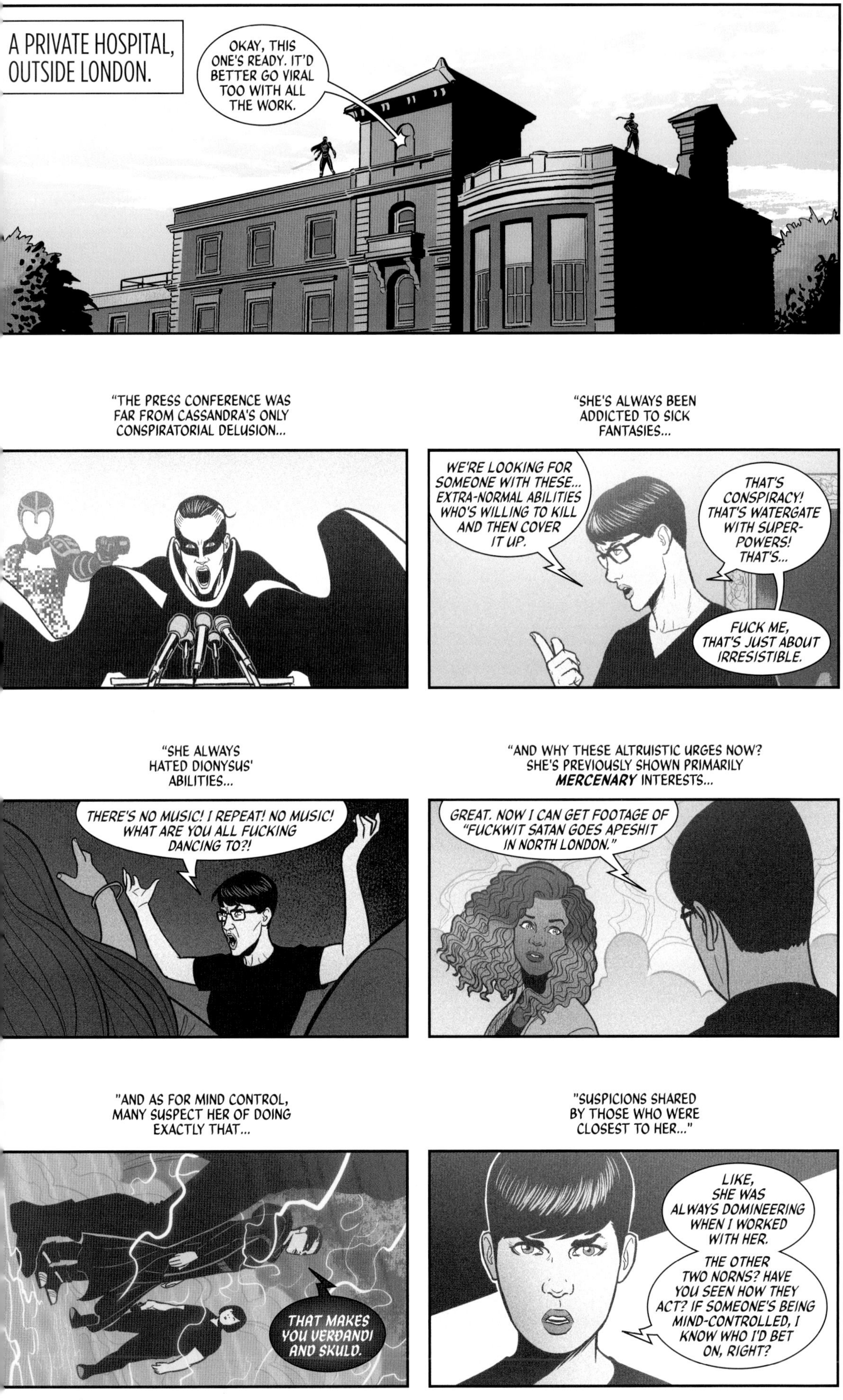
A PRIVATE HOSPITAL, OUTSIDE LONDON.
OKAY, THIS ONE'S READY. IT'D BETTER GO VIRAL TOO WITH ALL THE WORK.
"THE PRESS CONFERENCE WAS FAR FROM CASSANDRA'S ONLY CONSPIRATORIAL DELUSION...
"SHE'S ALWAYS BEEN ADDICTED TO SICK FANTASIES...
WE'RE LOOKING FOR SOMEONE WITH THESE... EXTRA-NORMAL ABILITIES WHO'S WILLING TO KILL AND THEN COVER IT UP.
THAT'S CONSPIRACY! THAT'S WATERGATE WITH SUPER-POWERS! THAT'S...
FUCK ME, THAT'S JUST ABOUT IRRESISTIBLE.
"SHE ALWAYS HATED DIONYSUS' ABILITIES...
THERE'S NO MUSIC! I REPEAT! NO MUSIC! WHAT ARE YOU ALL FUCKING DANCING TO?!
"AND WHY THESE ALTRUISTIC URGES NOW? SHE'S PREVIOUSLY SHOWN PRIMARILY ***MERCENARY*** INTERESTS...
GREAT. NOW I CAN GET FOOTAGE OF "FUCKWIT SATAN GOES APESHIT IN NORTH LONDON."
"AND AS FOR MIND CONTROL, MANY SUSPECT HER OF DOING EXACTLY THAT...
THAT MAKES YOU VERDANDI AND SKULD.
"SUSPICIONS SHARED BY THOSE WHO WERE CLOSEST TO HER..."
LIKE, SHE WAS ALWAYS DOMINEERING WHEN I WORKED WITH HER.
THE OTHER TWO NORNS? HAVE YOU SEEN HOW THEY ACT? IF SOMEONE'S BEING MIND-CONTROLLED, I KNOW WHO I'D BET ON, RIGHT?

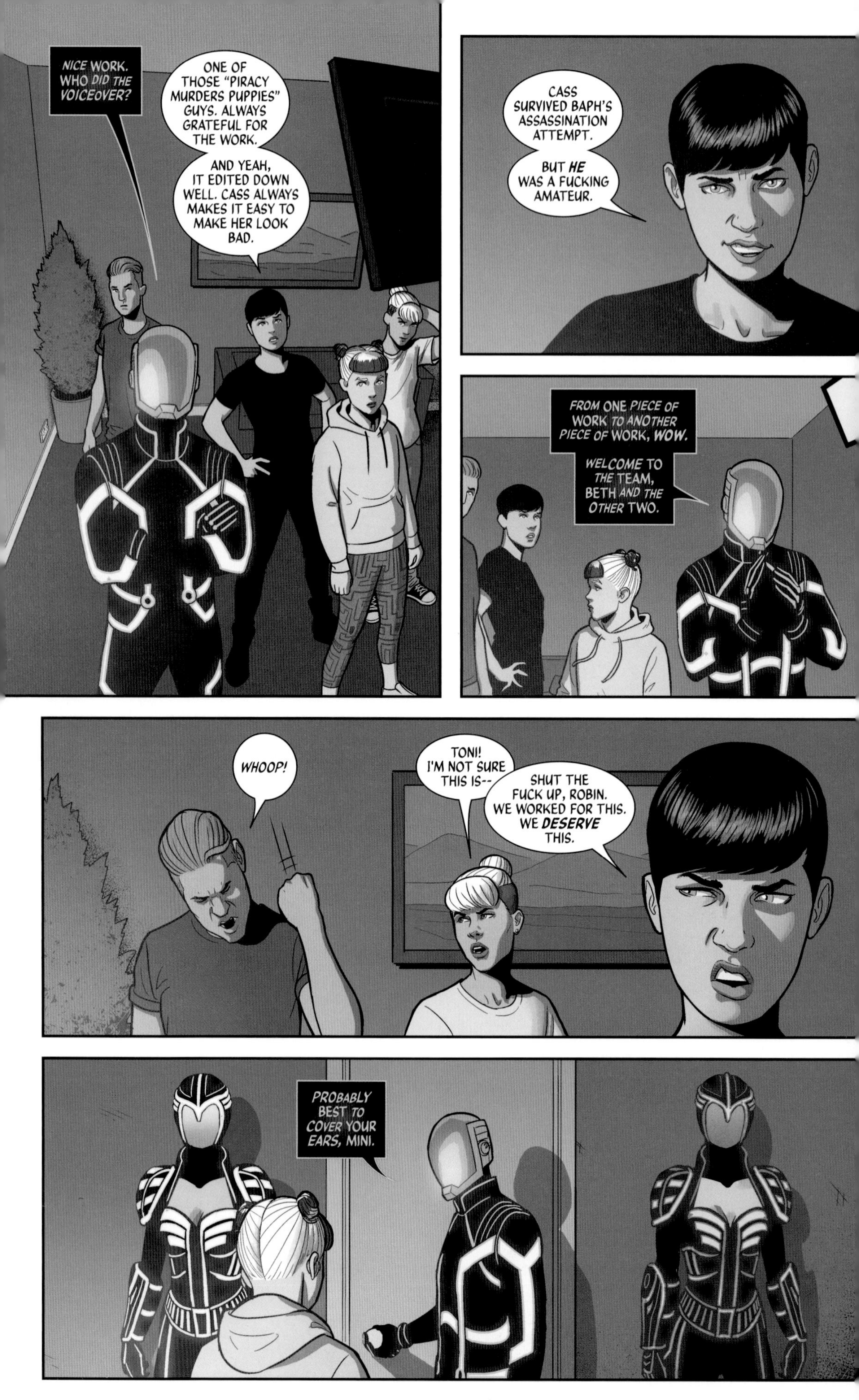
NICE WORK. WHO DID THE VOICEOVER?
ONE OF THOSE "PIRACY MURDERS PUPPIES" GUYS. ALWAYS GRATEFUL FOR THE WORK.
AND YEAH, IT EDITED DOWN WELL. CASS ALWAYS MAKES IT EASY TO MAKE HER LOOK BAD.
CASS SURVIVED BAPH'S ASSASSINATION ATTEMPT.
BUT HE WAS A FUCKING AMATEUR.
FROM ONE PIECE OF WORK TO ANOTHER PIECE OF WORK, WOW.
WELCOME TO THE TEAM, BETH AND THE OTHER TWO.
WHOOP!
TONI! I'M NOT SURE THIS IS--
SHUT THE FUCK UP, ROBIN. WE WORKED FOR THIS. WE DESERVE THIS.
PROBABLY BEST TO COVER YOUR EARS, MINI.

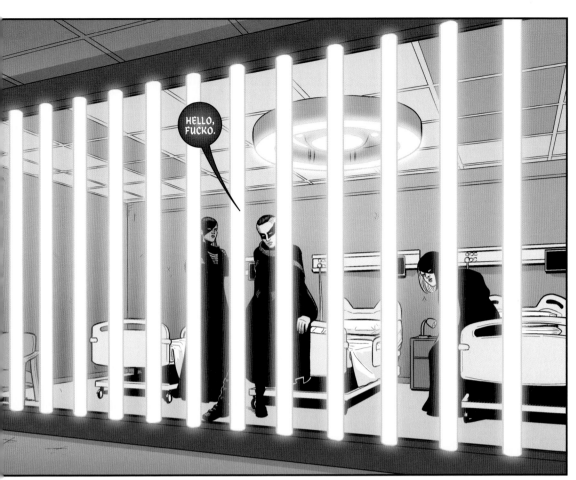

HELLO, FUCKO.

OKAY, CASS. WE'VE GOT A TO-DO LIST FOR YOU.

FIRST UP...

I'M NOT GOING TO VOLUNTARILY DO A DAMN THING YOU SAY.

ARE YOU GOING TO THREATEN ME?

DO I HAVE TO? YOU'RE SMART.

YOU KNOW HOW SUBTEXT WORKS...

CASS, HE'S REALLY MEAN. HE NEARLY SHOT ME.

PLEASE HELP HIM. I'M SCARED. I HAVE NO IDEA WHAT HE COULD DO...

UGH. YEAH, DON'T RISK BURNING UP ANY OF YOUR BRAIN CELLS TRYING TO THINK LIKE HIM.

OKAY... I WON'T HELP YOU HURT ANYONE ELSE, OR...

WHAT DO YOU NEED?

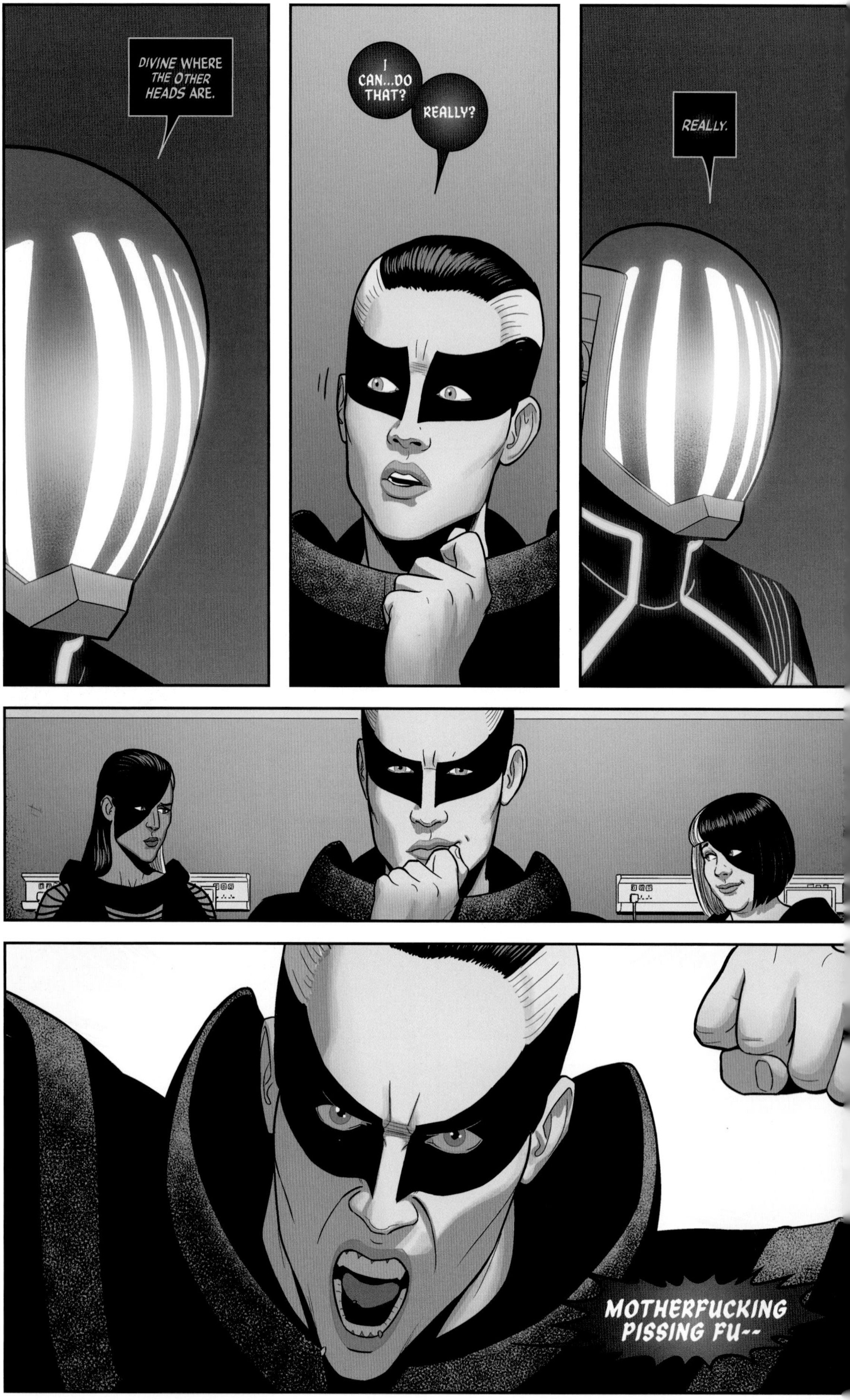
DIVINE WHERE THE OTHER HEADS ARE.
I CAN...DO THAT?
REALLY?
REALLY.
MOTHERFUCKING PISSING FU--

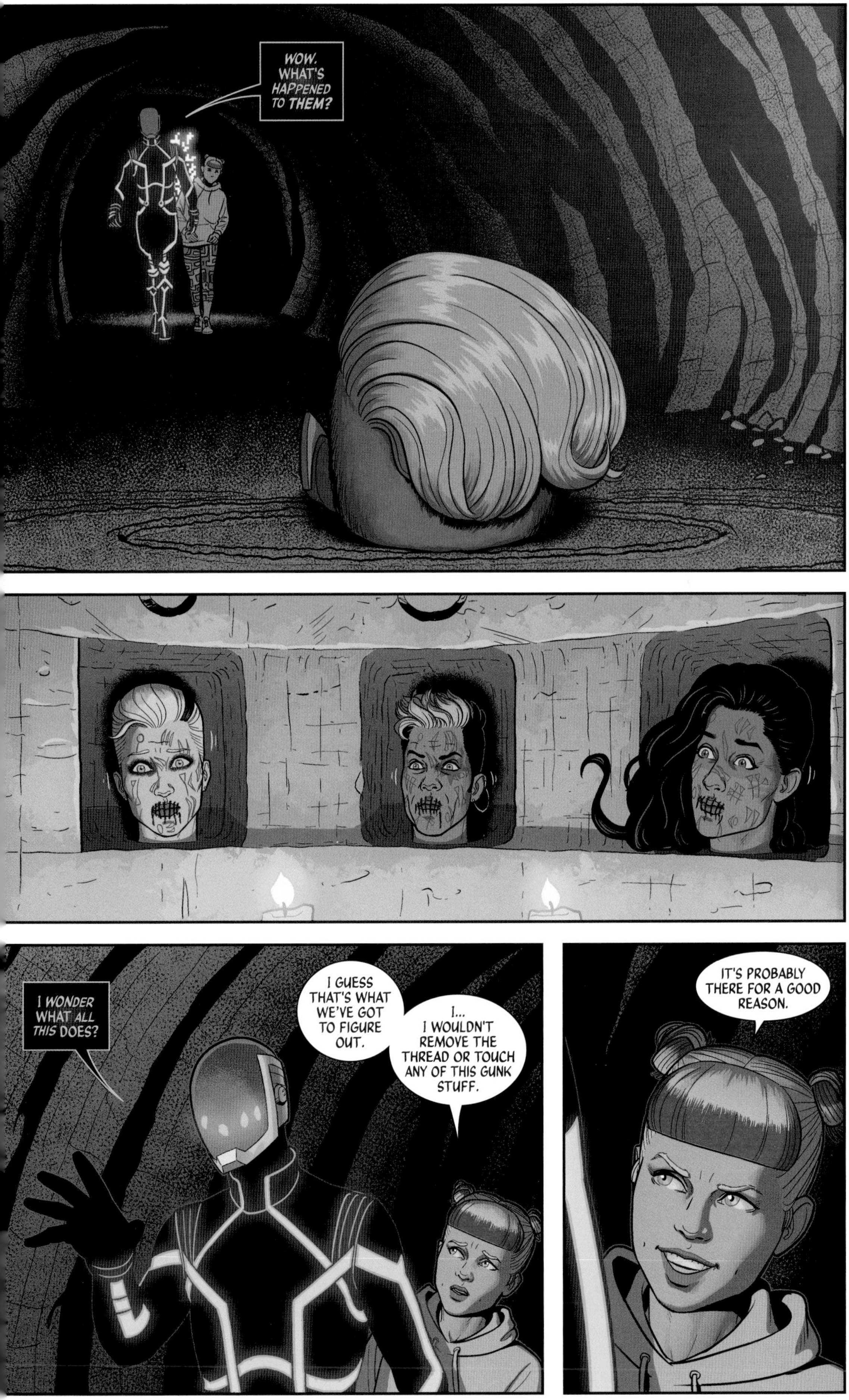
WOW. WHAT'S HAPPENED TO THEM?
I WONDER WHAT ALL THIS DOES?
I GUESS THAT'S WHAT WE'VE GOT TO FIGURE OUT.
I... I WOULDN'T REMOVE THE THREAD OR TOUCH ANY OF THIS GUNK STUFF.
IT'S PROBABLY THERE FOR A GOOD REASON.

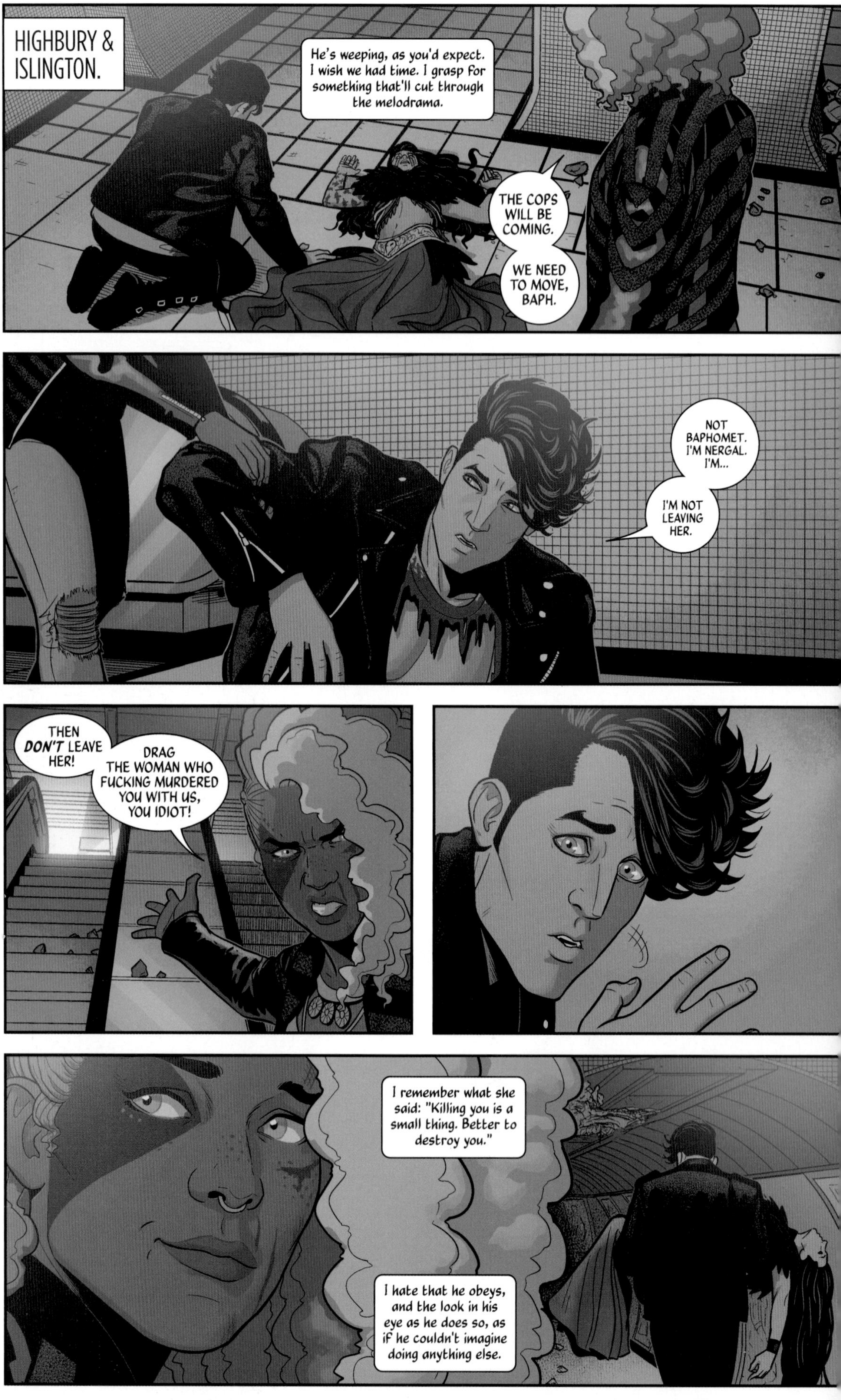
HIGHBURY & ISLINGTON.
He's weeping, as you'd expect. I wish we had time. I grasp for something that'll cut through the melodrama.
THE COPS WILL BE COMING.
WE NEED TO MOVE, BAPH.
NOT BAPHOMET. I'M NERGAL. I'M...
I'M NOT LEAVING HER.
THEN DON'T LEAVE HER!
DRAG THE WOMAN WHO FUCKING MURDERED YOU WITH US, YOU IDIOT!
I remember what she said: "Killing you is a small thing. Better to destroy you."
I hate that he obeys, and the look in his eye as he does so, as if he couldn't imagine doing anything else.

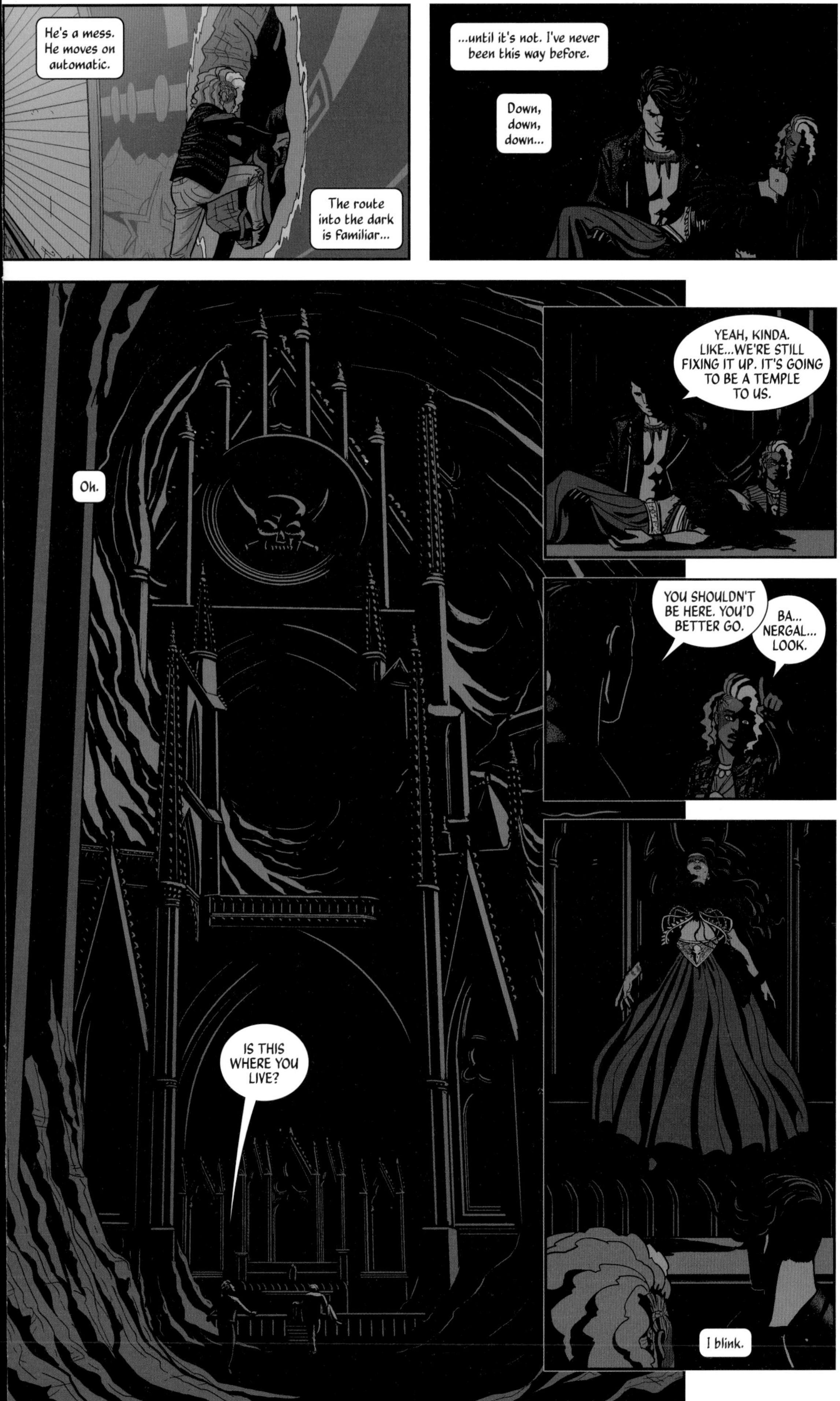
He's a mess. He moves on automatic.
The route into the dark is familiar...
...until it's not. I've never been this way before.
Down, down, down...
Oh.
IS THIS WHERE YOU LIVE?
YEAH, KINDA. LIKE...WE'RE STILL FIXING IT UP. IT'S GOING TO BE A TEMPLE TO US.
YOU SHOULDN'T BE HERE. YOU'D BETTER GO.
BA... NERGAL... LOOK.
I blink.

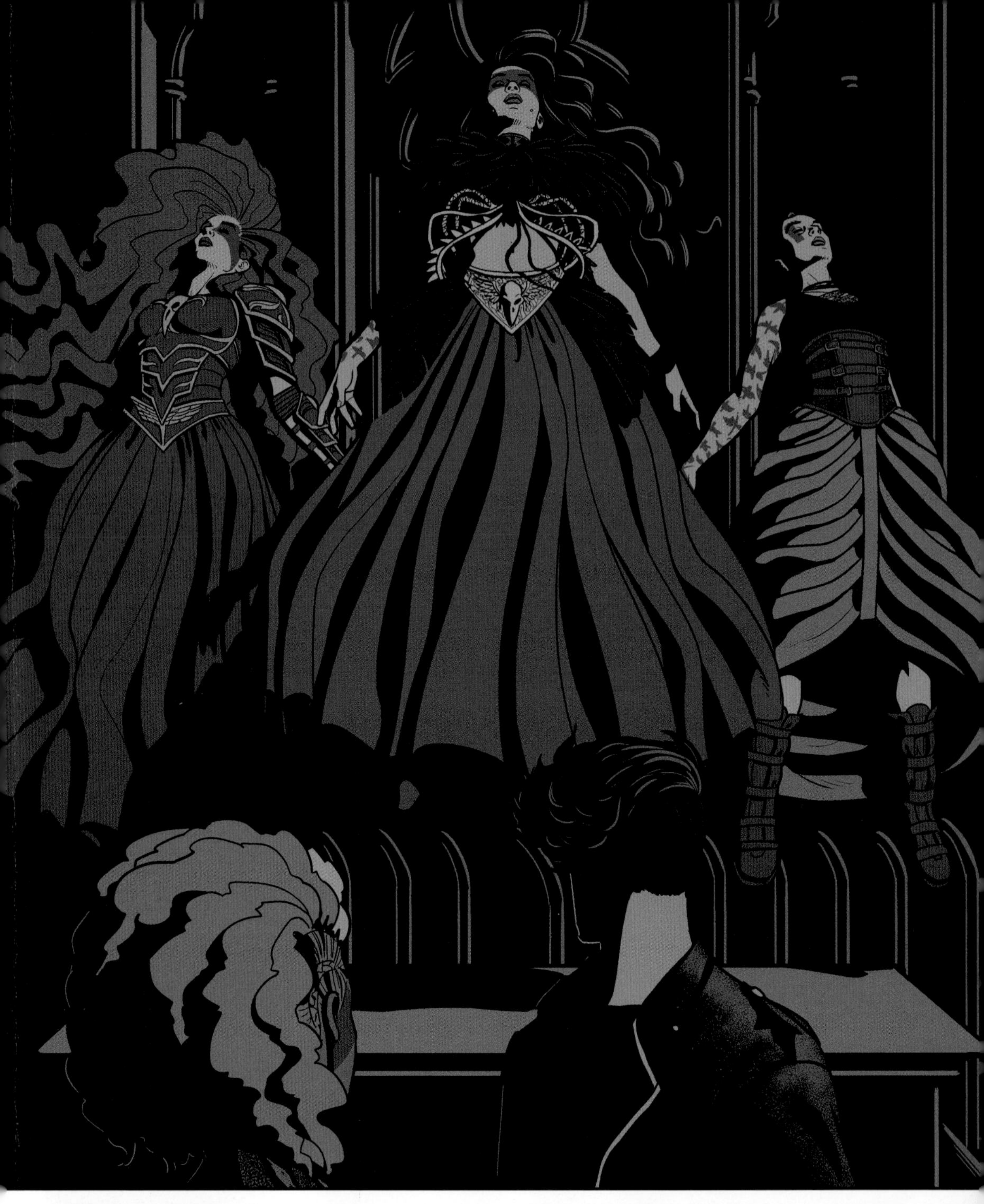

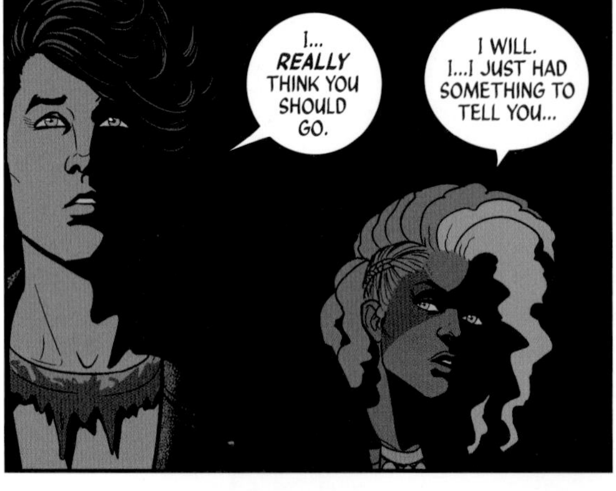
I... *REALLY* THINK YOU SHOULD GO.
I WILL. I...I JUST HAD SOMETHING TO TELL YOU...

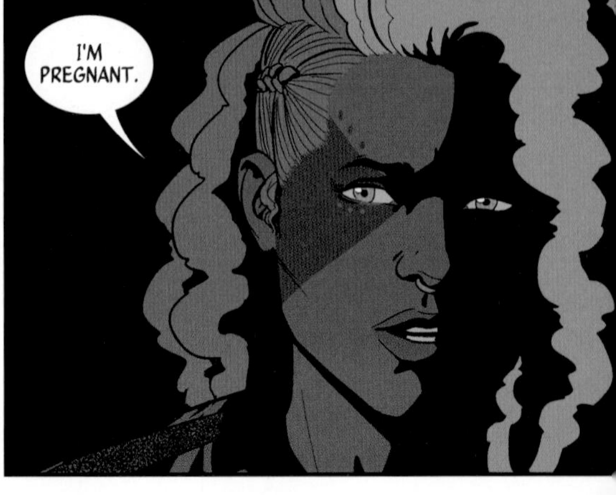
I'M PREGNANT.

SHIT. I... SHIT.

ARE YOU TELLING ME THIS AS I'M YOUR FRIEND OR... THE OTHER REASON?

I DUNNO. ONE, THE OTHER. MAYBE BOTH.

WHAT WOULD YOU DO?

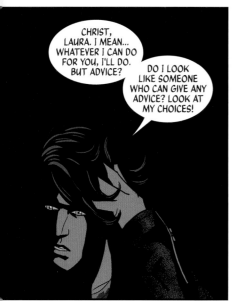

CHRIST, LAURA. I MEAN... WHATEVER I CAN DO FOR YOU, I'LL DO. BUT ADVICE?

DO I LOOK LIKE SOMEONE WHO CAN GIVE ANY ADVICE? LOOK AT MY CHOICES!

I'M GOING TO FINISH THIS TEMPLE TO THE THREE-FOLD CORPSE OF MY DEAD GIRLFRIEND WHO KILLED ME AND BROUGHT ME BACK.

I SAY THAT SENTENCE, AND I DON'T FUCKING BLINK. THAT'S MY LIFE. THAT'S MY CHOICE.

WHATEVER I DO?

DON'T.

We weren't talking about me being pregnant or him still being trapped any more.

We were talking about *everything*. And then...

I realised.

I couldn't say it aloud yet, but I knew.

THANK YOU.

I'M SORRY.

I'm not sure I can explain.

But I'll try.

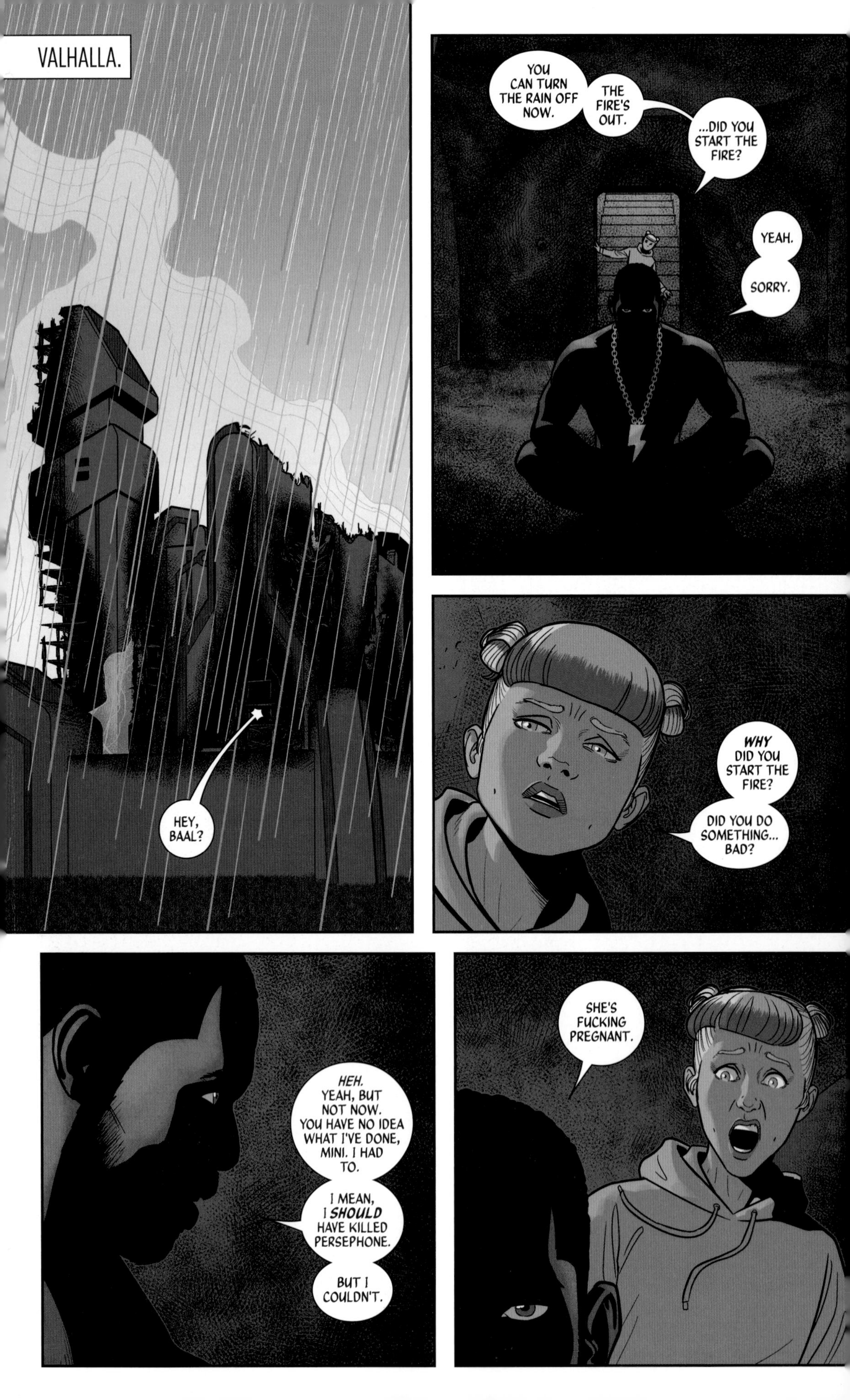
VALHALLA.
HEY, BAAL?
YOU CAN TURN THE RAIN OFF NOW.
THE FIRE'S OUT.
...DID YOU START THE FIRE?
YEAH.
SORRY.
WHY DID YOU START THE FIRE?
DID YOU DO SOMETHING... BAD?
HEH. YEAH, BUT NOT NOW. YOU HAVE NO IDEA WHAT I'VE DONE, MINI. I HAD TO.
I MEAN, I SHOULD HAVE KILLED PERSEPHONE.
BUT I COULDN'T.
SHE'S FUCKING PREGNANT.

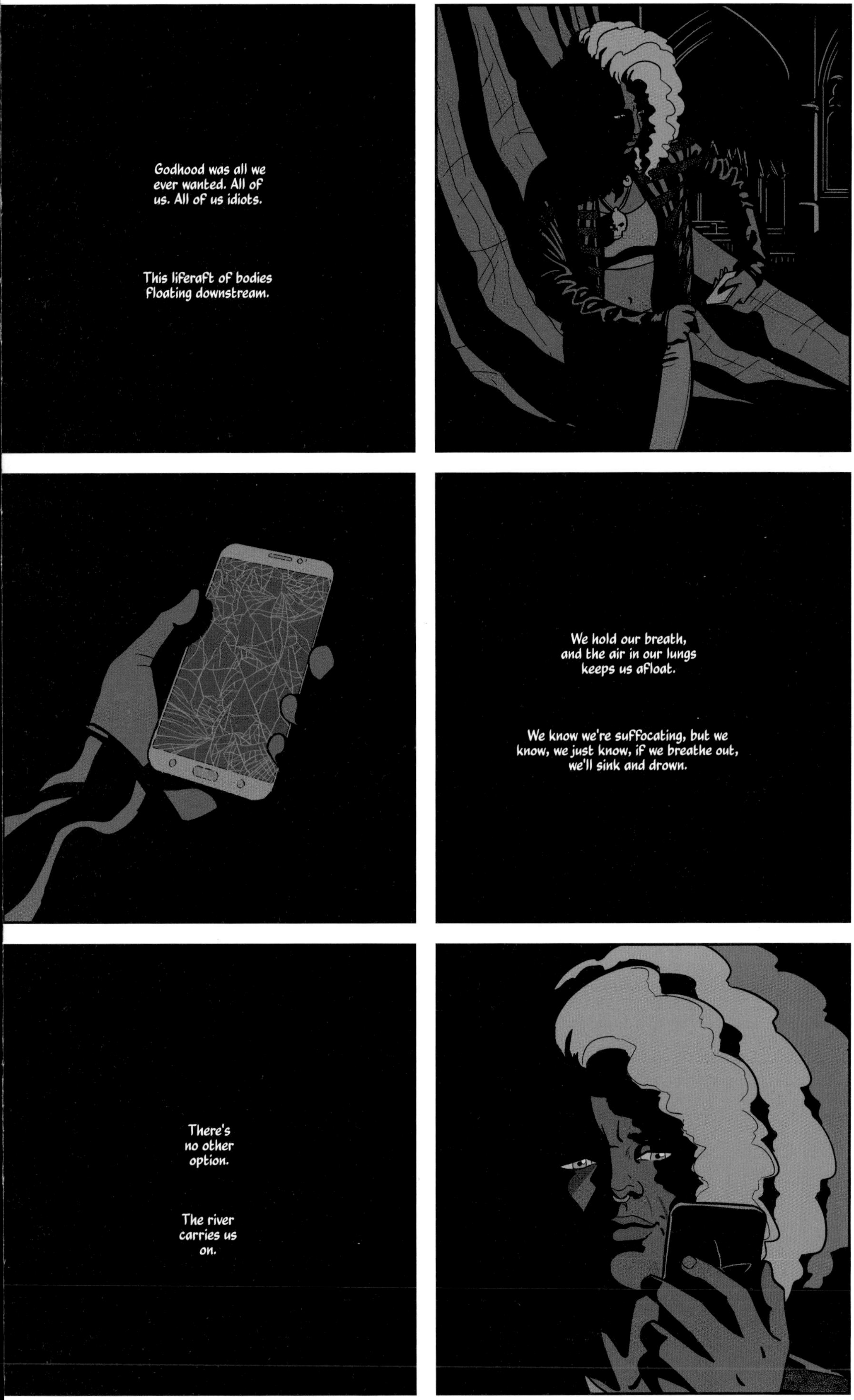
Godhood was all we ever wanted. All of us. All of us idiots.
This liferaft of bodies floating downstream.
We hold our breath, and the air in our lungs keeps us afloat.
We know we're suffocating, but we know, we just know, if we breathe out, we'll sink and drown.
There's no other option.
The river carries us on.

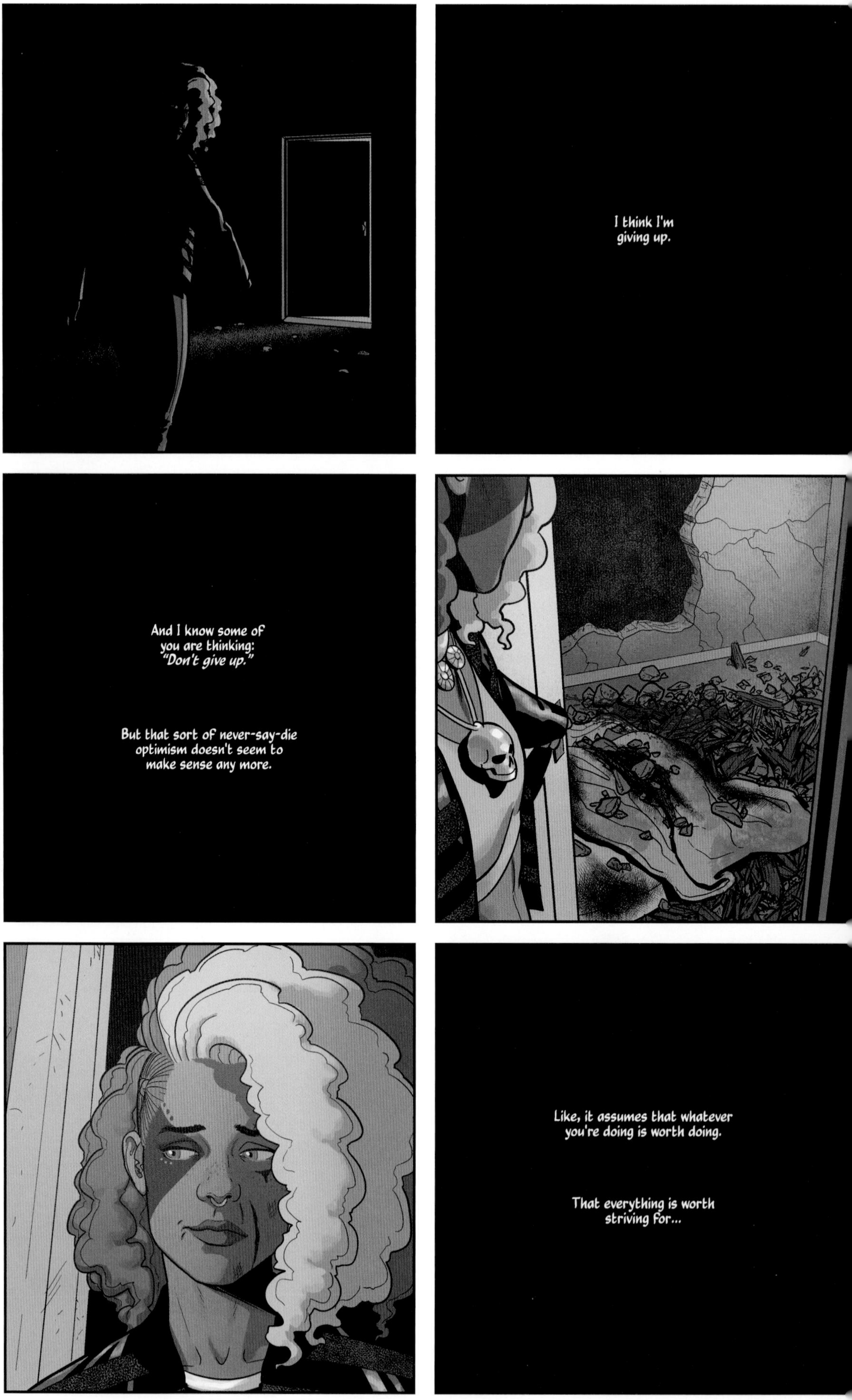
I think I'm giving up.
And I know some of you are thinking: "Don't give up."
But that sort of never-say-die optimism doesn't seem to make sense any more.
Like, it assumes that whatever you're doing is worth doing.
That everything is worth striving for...

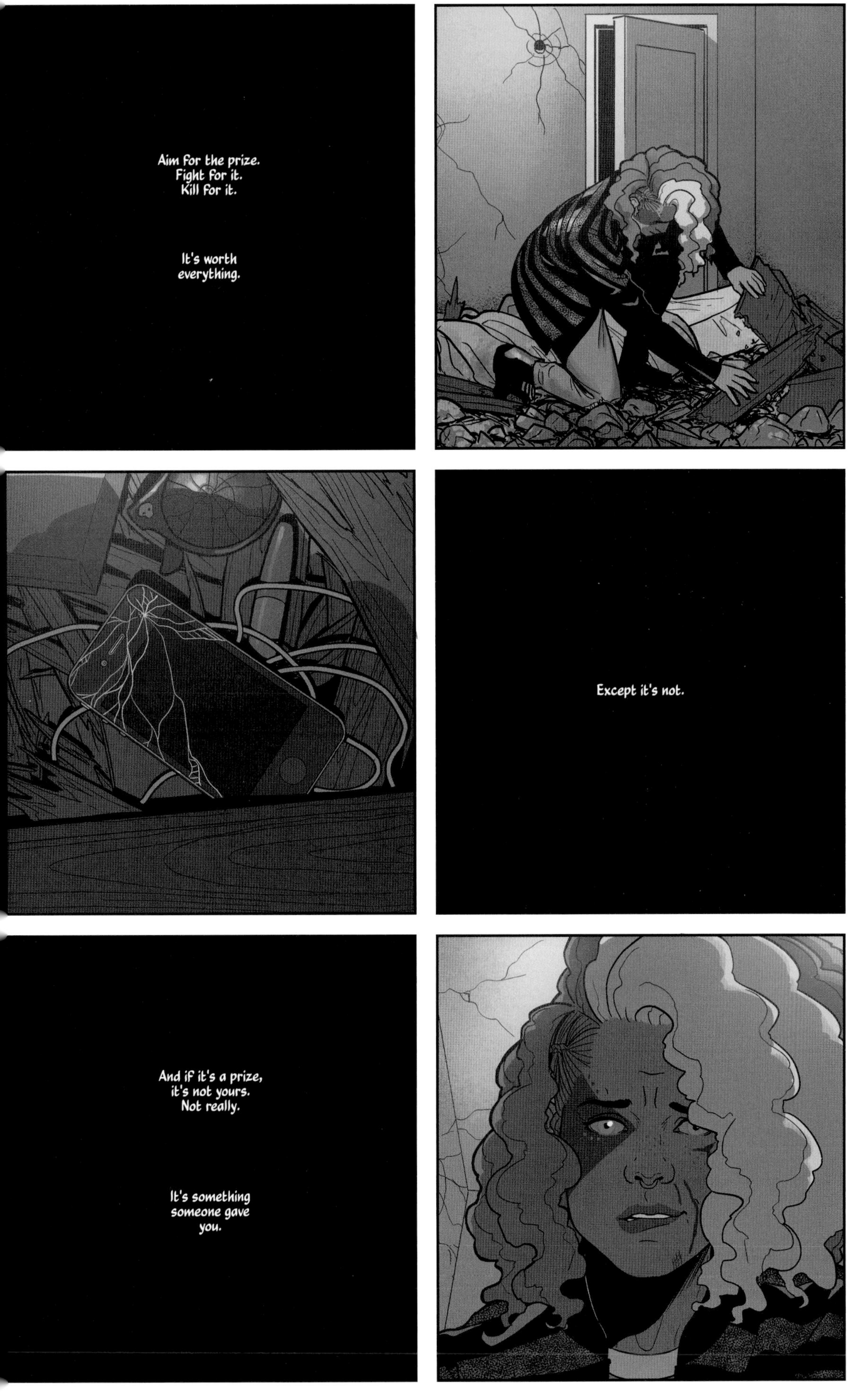
Aim for the prize.
Fight for it.
Kill for it.
It's worth everything.
Except it's not.
And if it's a prize, it's not yours. Not really.
It's something someone gave you.

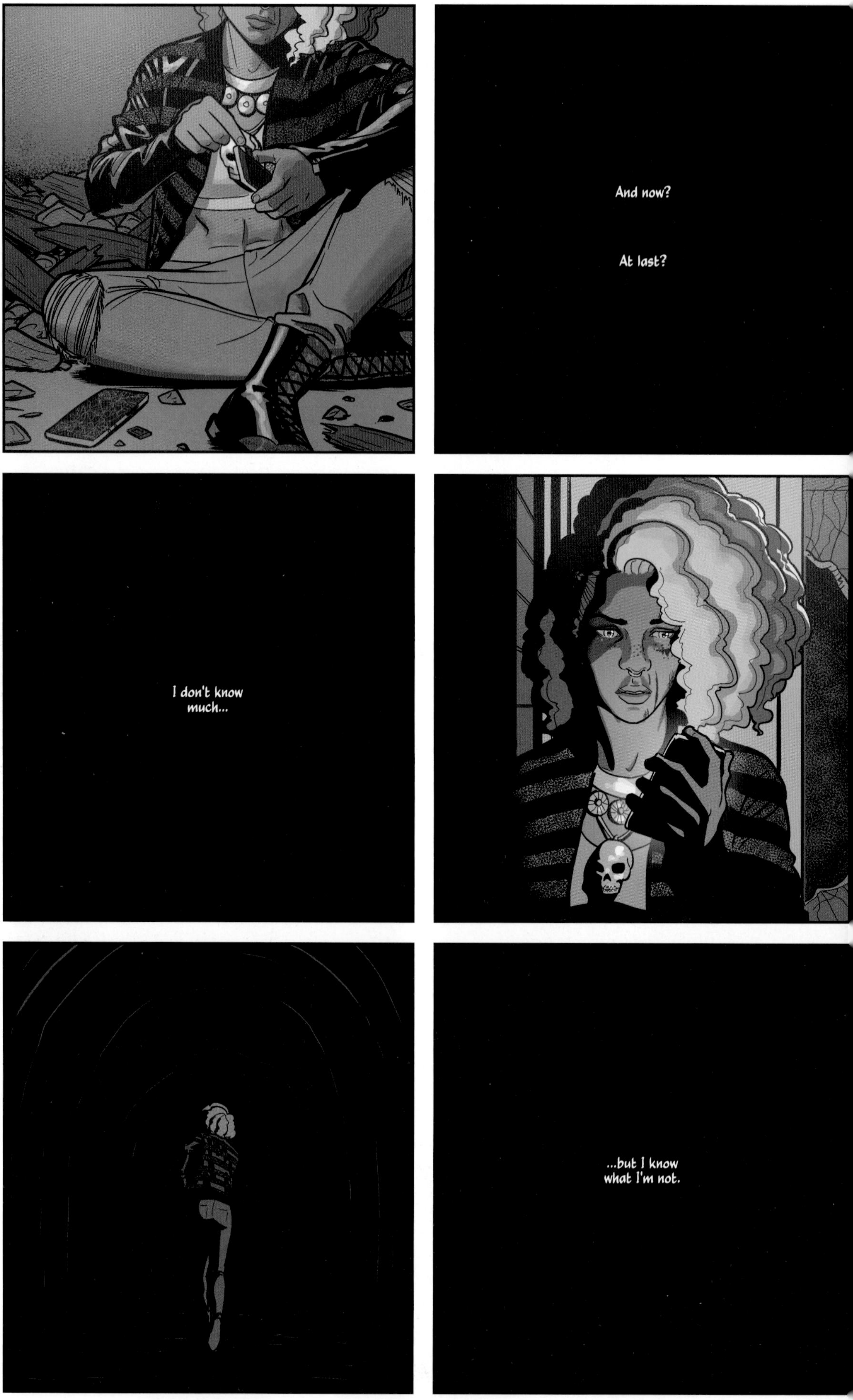
And now?
At last?
I don't know much...
...but I know what I'm not.

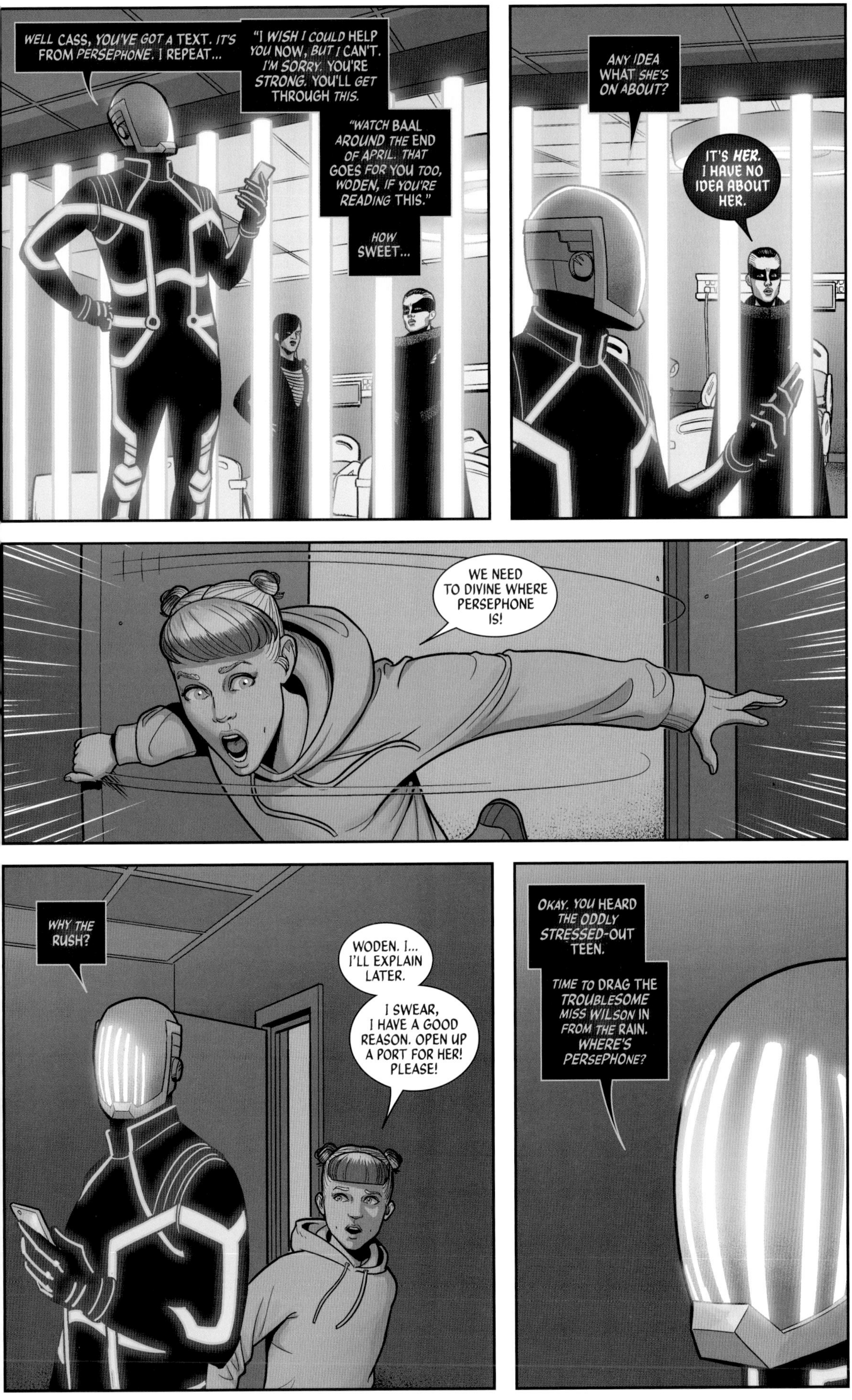
WELL CASS, YOU'VE GOT A TEXT. IT'S FROM PERSEPHONE. I REPEAT...
"I WISH I COULD HELP YOU NOW, BUT I CAN'T. I'M SORRY. YOU'RE STRONG. YOU'LL GET THROUGH THIS.
"WATCH BAAL AROUND THE END OF APRIL. THAT GOES FOR YOU TOO, WODEN, IF YOU'RE READING THIS."
HOW SWEET...
ANY IDEA WHAT SHE'S ON ABOUT?
IT'S HER. I HAVE NO IDEA ABOUT HER.
WE NEED TO DIVINE WHERE PERSEPHONE IS!
WHY THE RUSH?
WODEN. I... I'LL EXPLAIN LATER.
I SWEAR, I HAVE A GOOD REASON. OPEN UP A PORT FOR HER! PLEASE!
OKAY. YOU HEARD THE ODDLY STRESSED-OUT TEEN.
TIME TO DRAG THE TROUBLESOME MISS WILSON IN FROM THE RAIN. WHERE'S PERSEPHONE?

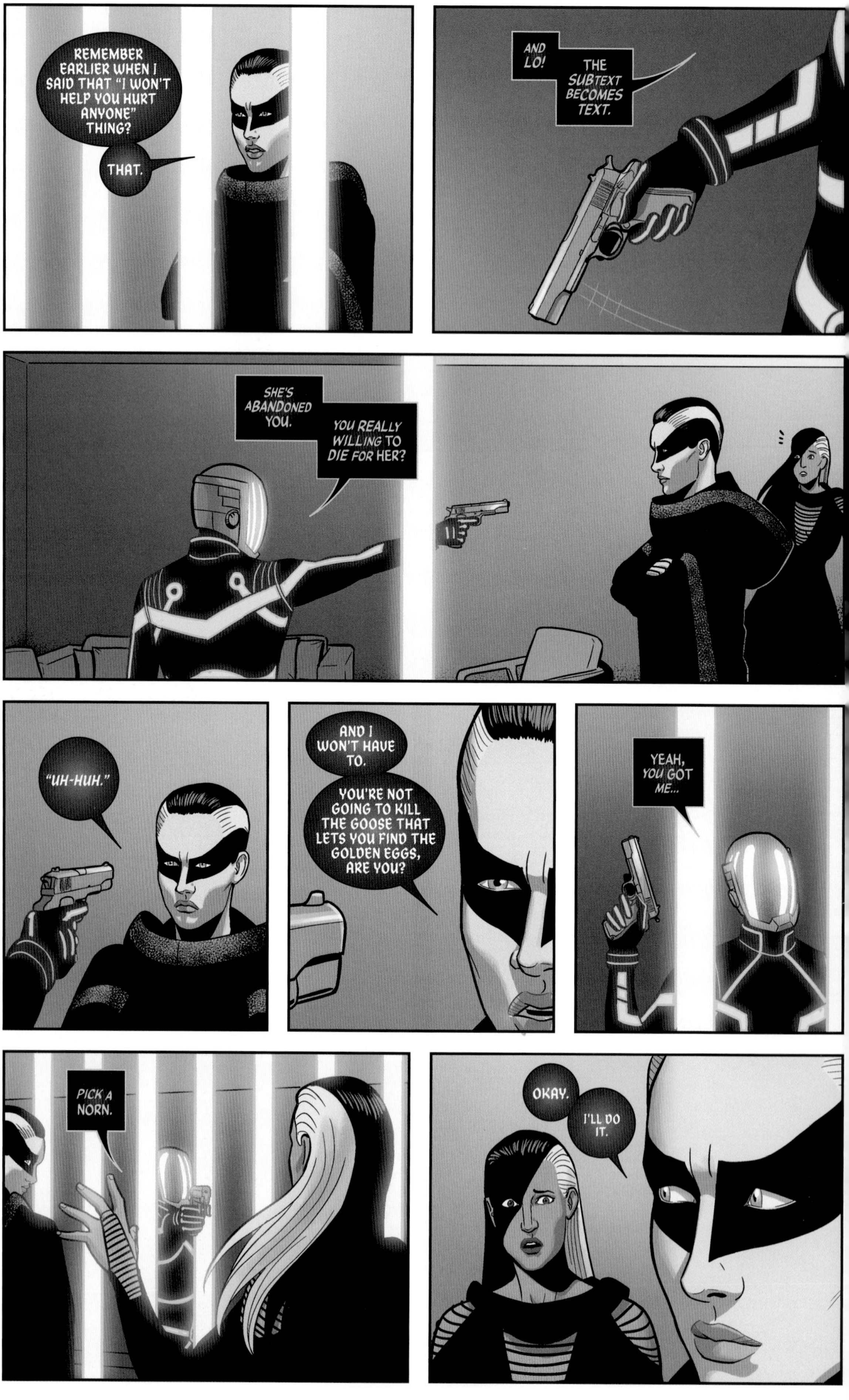
REMEMBER EARLIER WHEN I SAID THAT "I WON'T HELP YOU HURT ANYONE" THING?
THAT.
AND LO!
THE SUBTEXT BECOMES TEXT.
SHE'S ABANDONED YOU.
YOU REALLY WILLING TO DIE FOR HER?
"UH-HUH."
AND I WON'T HAVE TO.
YOU'RE NOT GOING TO KILL THE GOOSE THAT LETS YOU FIND THE GOLDEN EGGS, ARE YOU?
YEAH, YOU GOT ME...
PICK A NORN.
OKAY.
I'LL DO IT.

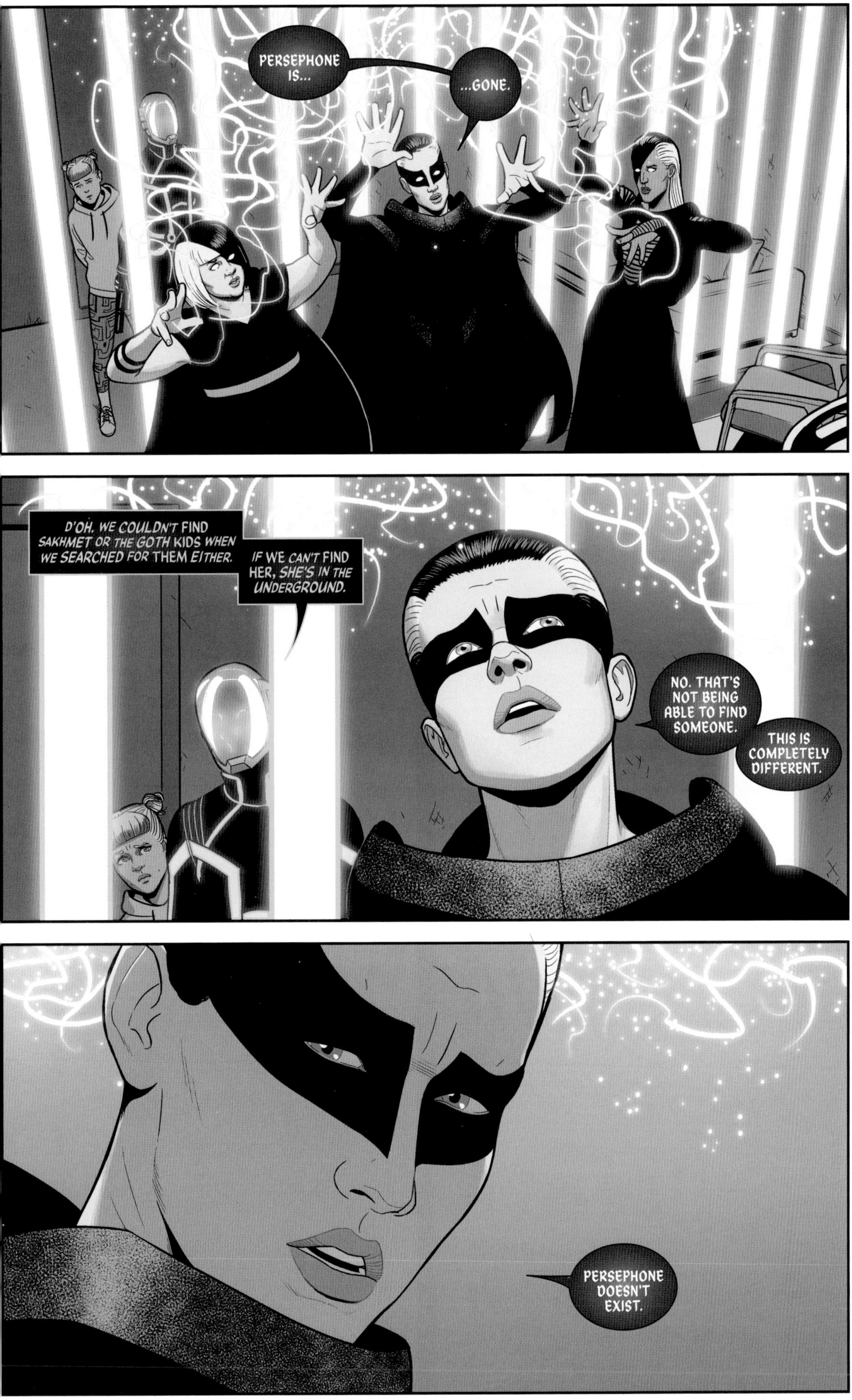
PERSEPHONE IS...
...GONE.
D'OH. WE COULDN'T FIND SAKHMET OR THE GOTH KIDS WHEN WE SEARCHED FOR THEM EITHER.
IF WE CAN'T FIND HER, SHE'S IN THE UNDERGROUND.
NO. THAT'S NOT BEING ABLE TO FIND SOMEONE.
THIS IS COMPLETELY DIFFERENT.
PERSEPHONE DOESN'T EXIST.

THE BOOK
I HAVE OPENED

9 MARCH 2015

THE
WICKED
+
DIVINE
THE

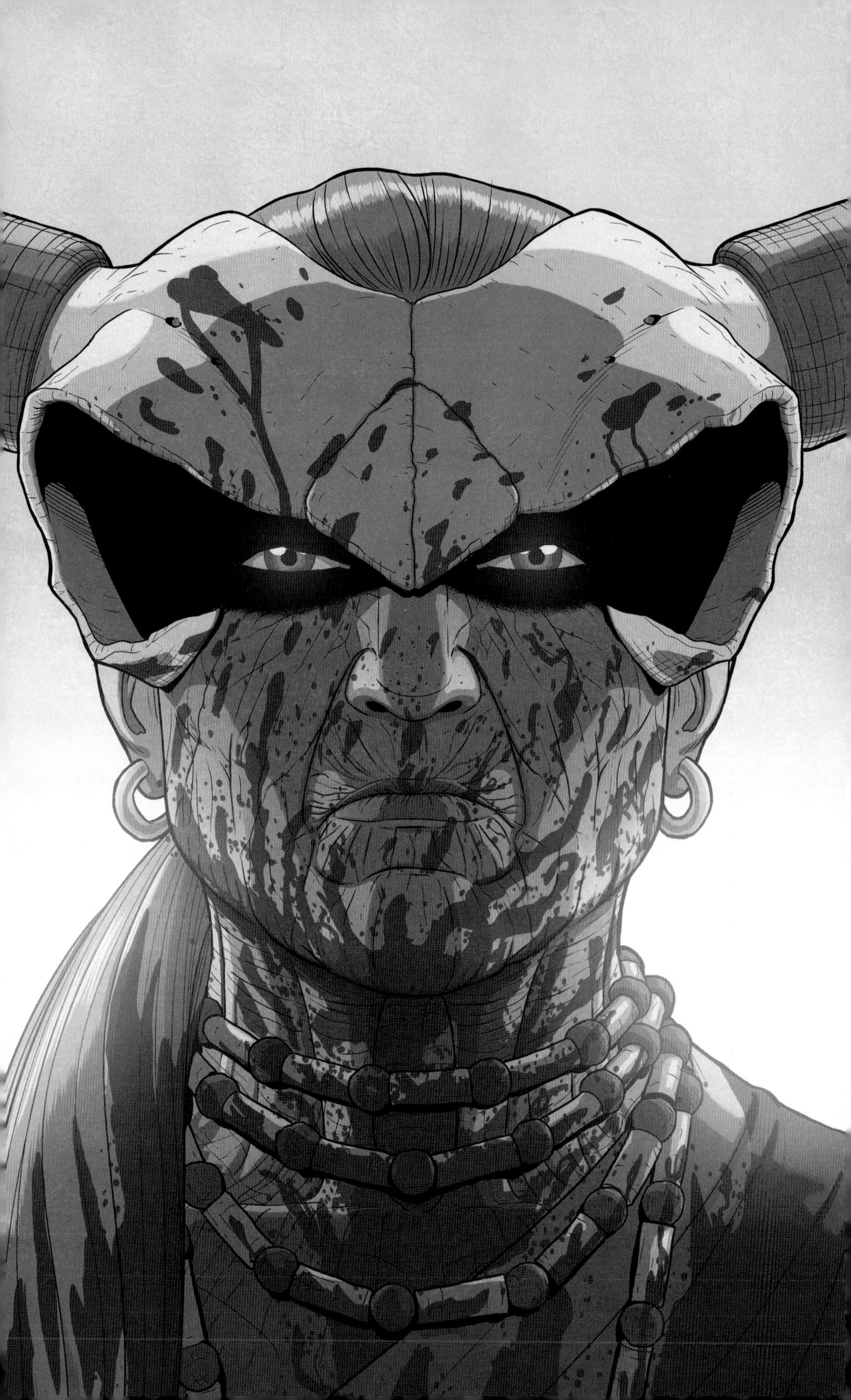

Ten days later.

A FORTY-SOMETHING MAN PRETENDING TO BE A FUCKING TEENAGER...

...THAT'S WHAT I'VE NEVER GOT.

HOW CAN YOU EVEN *DO* THAT?

ARE *YOU* SAYING YOU'VE NEVER *READ* A *NOVEL*? TRUST ME. IT'S EASIER THAN A *CHILD PLAYING* A GROWN-UP.

YOU JUST ABANDON YOUR *SUPEREGO'S* RESTRAINTS AND PEPPER IN A *LITTLE SLANG.*

ANYONE CAN BE A CHILD.

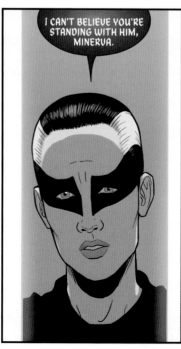

I CAN'T BELIEVE YOU'RE STANDING WITH HIM, MINERVA.

I'M SORRY.

HOW'S THE POWER-MIMICKING? ARE YOU STILL WORKING ON DUPLICATING DIO?

YES. I COULD SAMPLE HIM WHEN HE WAS HERE, BUT NOW HE'S GONE, I'M JUST LEFT WITH THE READINGS FROM THE GIG.

I'D HAVE HAD MORE IF BAAL HADN'T BURNED DOWN VALHALLA...

WHERE IS BAAL ANYWAY?

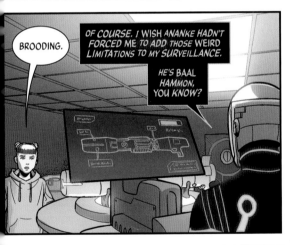

BROODING.

OF COURSE. I WISH ANANKE HADN'T FORCED ME TO ADD THOSE WEIRD LIMITATIONS TO MY SURVEILLANCE.

HE'S BAAL HAMMON, YOU KNOW?

YEAH, I KNOW. HE TOLD ME.

OF COURSE HE DID. MY FEEDS ALWAYS CUT OFF AT WEIRD TIMES. I'VE GOT ALL THESE BLANKS. EVERYONE HAS TO HAVE THEIR FUCKING SECRETS. WHAT IS HE UP TO?

I DUNNO. HE SAYS HE'LL BE THERE FOR HIS BIG RITUAL.

YEAH, NO SURPRISE. HIM AND HIS GREAT DARKNESS...

HEY, WODEN. I WAS WONDERING...

...IF YOU DO FIND A WAY TO COPY DIO'S POWERS, ARE YOU GOING TO MAKE CASSANDRA, LIKE...DO YOU?

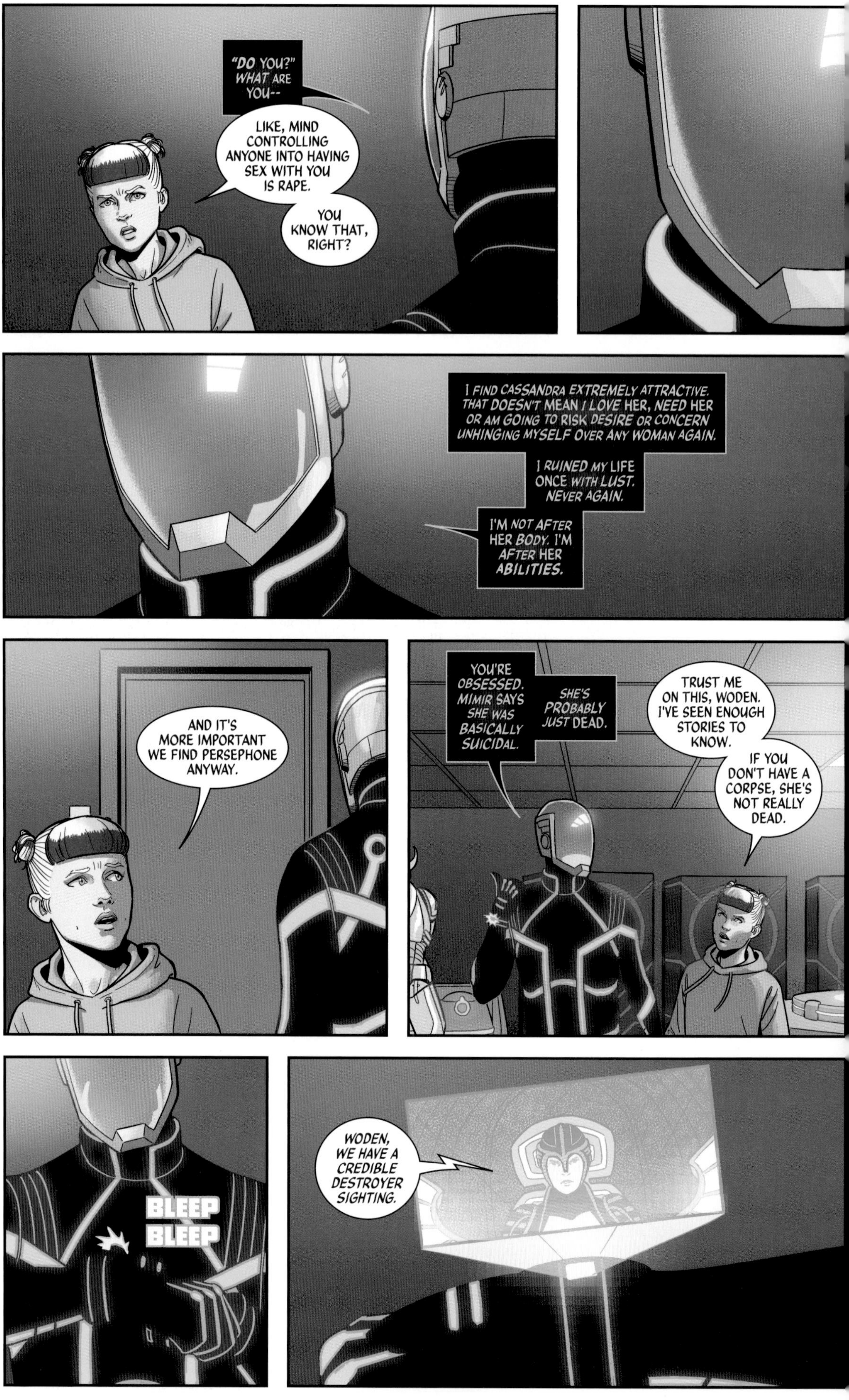
"DO YOU?" WHAT ARE YOU--
LIKE, MIND CONTROLLING ANYONE INTO HAVING SEX WITH YOU IS RAPE.
YOU KNOW THAT, RIGHT?
I FIND CASSANDRA EXTREMELY ATTRACTIVE. THAT DOESN'T MEAN I LOVE HER, NEED HER OR AM GOING TO RISK DESIRE OR CONCERN UNHINGING MYSELF OVER ANY WOMAN AGAIN.
I RUINED MY LIFE ONCE WITH LUST. NEVER AGAIN.
I'M NOT AFTER HER BODY. I'M AFTER HER ABILITIES.
AND IT'S MORE IMPORTANT WE FIND PERSEPHONE ANYWAY.
YOU'RE OBSESSED. MIMIR SAYS SHE WAS BASICALLY SUICIDAL.
SHE'S PROBABLY JUST DEAD.
TRUST ME ON THIS, WODEN. I'VE SEEN ENOUGH STORIES TO KNOW.
IF YOU DON'T HAVE A CORPSE, SHE'S NOT REALLY DEAD.
BLEEP BLEEP
WODEN, WE HAVE A CREDIBLE DESTROYER SIGHTING.

IT'S TIME TO SEND OUT THE NEW KIDS. THEY'VE GOT SOMETHING TO PROVE.

CRAP! I STILL NEED TO FINISH GETTING THIS BABY READY.

YOU GO BRIEF THEM. I CAN FINISH THE PREP.

OKAY. IT SHOULD JUST NEED POWERING UP. IT'S CALIBRATED TO STUN.

BRUNHILDE, TELL BETH'S CREW TO PREP FOR SHOWTIME.

WOULDN'T IT BE BEST FOR YOU TO GO ALONG WITH THEM? YOU'VE GIVEN THEM THE OUTFITS, BUT THEY'RE HARDLY EXPERIENCED...

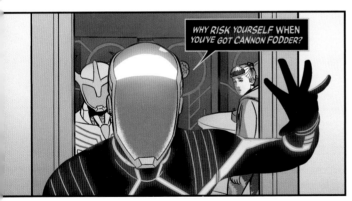

WHY RISK YOURSELF WHEN YOU'VE GOT CANNON FODDER?

HMM.

YOU'RE LEARNING.

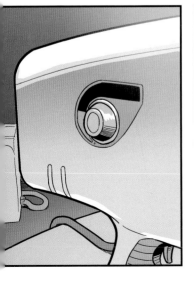

WARNING! LETHAL

PLEASE.

SHE CAN'T WIN.

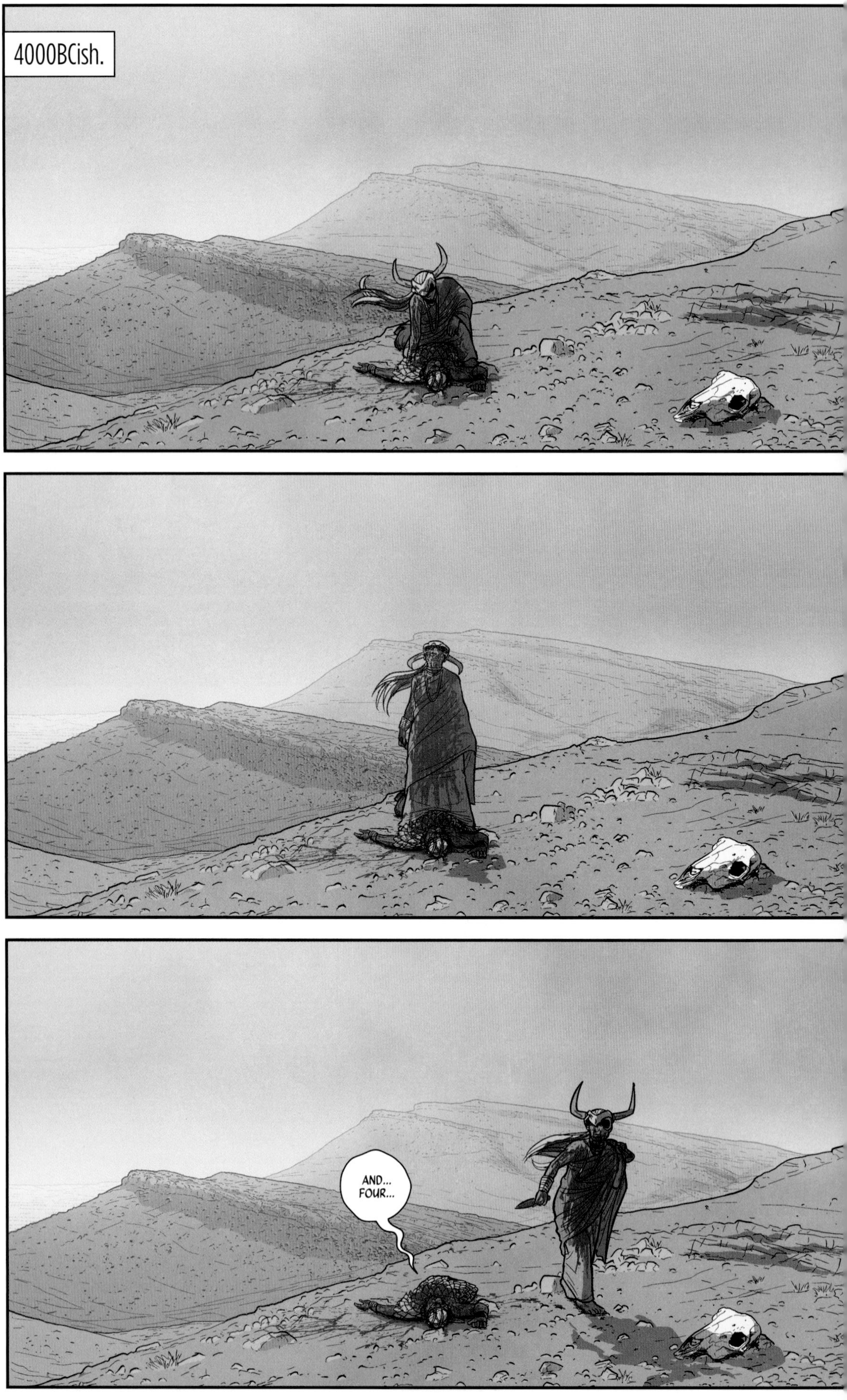
4000BCish.
AND... FOUR...

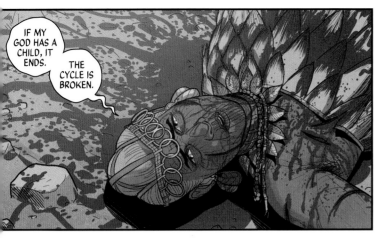

IF MY GOD HAS A CHILD, IT ENDS.

THE CYCLE IS BROKEN.

AND THEN A GREAT DARKNESS WILL CLAIM YOU, SISTER.

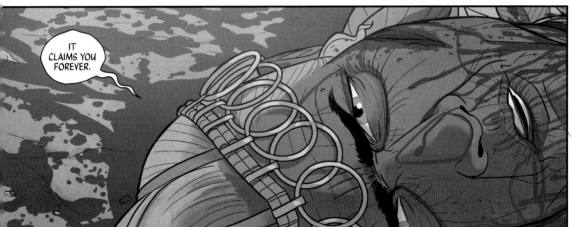

IT CLAIMS YOU FOREVER.

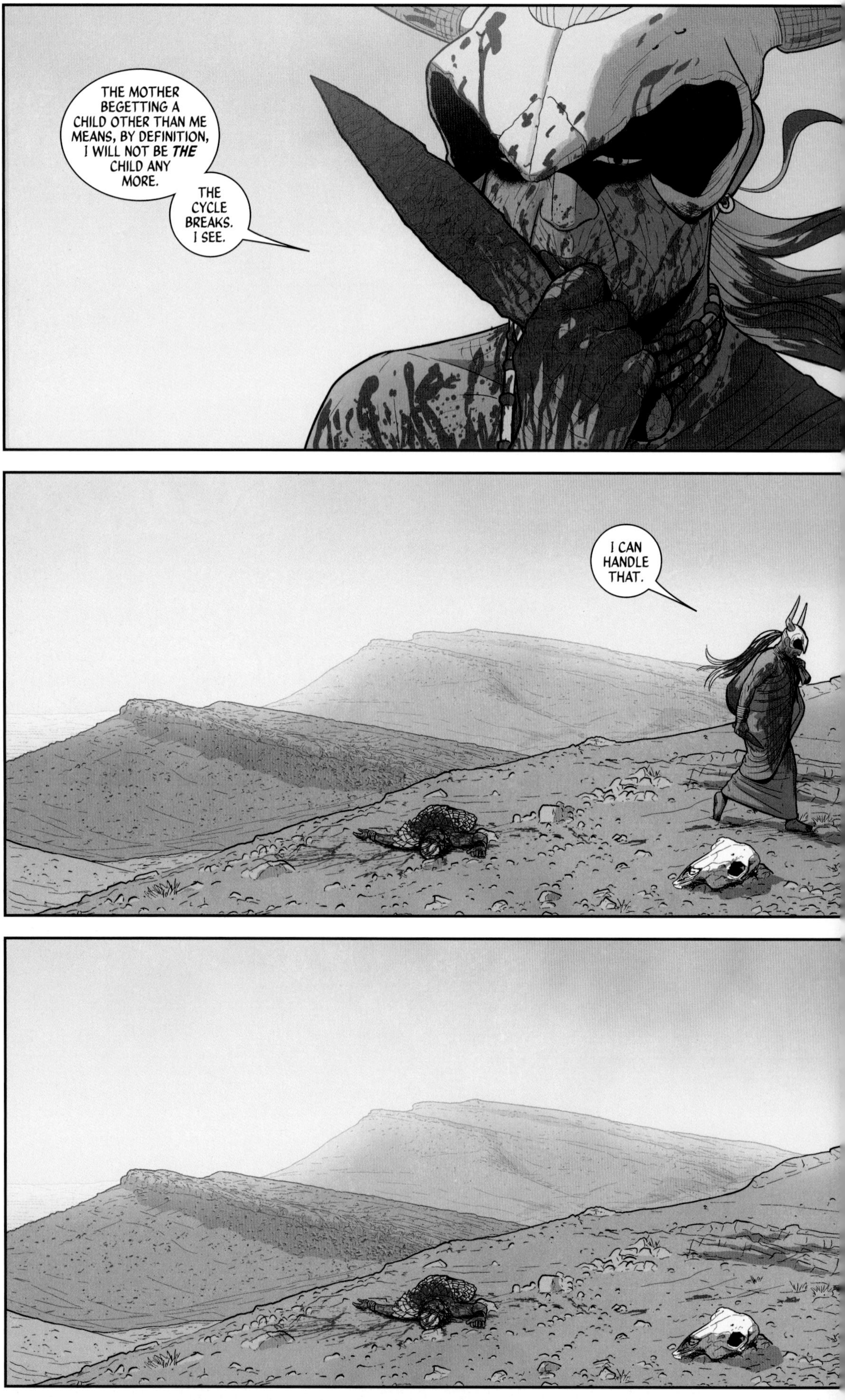
THE MOTHER BEGETTING A CHILD OTHER THAN ME MEANS, BY DEFINITION, I WILL NOT BE *THE* CHILD ANY MORE.
THE CYCLE BREAKS. I SEE.
I CAN HANDLE THAT.

LOW

19 MARCH 2015

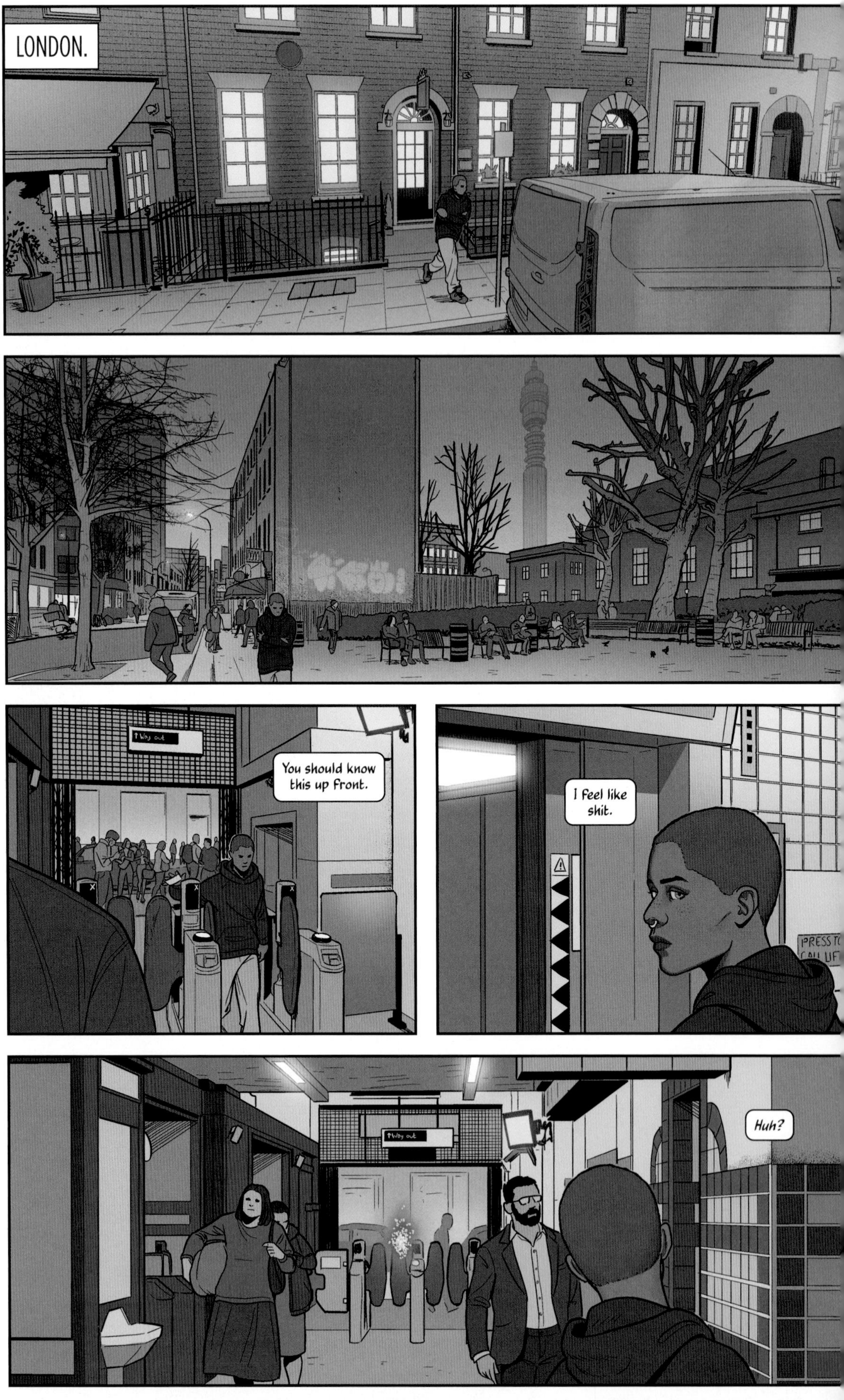
LONDON.
Way out
You should know this up front.
I feel like shit.
Way out
Huh?

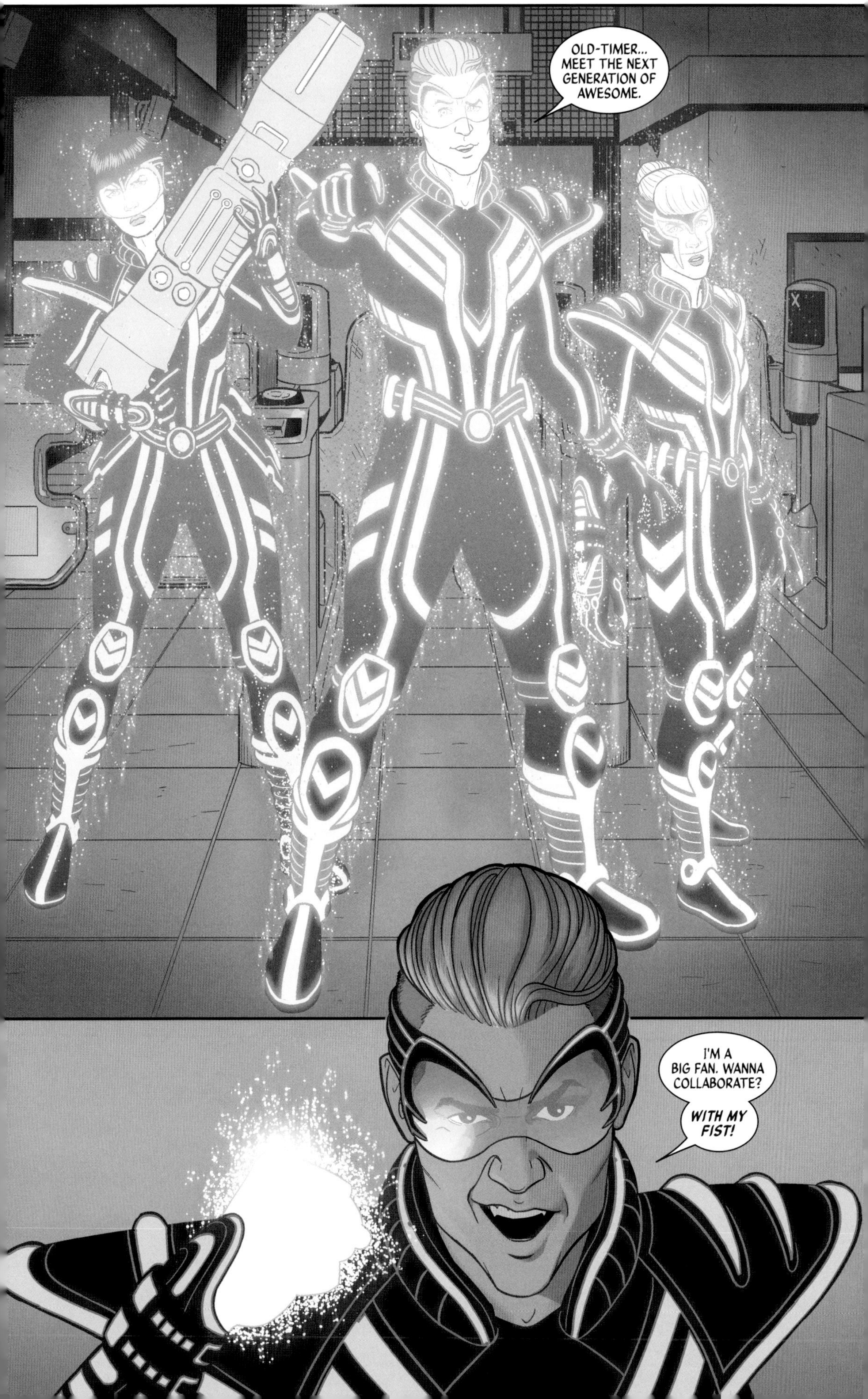
OLD-TIMER... MEET THE NEXT GENERATION OF AWESOME.
I'M A BIG FAN. WANNA COLLABORATE?
WITH MY FIST!

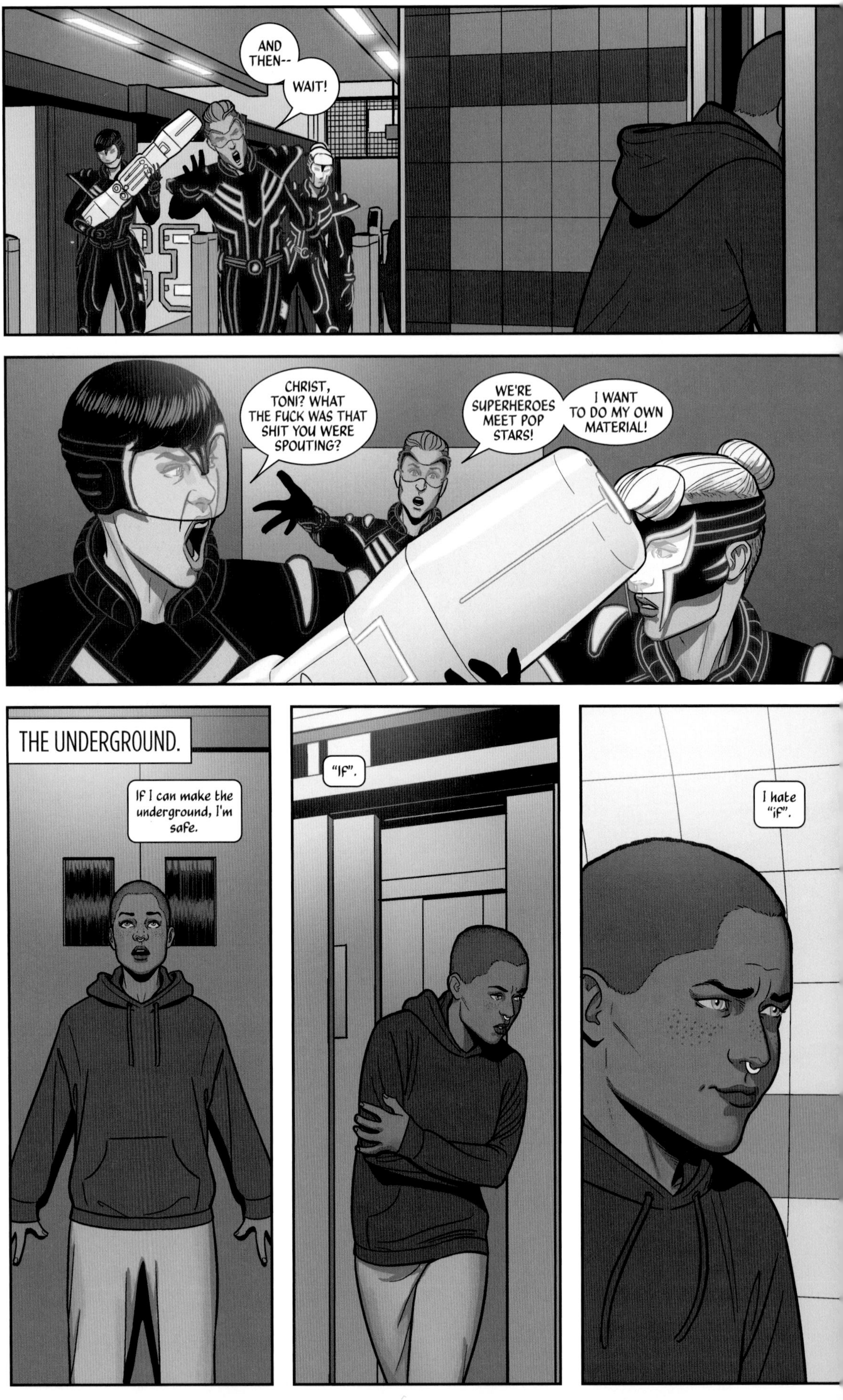
AND THEN--
WAIT!
CHRIST, TONI? WHAT THE FUCK WAS THAT SHIT YOU WERE SPOUTING?
WE'RE SUPERHEROES MEET POP STARS!
I WANT TO DO MY OWN MATERIAL!
THE UNDERGROUND.
If I can make the underground, I'm safe.
"If".
I hate "if".

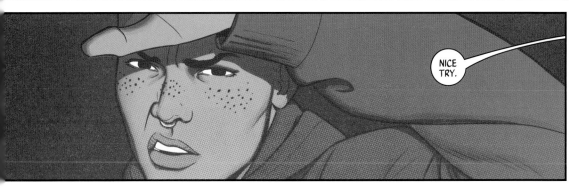

NICE TRY.

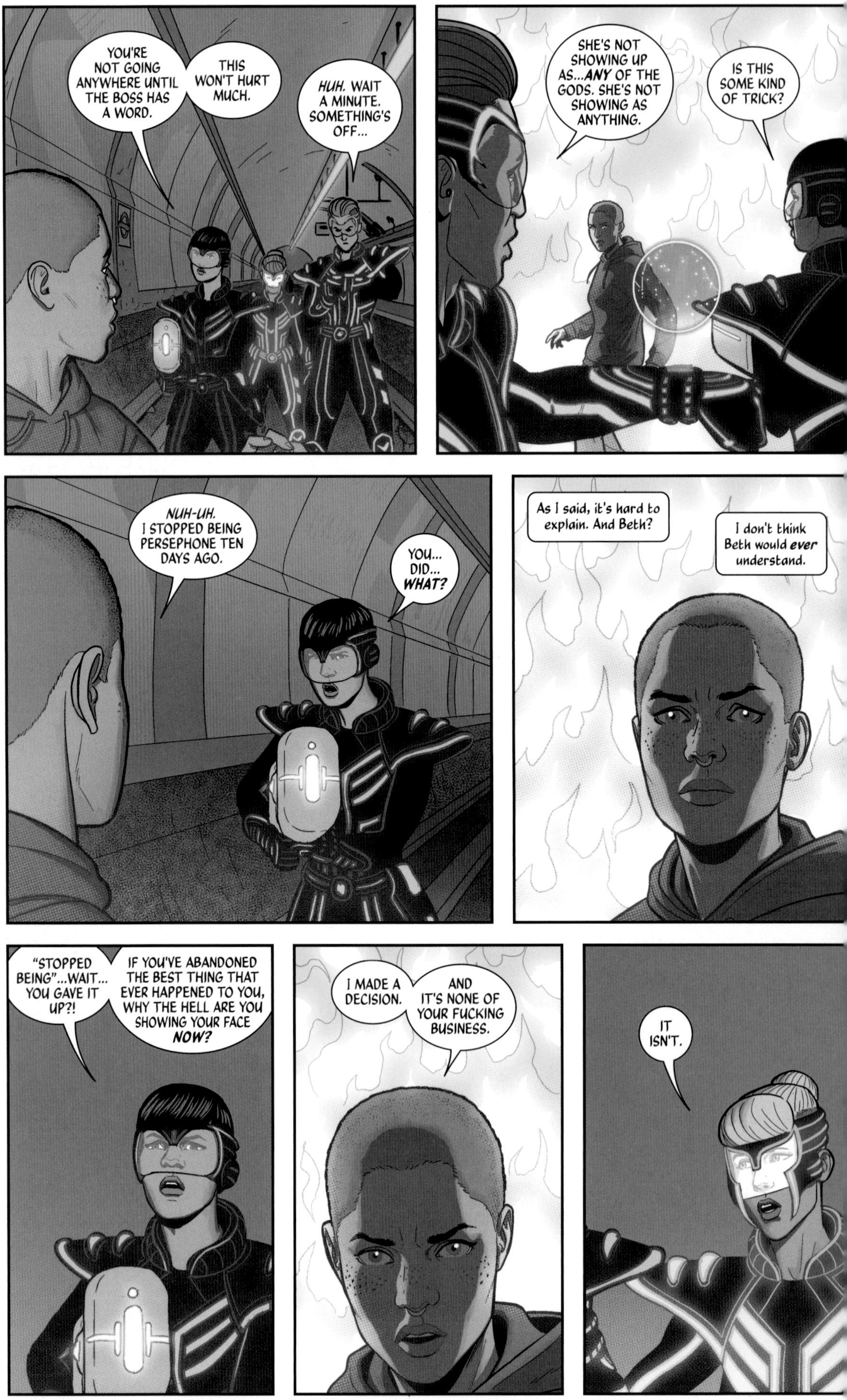

YOU'RE NOT GOING ANYWHERE UNTIL THE BOSS HAS A WORD.
THIS WON'T HURT MUCH.
HUH. WAIT A MINUTE. SOMETHING'S OFF...
SHE'S NOT SHOWING UP AS...***ANY*** OF THE GODS. SHE'S NOT SHOWING AS ANYTHING.
IS THIS SOME KIND OF TRICK?
NUH-UH. I STOPPED BEING PERSEPHONE TEN DAYS AGO.
YOU... DID... ***WHAT?***
As I said, it's hard to explain. And Beth?
I don't think Beth would ***ever*** understand.
"STOPPED BEING"...WAIT... YOU GAVE IT UP?!
IF YOU'VE ABANDONED THE BEST THING THAT EVER HAPPENED TO YOU, WHY THE HELL ARE YOU SHOWING YOUR FACE ***NOW?***
I MADE A DECISION.
AND IT'S NONE OF YOUR FUCKING BUSINESS.
IT ISN'T.

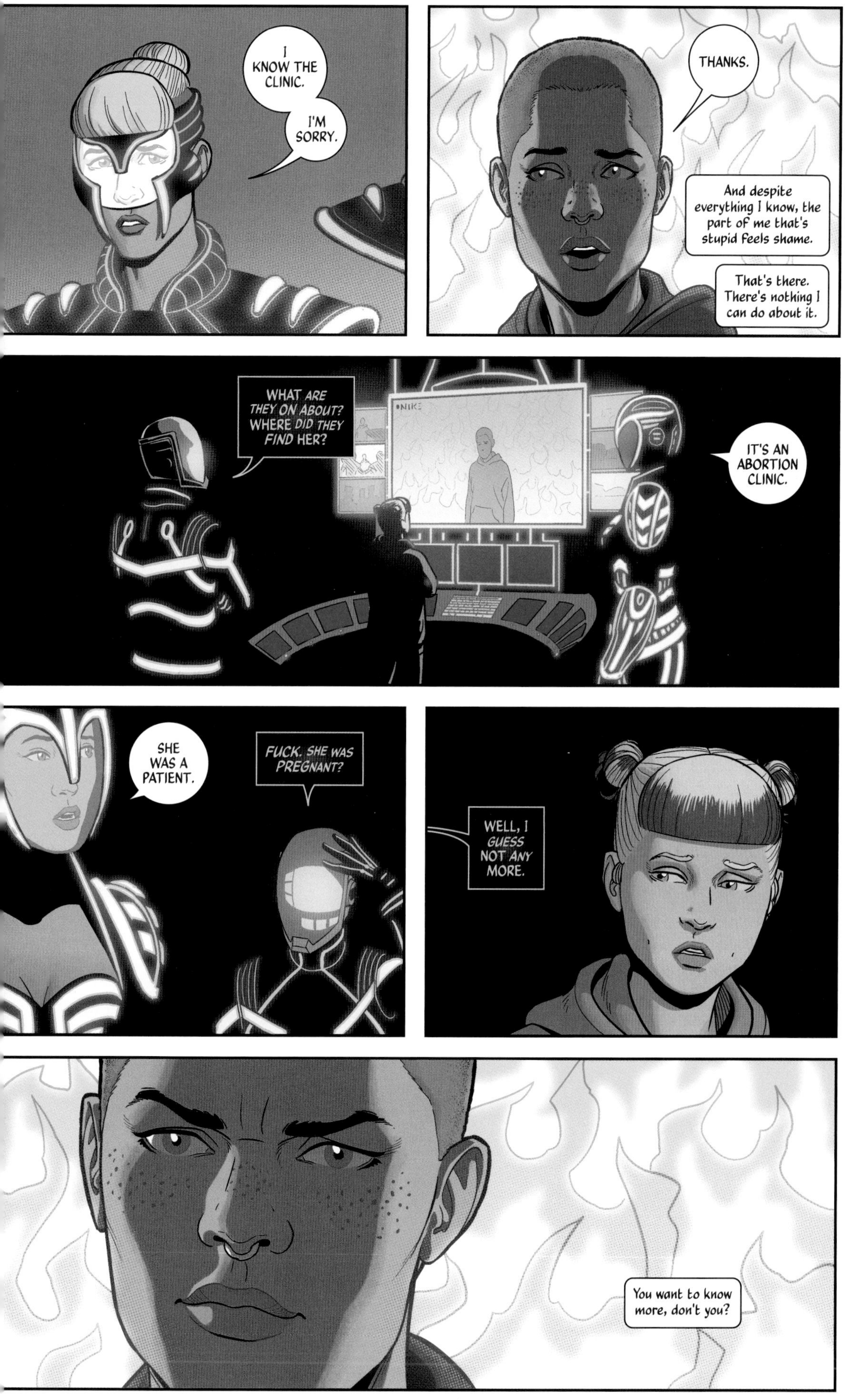
I KNOW THE CLINIC.
I'M SORRY.
THANKS.
And despite everything I know, the part of me that's stupid feels shame.
That's there. There's nothing I can do about it.
WHAT ARE THEY ON ABOUT? WHERE DID THEY FIND HER?
IT'S AN ABORTION CLINIC.
SHE WAS A PATIENT.
FUCK. SHE WAS PREGNANT?
WELL, I GUESS NOT ANY MORE.
You want to know more, don't you?

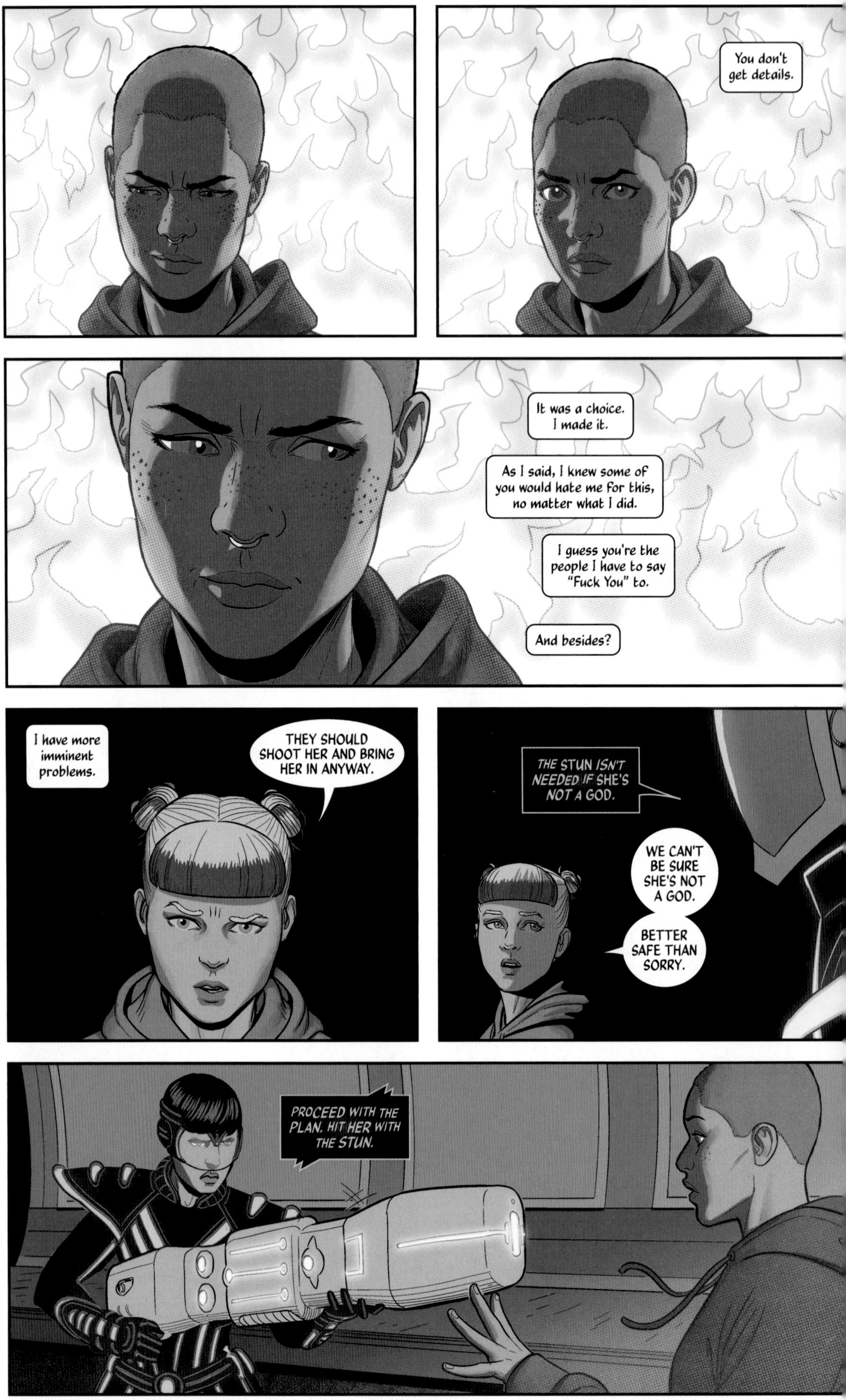
You don't get details.
It was a choice. I made it.
As I said, I knew some of you would hate me for this, no matter what I did.
I guess you're the people I have to say "Fuck You" to.
And besides?
I have more imminent problems.
THEY SHOULD SHOOT HER AND BRING HER IN ANYWAY.
THE STUN ISN'T NEEDED IF SHE'S NOT A GOD.
WE CAN'T BE SURE SHE'S NOT A GOD.
BETTER SAFE THAN SORRY.
PROCEED WITH THE PLAN. HIT HER WITH THE STUN.

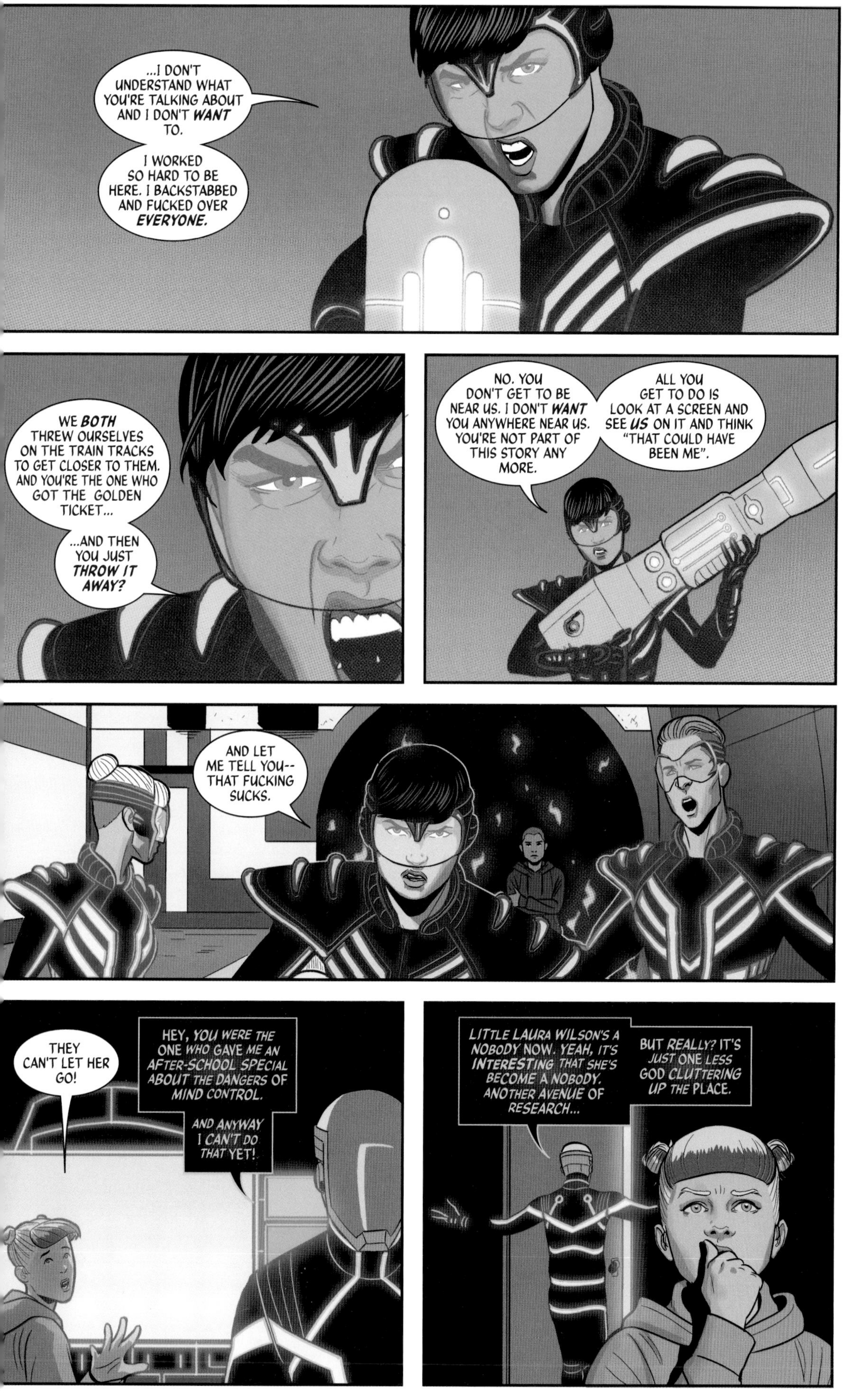
...I DON'T UNDERSTAND WHAT YOU'RE TALKING ABOUT AND I DON'T WANT TO.
I WORKED SO HARD TO BE HERE. I BACKSTABBED AND FUCKED OVER EVERYONE.
WE BOTH THREW OURSELVES ON THE TRAIN TRACKS TO GET CLOSER TO THEM. AND YOU'RE THE ONE WHO GOT THE GOLDEN TICKET...
...AND THEN YOU JUST THROW IT AWAY?
NO. YOU DON'T GET TO BE NEAR US. I DON'T WANT YOU ANYWHERE NEAR US. YOU'RE NOT PART OF THIS STORY ANY MORE.
ALL YOU GET TO DO IS LOOK AT A SCREEN AND SEE US ON IT AND THINK "THAT COULD HAVE BEEN ME".
AND LET ME TELL YOU-- THAT FUCKING SUCKS.
THEY CAN'T LET HER GO!
HEY, YOU WERE THE ONE WHO GAVE ME AN AFTER-SCHOOL SPECIAL ABOUT THE DANGERS OF MIND CONTROL.
AND ANYWAY I CAN'T DO THAT YET!
LITTLE LAURA WILSON'S A NOBODY NOW. YEAH, IT'S INTERESTING THAT SHE'S BECOME A NOBODY. ANOTHER AVENUE OF RESEARCH...
BUT REALLY? IT'S JUST ONE LESS GOD CLUTTERING UP THE PLACE.

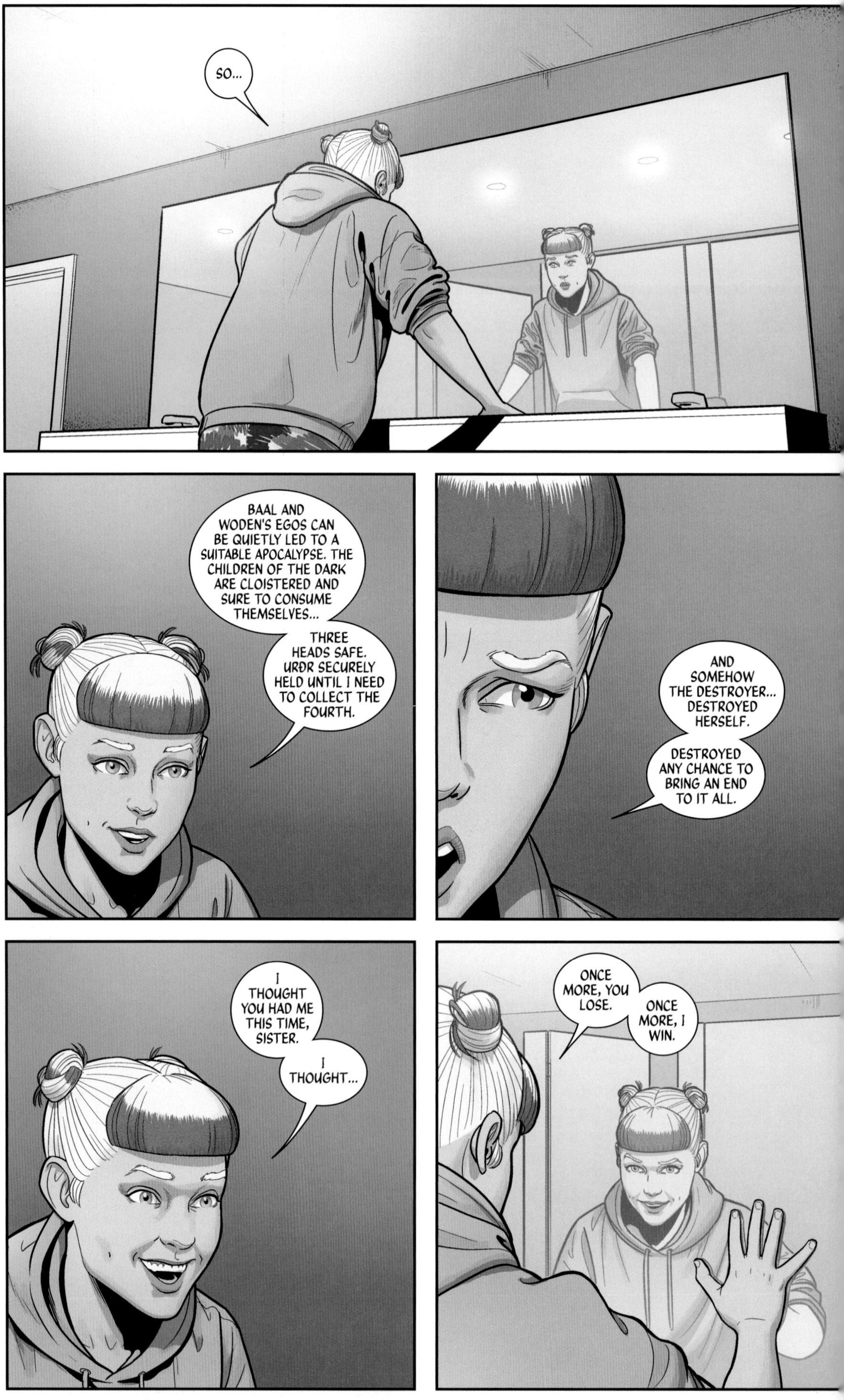
SO...
BAAL AND WODEN'S EGOS CAN BE QUIETLY LED TO A SUITABLE APOCALYPSE. THE CHILDREN OF THE DARK ARE CLOISTERED AND SURE TO CONSUME THEMSELVES...
THREE HEADS SAFE. URÐR SECURELY HELD UNTIL I NEED TO COLLECT THE FOURTH.
AND SOMEHOW THE DESTROYER... DESTROYED HERSELF.
DESTROYED ANY CHANCE TO BRING AN END TO IT ALL.
I THOUGHT YOU HAD ME THIS TIME, SISTER.
I THOUGHT...
ONCE MORE, YOU LOSE.
ONCE MORE, I WIN.

MY LONG CON
IS LONGER THAN
YOUR LONG CON

4000BCish

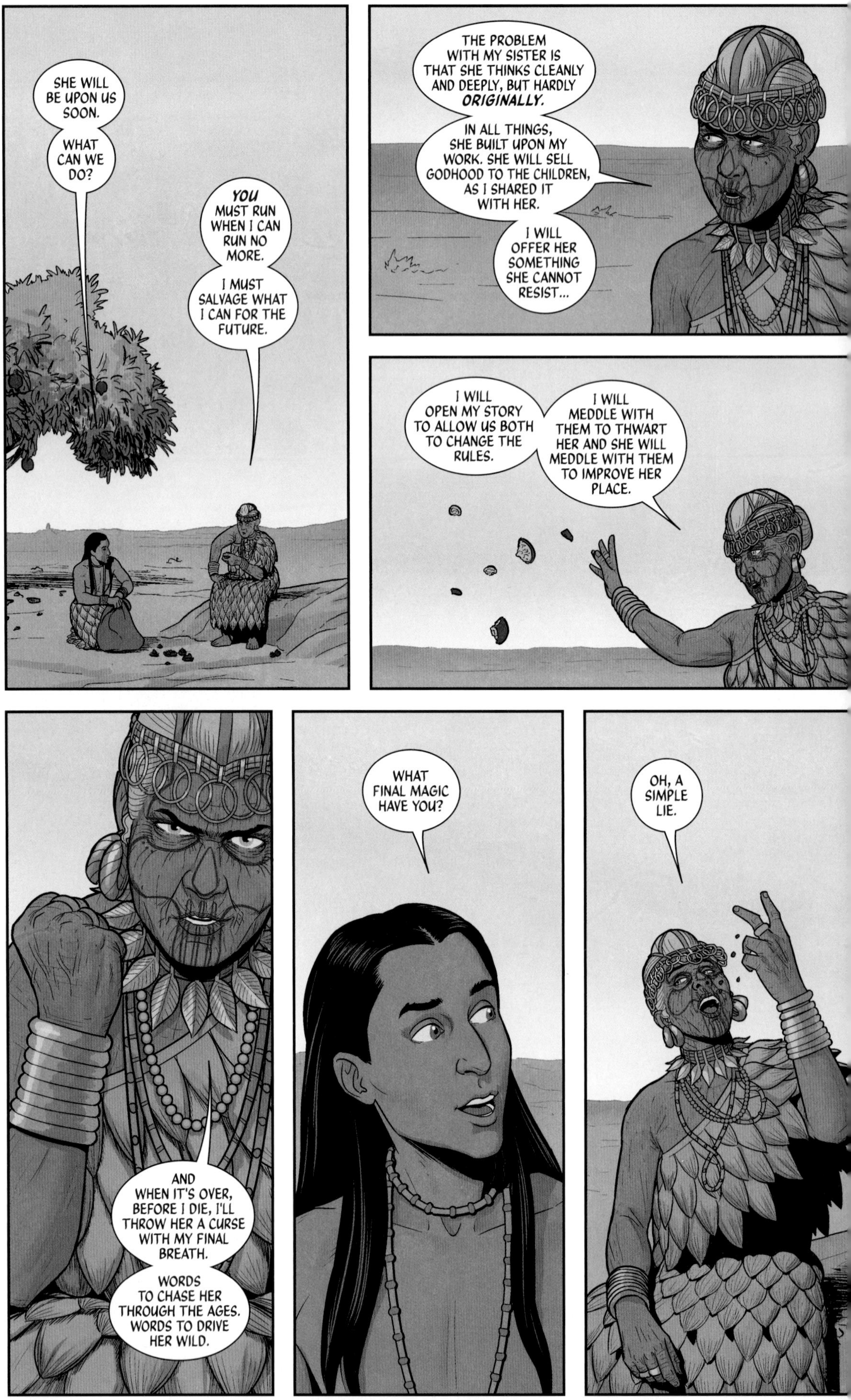
SHE WILL BE UPON US SOON.
WHAT CAN WE DO?
YOU MUST RUN WHEN I CAN RUN NO MORE.
I MUST SALVAGE WHAT I CAN FOR THE FUTURE.
THE PROBLEM WITH MY SISTER IS THAT SHE THINKS CLEANLY AND DEEPLY, BUT HARDLY ***ORIGINALLY.***
IN ALL THINGS, SHE BUILT UPON MY WORK. SHE WILL SELL GODHOOD TO THE CHILDREN, AS I SHARED IT WITH HER.
I WILL OFFER HER SOMETHING SHE CANNOT RESIST...
I WILL OPEN MY STORY TO ALLOW US BOTH TO CHANGE THE RULES.
I WILL MEDDLE WITH THEM TO THWART HER AND SHE WILL MEDDLE WITH THEM TO IMPROVE HER PLACE.
AND WHEN IT'S OVER, BEFORE I DIE, I'LL THROW HER A CURSE WITH MY FINAL BREATH.
WORDS TO CHASE HER THROUGH THE AGES. WORDS TO DRIVE HER WILD.
WHAT FINAL MAGIC HAVE YOU?
OH, A SIMPLE LIE.

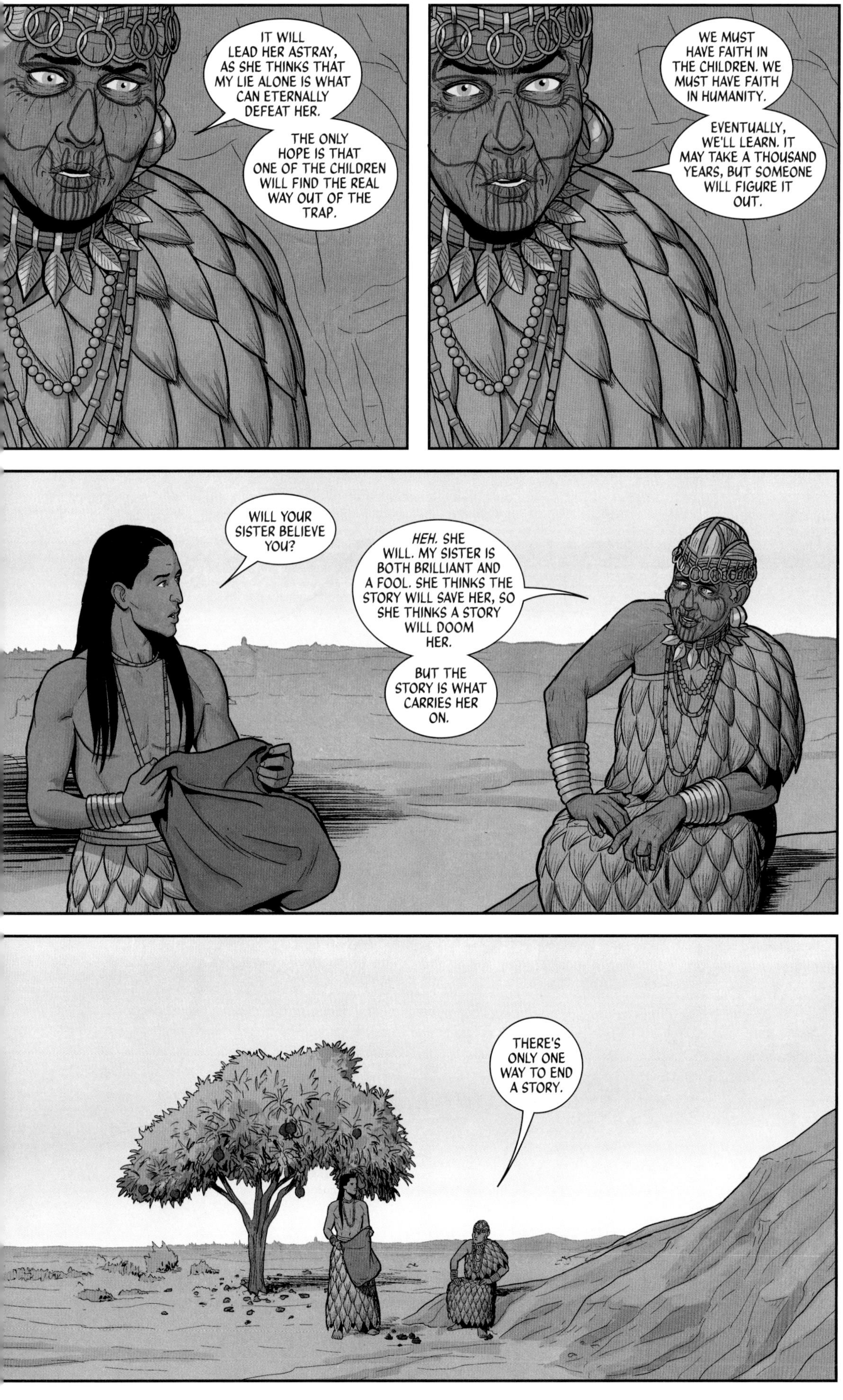
IT WILL LEAD HER ASTRAY, AS SHE THINKS THAT MY LIE ALONE IS WHAT CAN ETERNALLY DEFEAT HER.
THE ONLY HOPE IS THAT ONE OF THE CHILDREN WILL FIND THE REAL WAY OUT OF THE TRAP.
WE MUST HAVE FAITH IN THE CHILDREN. WE MUST HAVE FAITH IN HUMANITY.
EVENTUALLY, WE'LL LEARN. IT MAY TAKE A THOUSAND YEARS, BUT SOMEONE WILL FIGURE IT OUT.
WILL YOUR SISTER BELIEVE YOU?
HEH. SHE WILL. MY SISTER IS BOTH BRILLIANT AND A FOOL. SHE THINKS THE STORY WILL SAVE HER, SO SHE THINKS A STORY WILL DOOM HER.
BUT THE STORY IS WHAT CARRIES HER ON.
THERE'S ONLY ONE WAY TO END A STORY.

So, what happened after Baph and Morri? After Sakhmet. After Baal. After Dio. After...everything.

This addict had her moment of clarity.

I could see everything.

I got it.

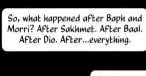

I'm not a god.

Not in a self-hating way. Not in an I-can't-achieve way. Not "I'm unworthy".

Just...*I'm not a god.* I'm really not a fucking god.

I knew it.

And then I wasn't.

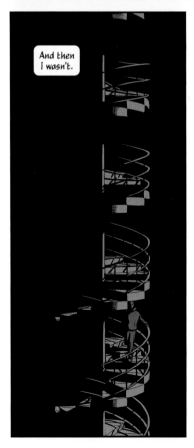

It was like sobering up. It was like hitting bottom.

Don't get me wrong. I cried. I lay in the darkness for days.

But I knew I was going to get up eventually. When I did, I looked at the mess of my life.

I started making changes.

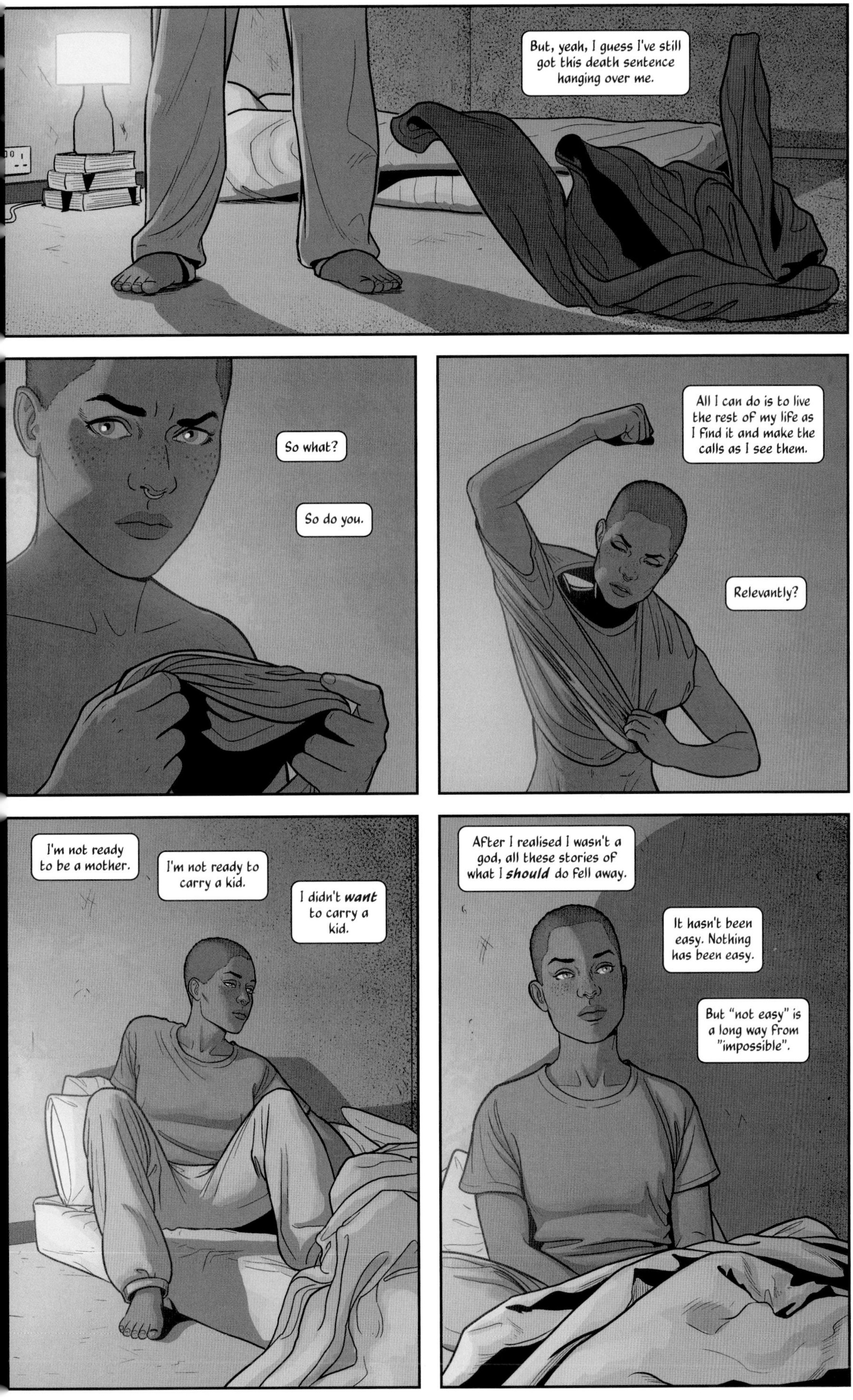

But, yeah, I guess I've still got this death sentence hanging over me.
So what?
So do you.
All I can do is to live the rest of my life as I find it and make the calls as I see them.
Relevantly?
I'm not ready to be a mother.
I'm not ready to carry a kid.
I didn't *want* to carry a kid.
After I realised I wasn't a god, all these stories of what I *should* do fell away.
It hasn't been easy. Nothing has been easy.
But "not easy" is a long way from "impossible".

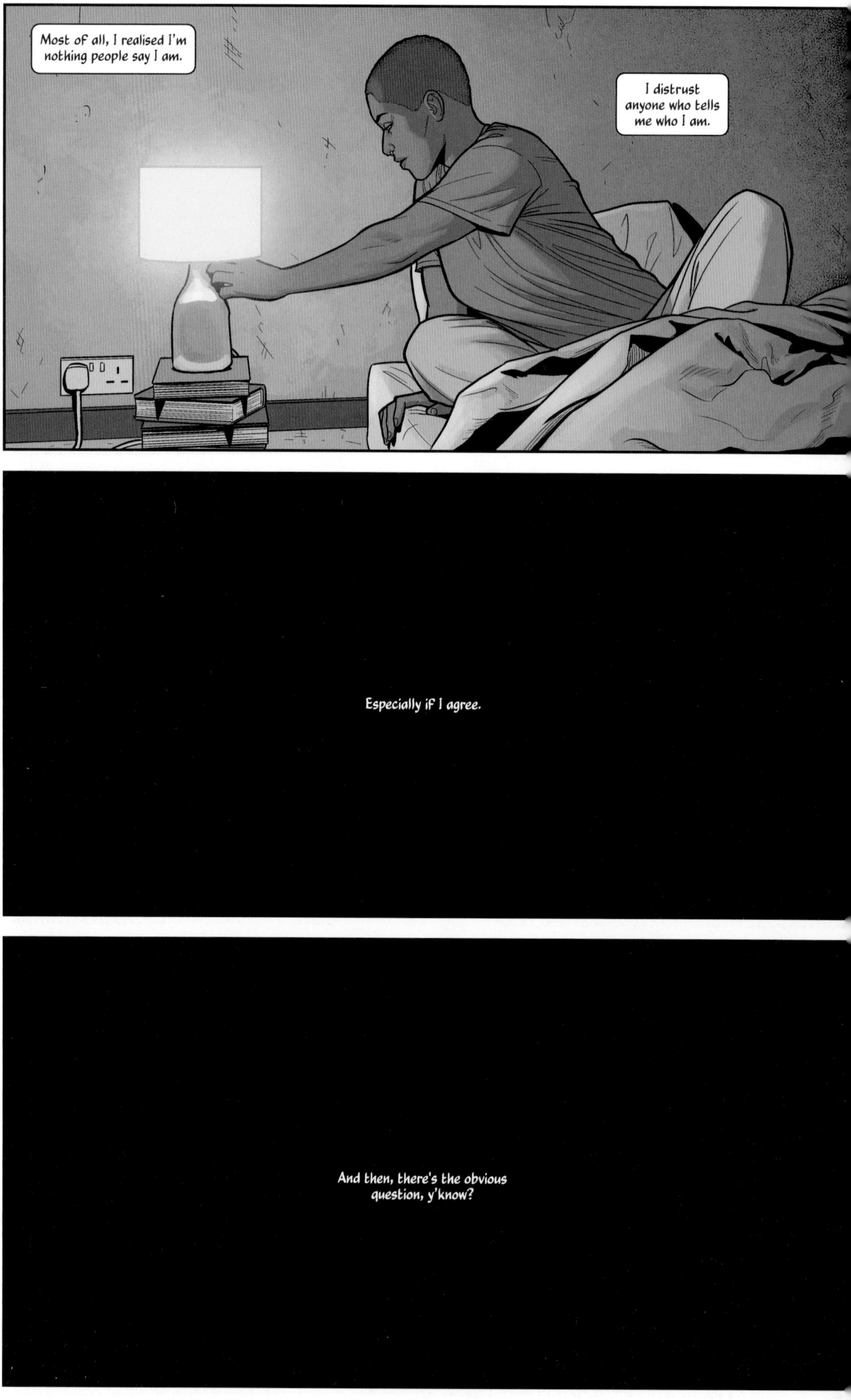
Most of all, I realised I'm nothing people say I am.
I distrust anyone who tells me who I am.
Especially if I agree.
And then, there's the obvious question, y'know?

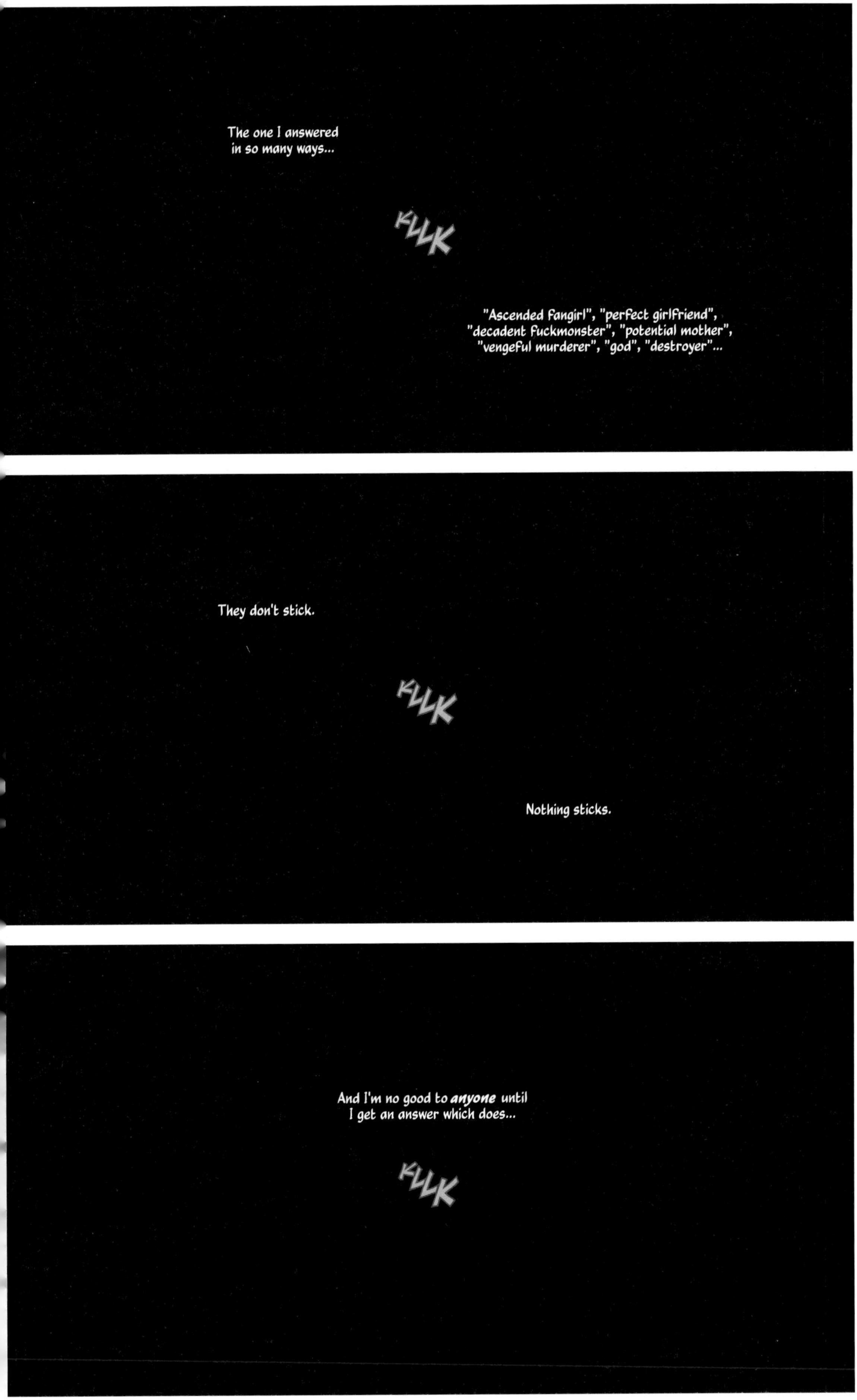
The one I answered in so many ways...
KLLK
"Ascended fangirl", "perfect girlfriend", "decadent fuckmonster", "potential mother", "vengeful murderer", "god", "destroyer"...
They don't stick.
KLLK
Nothing sticks.
And I'm no good to ***anyone*** until I get an answer which does...
KLLK

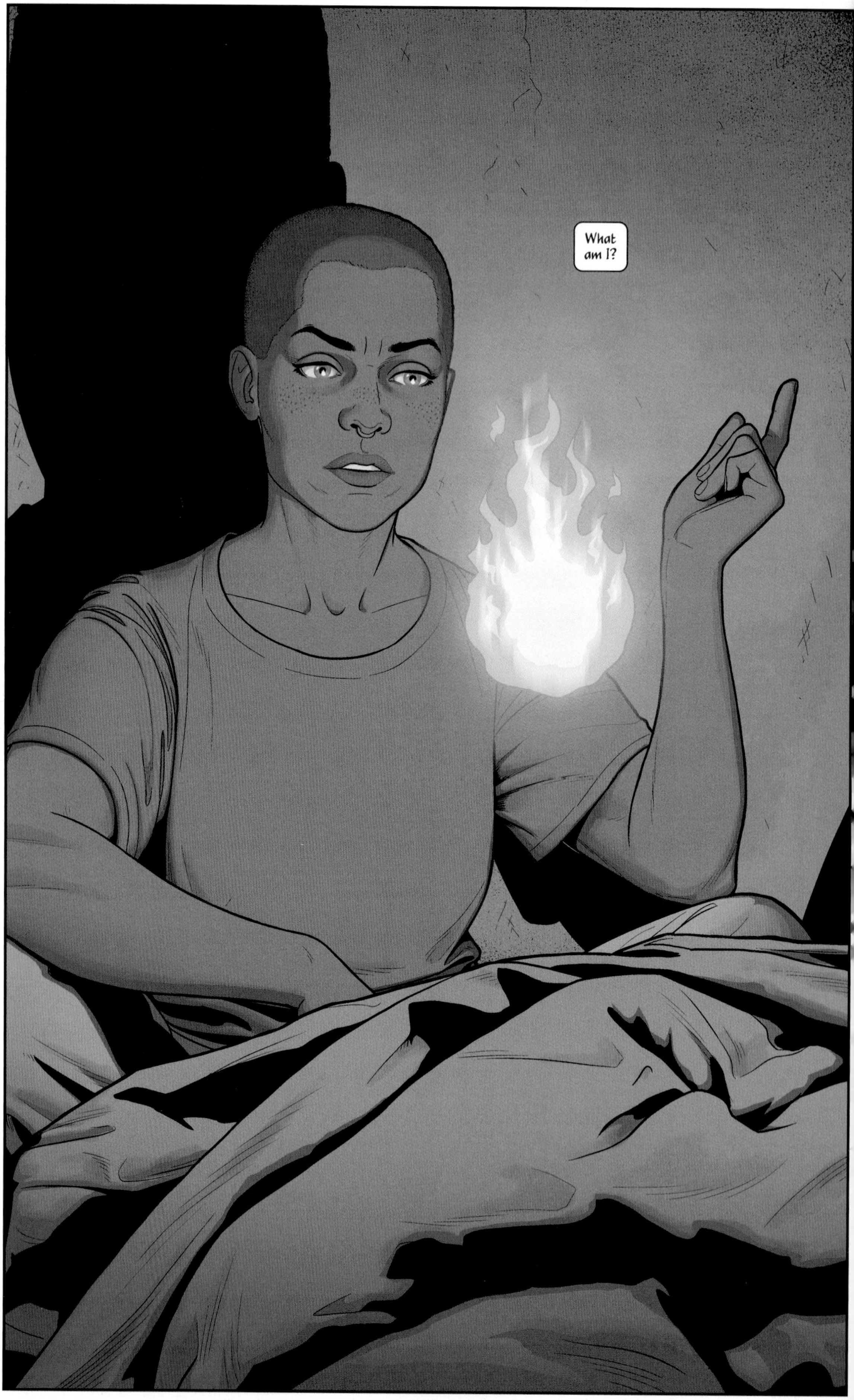
What am I?

CAN'T START
A FIRE

19 MARCH 2015

VARIANT ART

As we approach the end of *WicDiv*, we're increasingly proud of what the variant covers showcase. We've been doing this for four years, and the variants are a snapshot of some of the finest people working in the visual comics arts of the period. You want to know what 2014–2019 was like in comics? I hope you'll be able to just flick through our galleries. It's been fun to curate. We're still considering whether or not we should do an art book collecting them all when it's over. Anyway — once more, our talented friends. We salute them.

Jamie McKelvie & Matthew Wilson
Issue 34 virgin wraparound cover

Daniel Warren Johnson & Mike Spicer
Issue 34 cover

Yoshi Yoshitani
Issue 35 cover

Babs Tarr
Issue 36 cover

Erica Henderson
Issue 37 cover

Cliff Chiang
Issue 38 cover

Phil Jimenez & Dee Cunniffe
Issue 39 cover

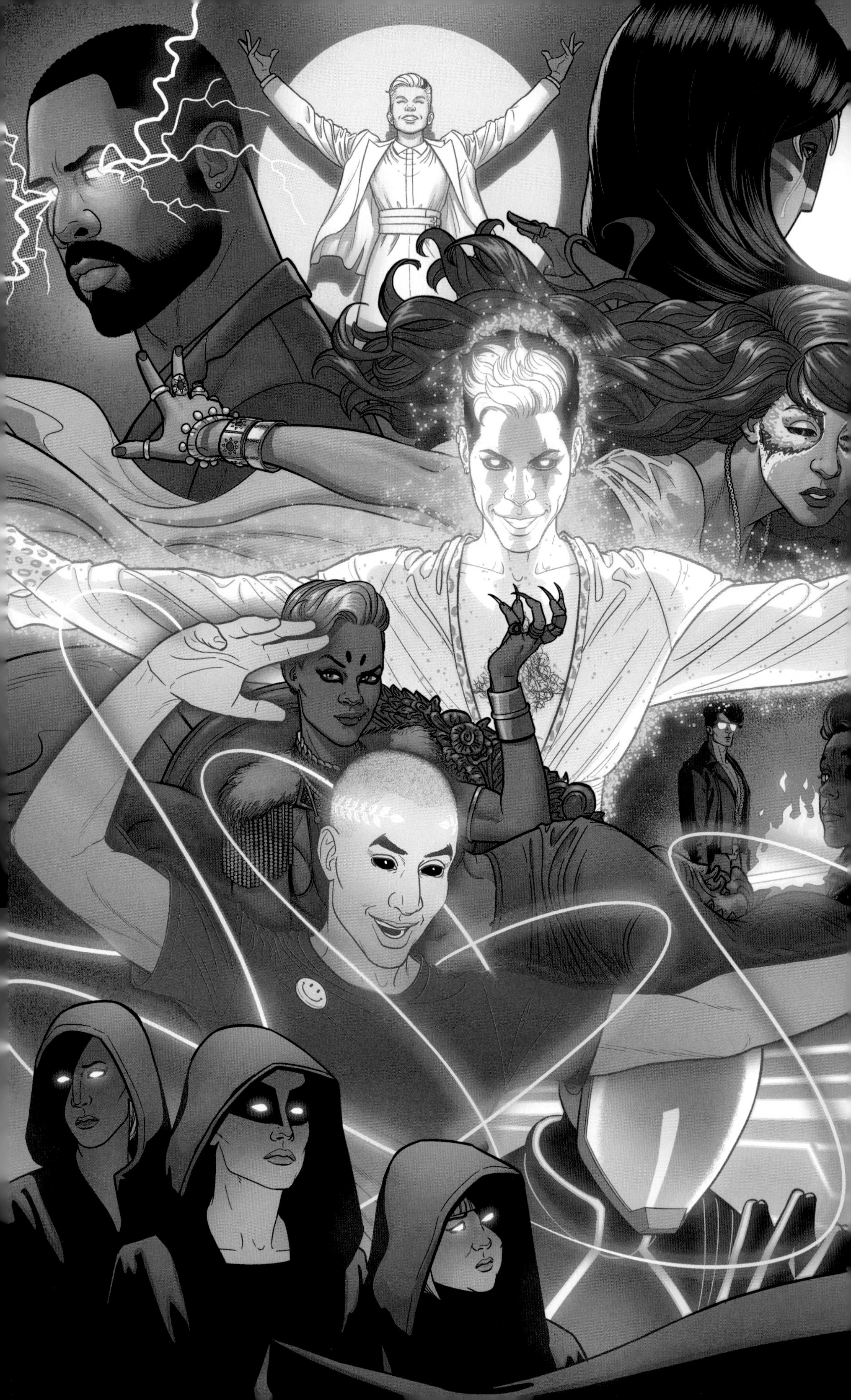

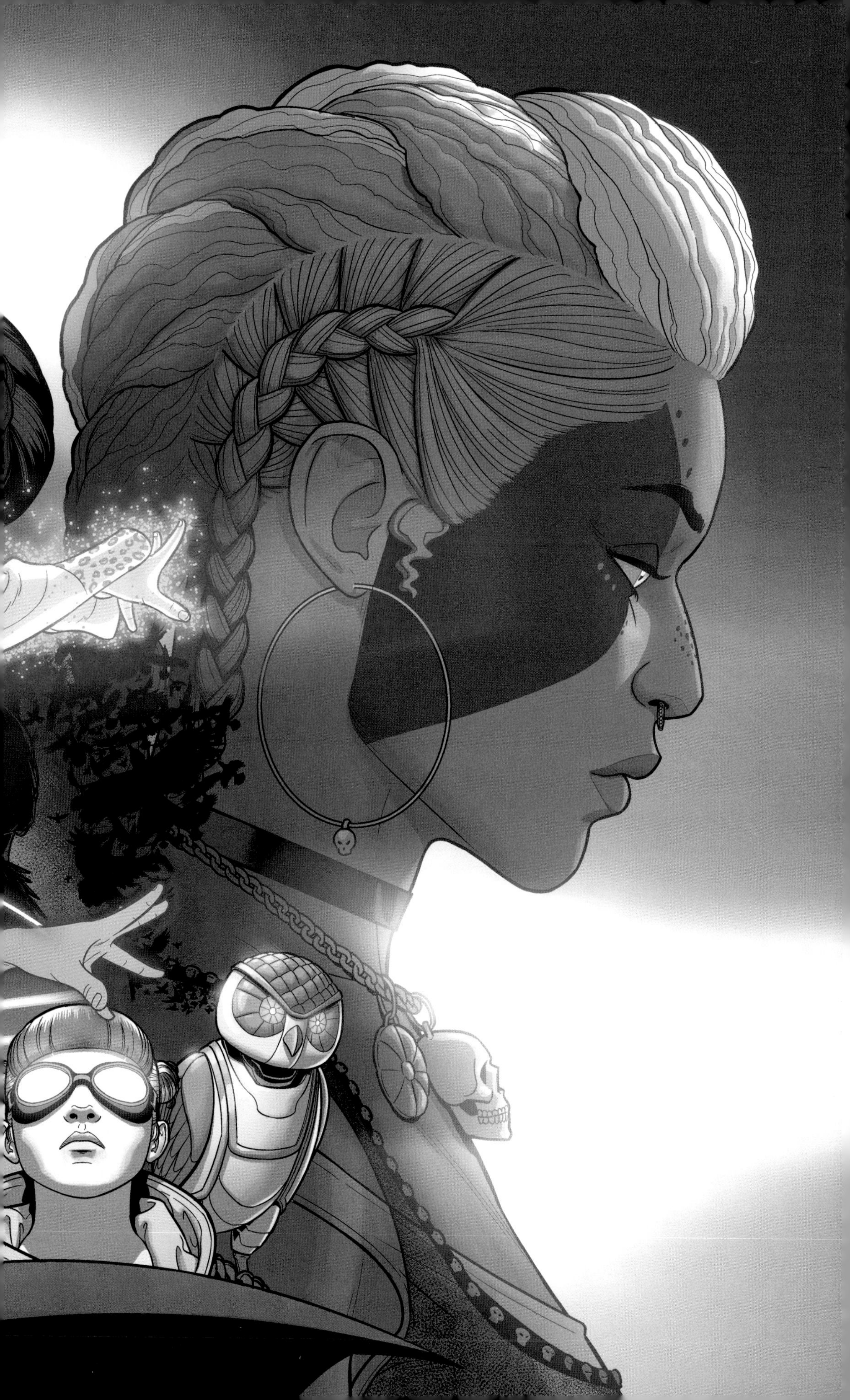

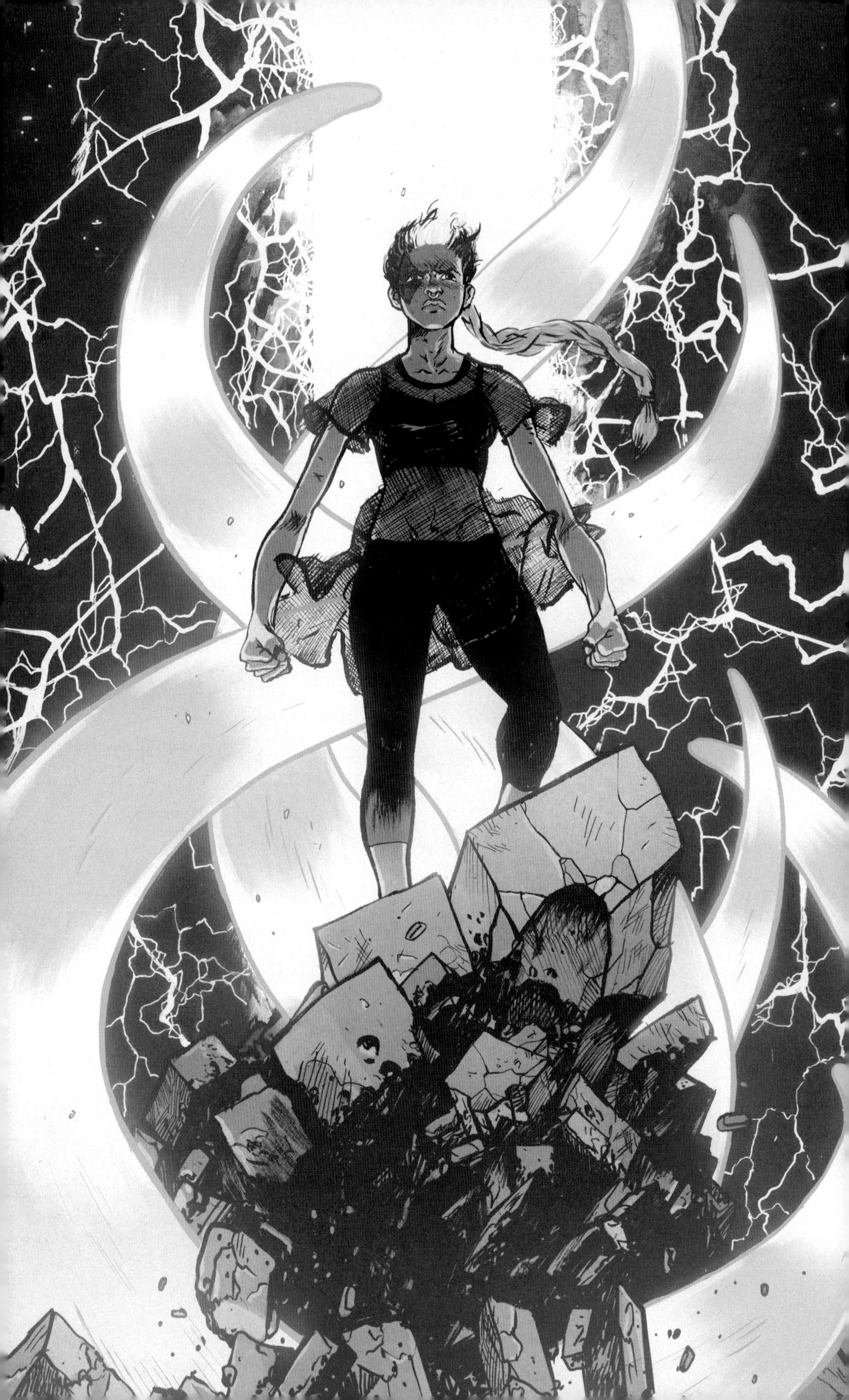

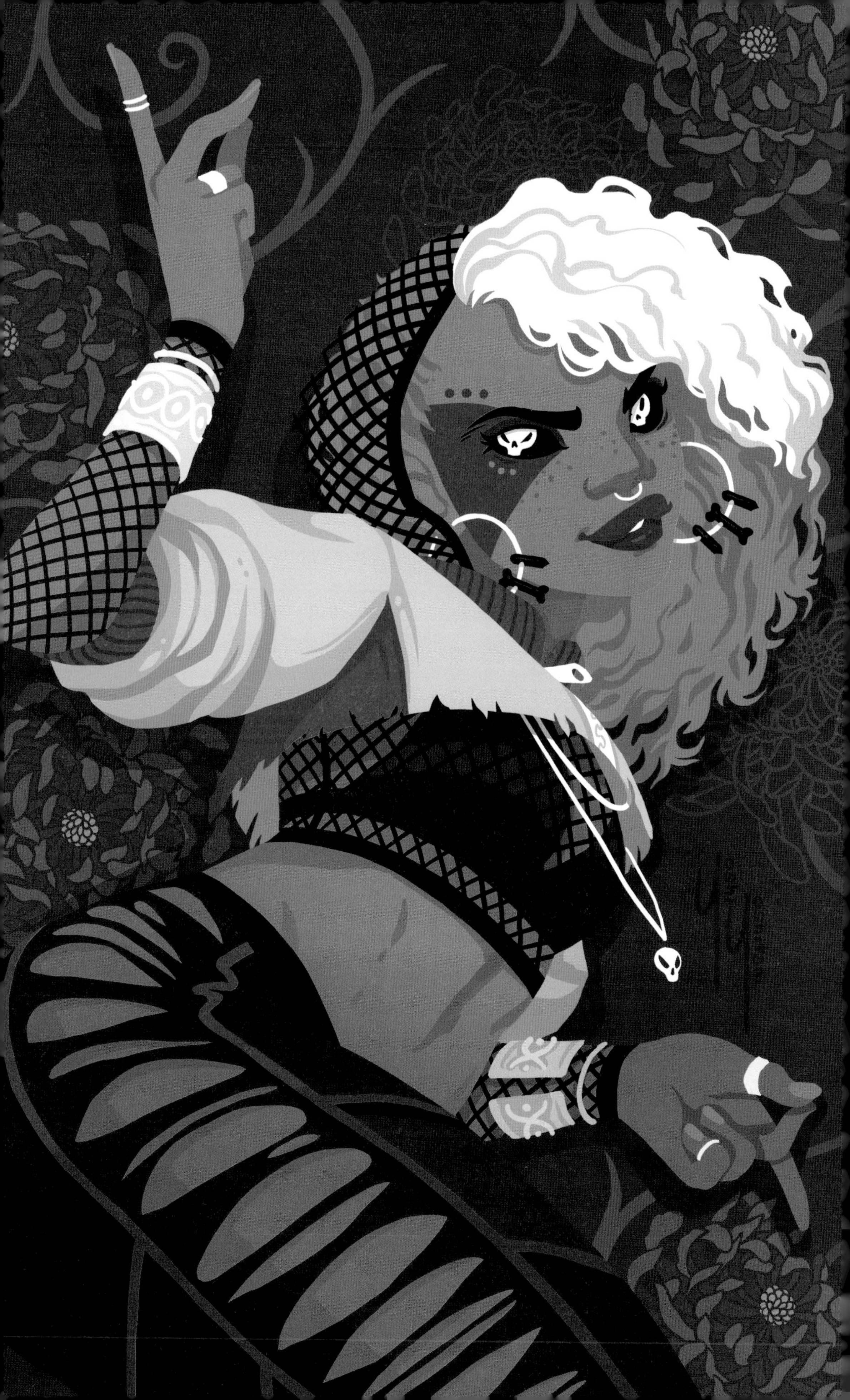

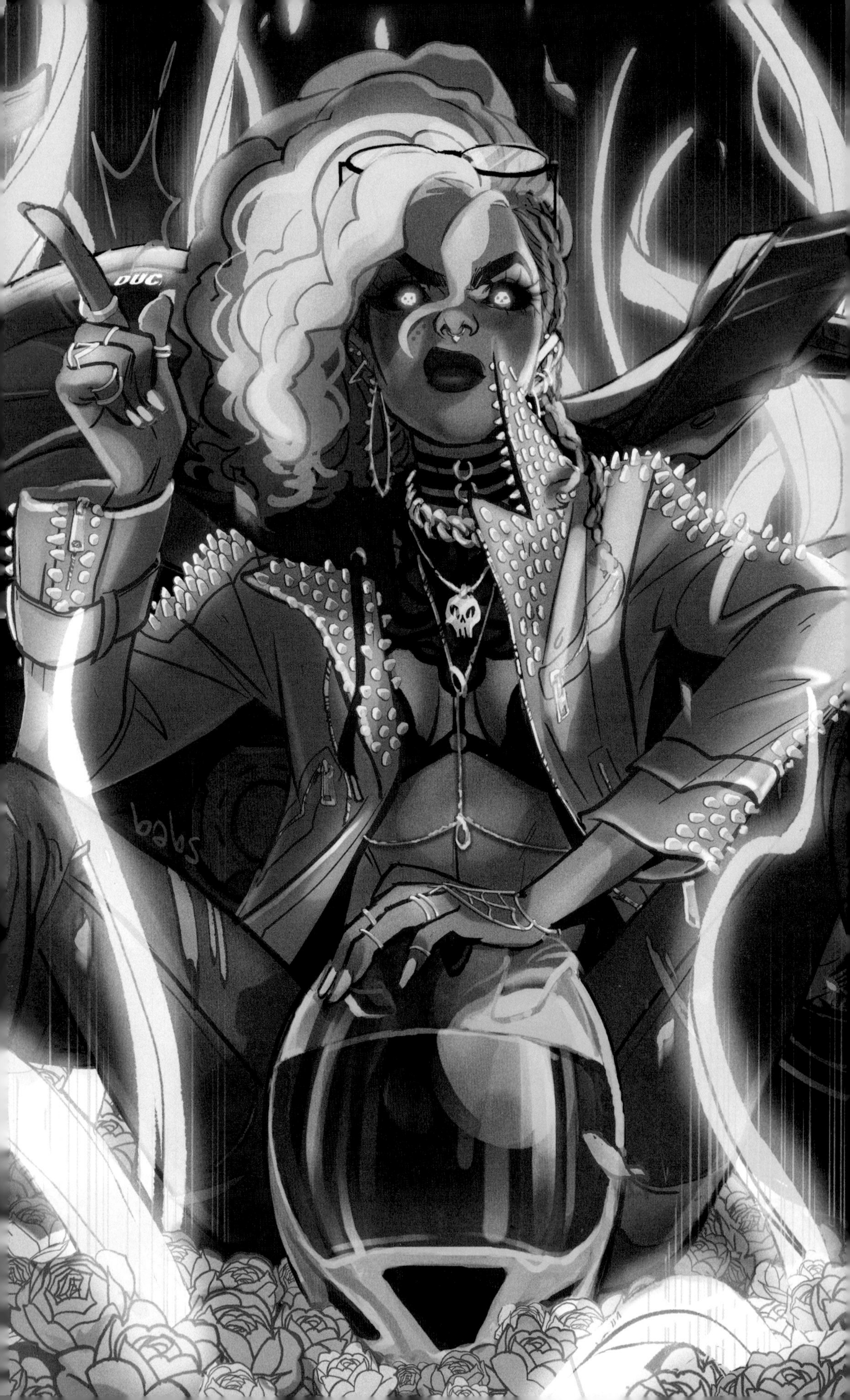
DUC
babs

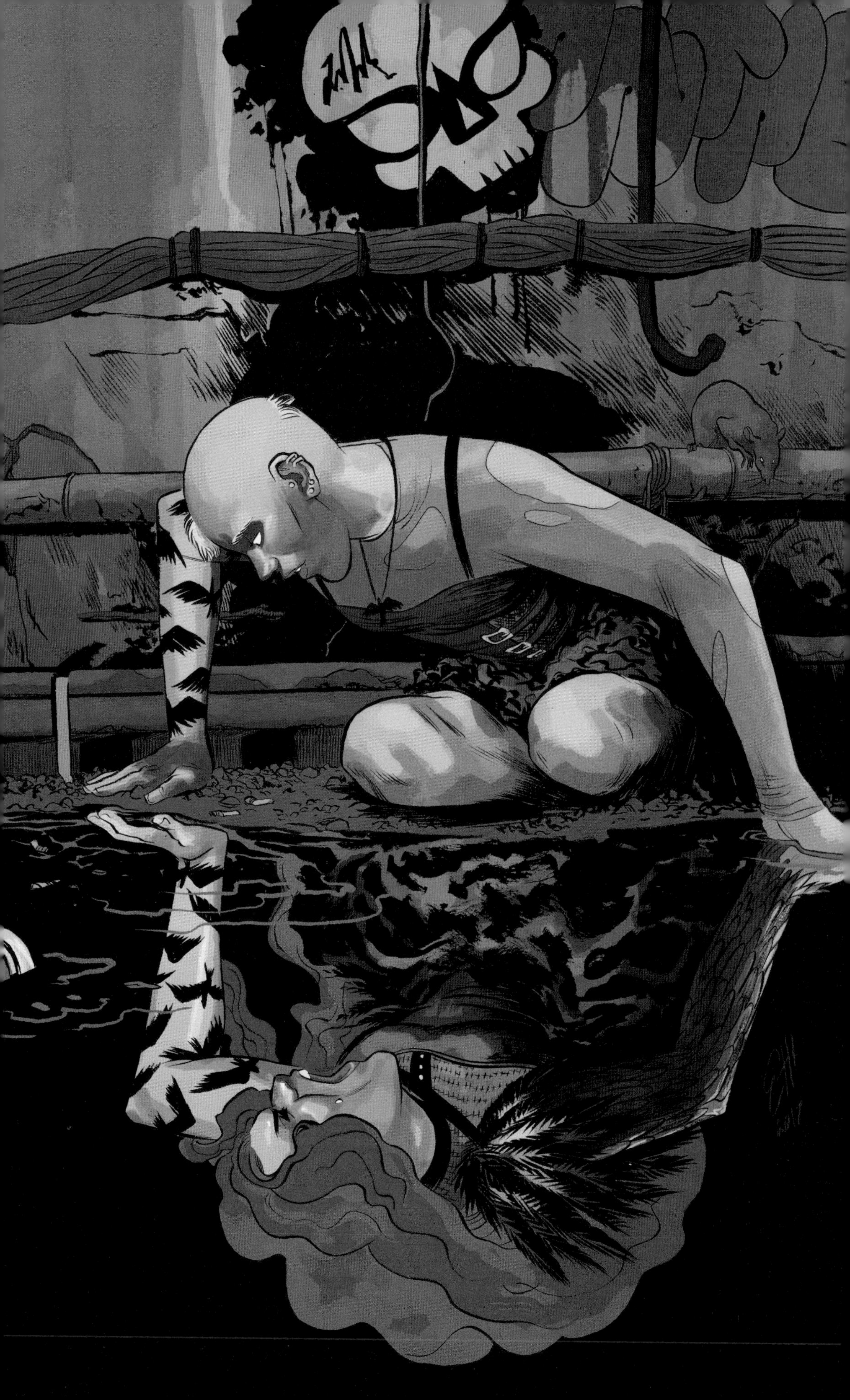

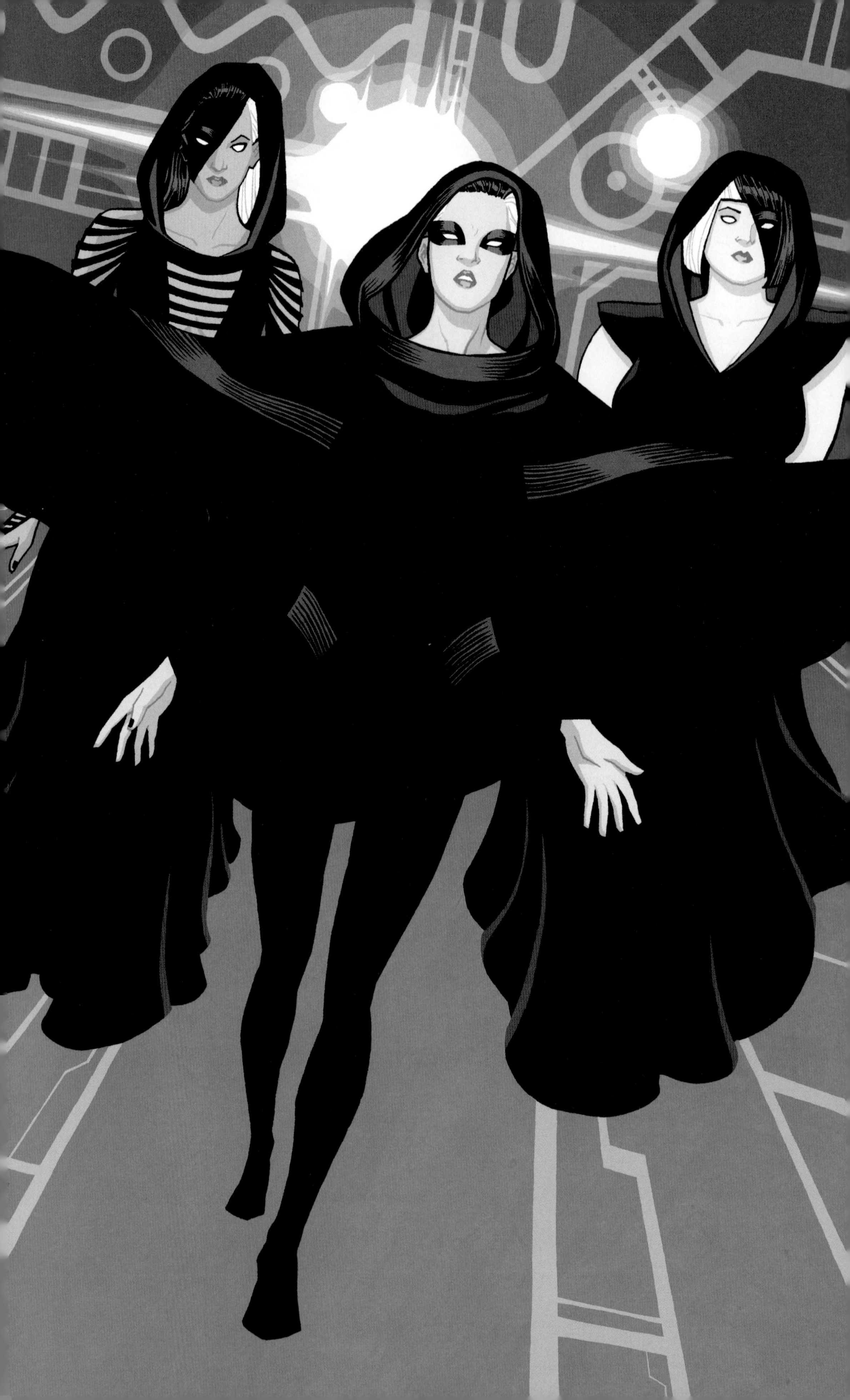

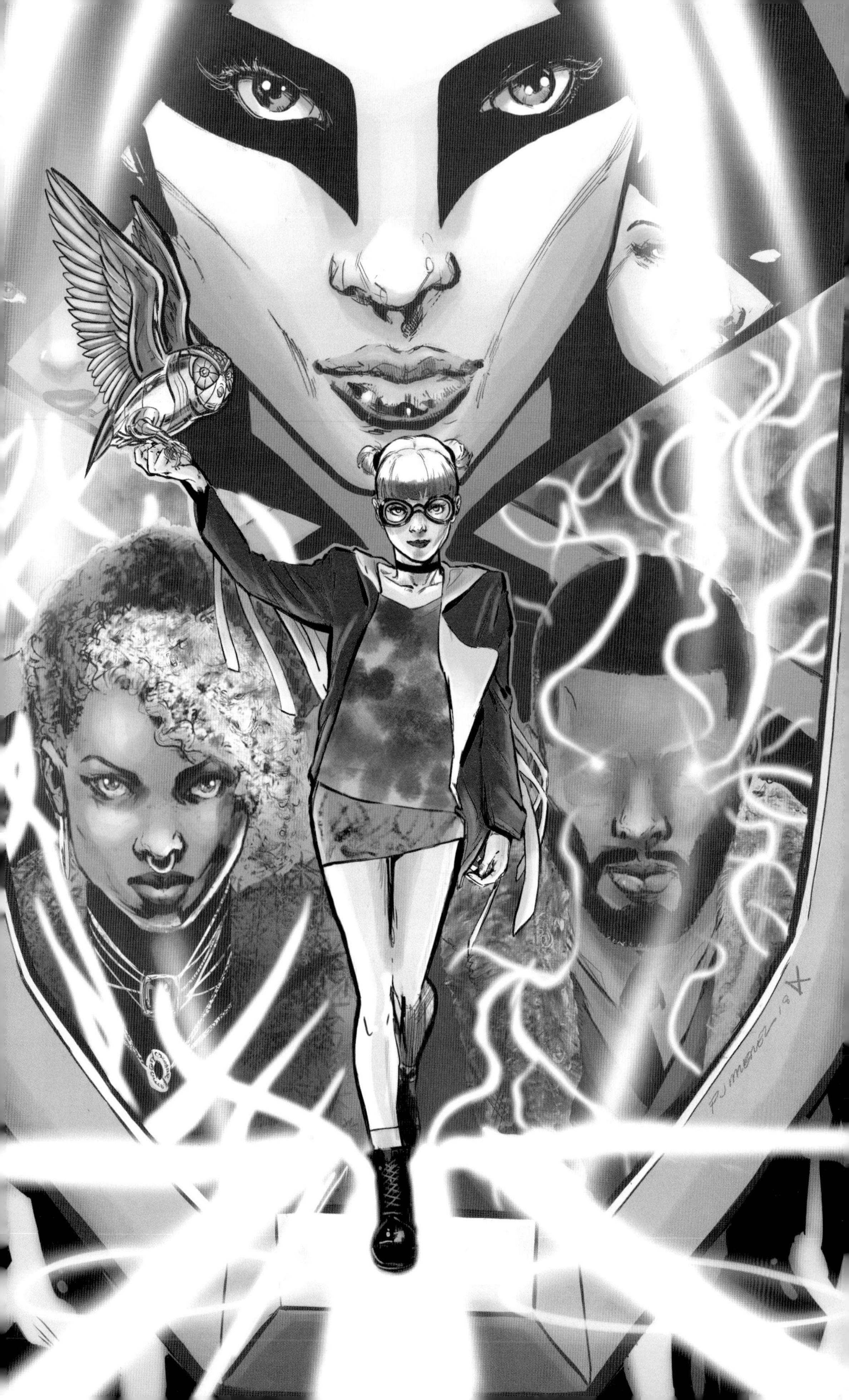

MAKING OF

As creators, we lean towards a fairly frank discussion of craft, so we like to showcase bits and pieces of things we generated while doing this book. This time, we thought it'd be fun to show a flatplan for an issue (an essential part of planning it) and a few pages of script. Issue 36 was a nightmare to do, so a sliver of the script is hopefully interesting to see. It only is a sliver, of course.

Flatplan
Issue 34

Script Pages
Issue 36 and Issue 34

FLATPLAN

Jamie works in Manga Studio, which means things like this are easy, allowing him to keep an overview of the whole shape of an issue. This is handy when Kieron has got a page turn wrong, so Jamie can tell Kieron when he's gone awry. This barely ever happens. Page turns are, in paper comics, one of the basic units of storytelling. If you want to surprise someone with a piece of visual information, you put it over the page turn, so it's not spoiled by readers' peripheral vision.

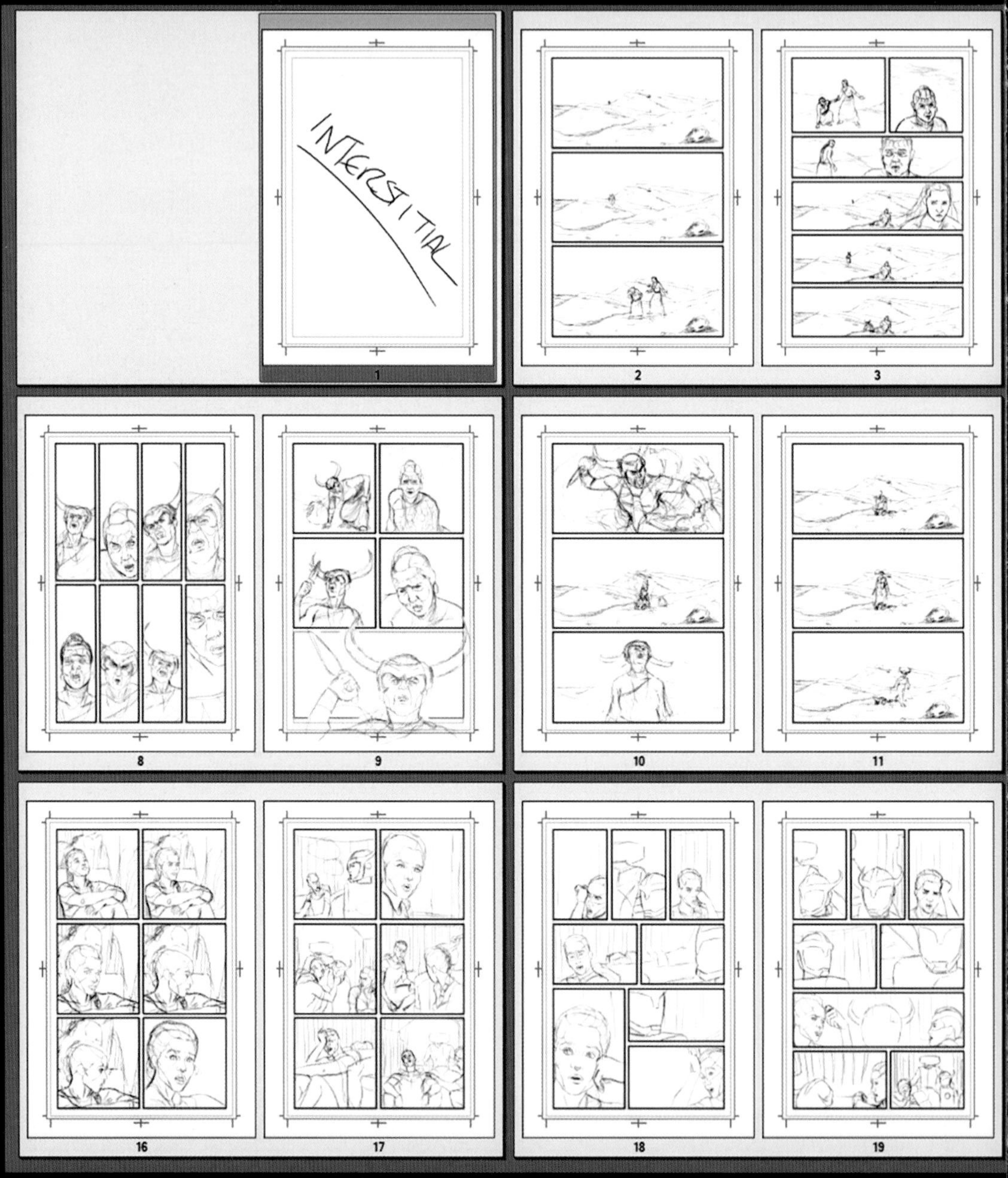
INTERSTITIAL
1
2
3
8
9
10
11
16
17
18
19

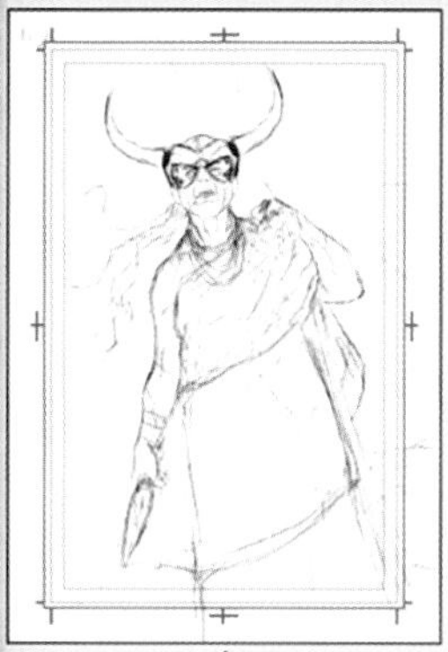

4

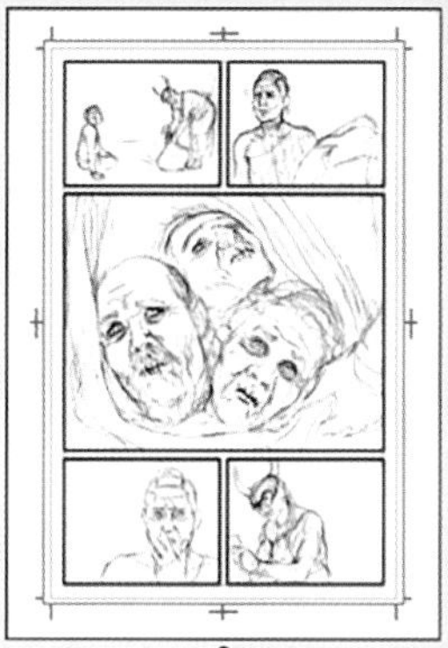

5

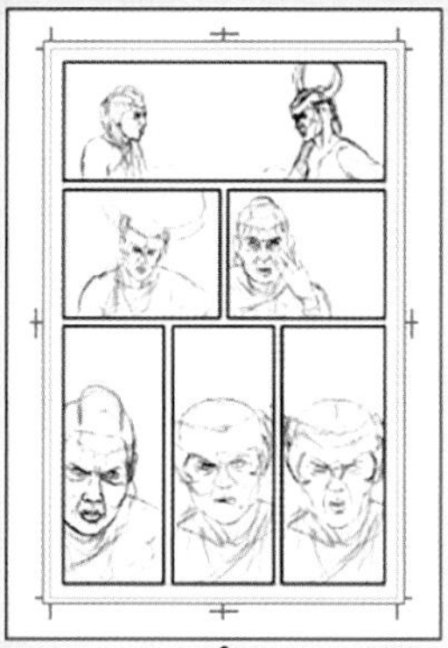

6

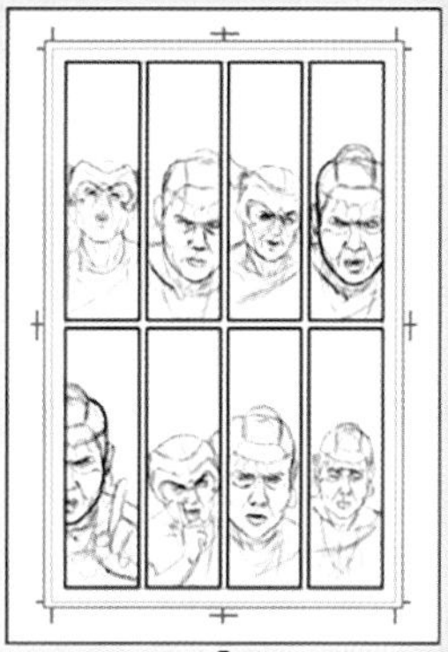

7

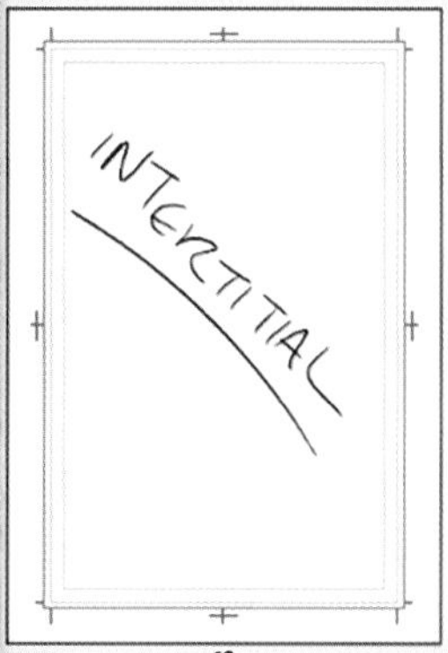
INTERSTITIAL

12

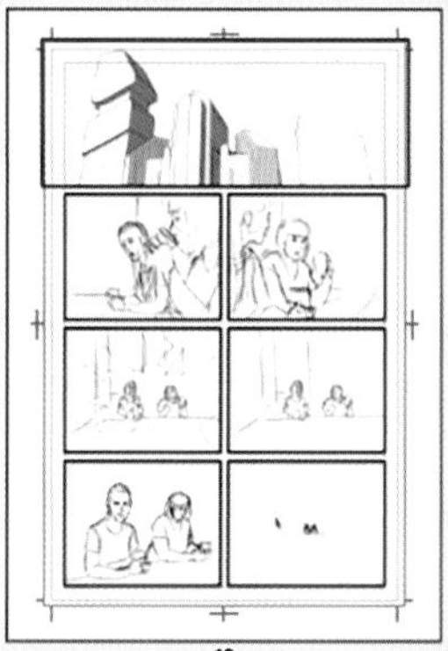

13

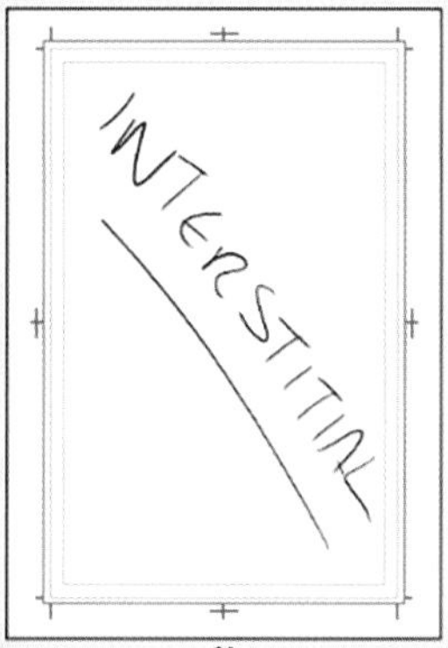
INTERSTITIAL

14

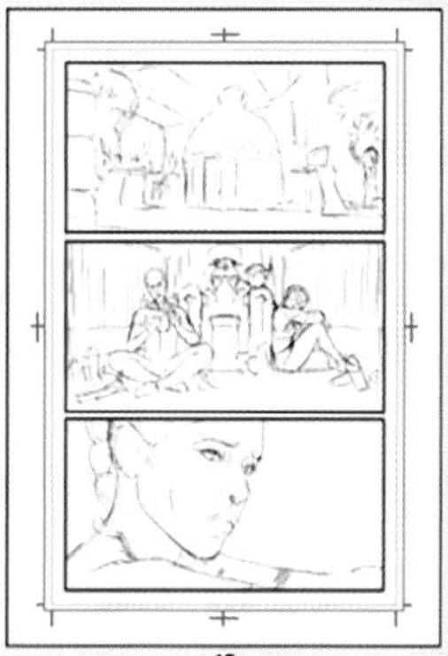

15

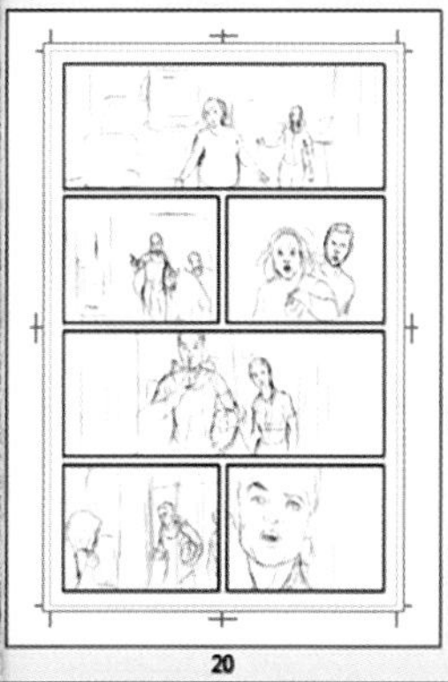

20

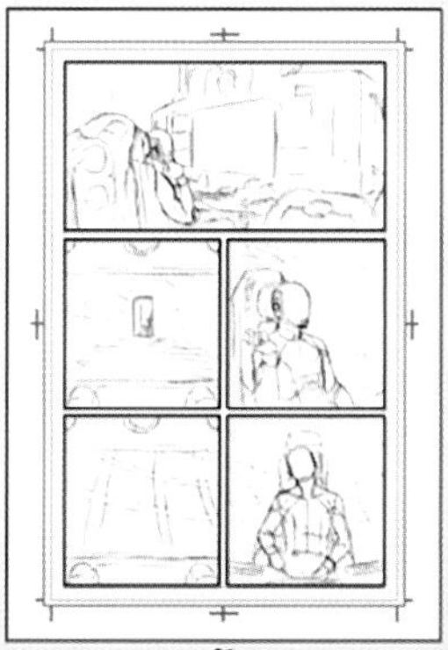

21

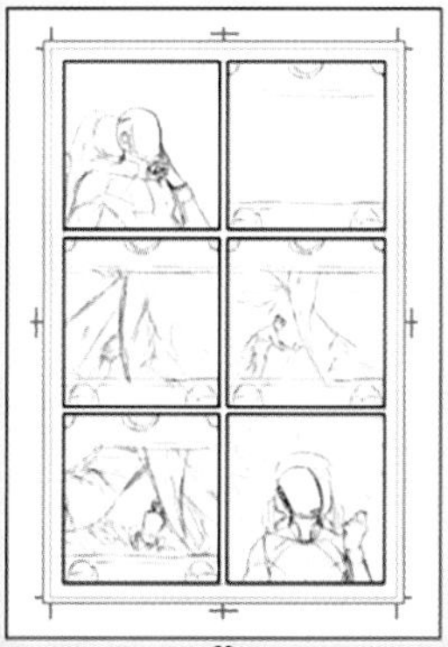

22

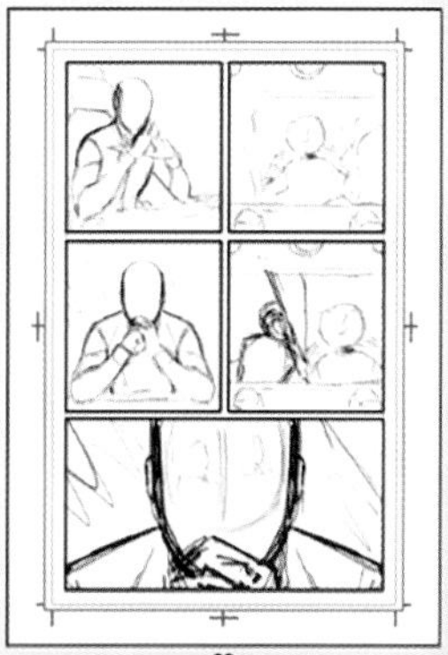

23

SCRIPT PAGES

Image Plus magazine was doing a "writing for comics" article, and asked if we had some sample pages for them, expressly interested in how on earth we managed to do issue 36. Frankly, it's not something we could easily show in a script, but we selected some pages, and lobbed over some more normal pages too. It was printed next to Jonathan Hickman's Marvel Method script for an issue of the amazing *East of West*. Kieron had done panels longer than Hickman's script. Comics is amazing.

(The work process is inverted in Marvel Method — scripting is done after an artist interprets the pages.)

Anyway — our scripts are often conversations, and *WicDiv* 36 was moreso. The format of the first half of this issue is explained at length (like, using multiple pages) at the start of the sequence. The later entries are described as such — in terms of a scene, and the period(s) we're riffing on, and my initial suggestions of what we were thinking of. You'll note that many include multiple options, and a lot of research and choices followed this stage. But this is where we started. Oh — and highlighted things were notes added later. And it has been slightly edited, for the record.

Of course, this is also just the tip of the iceberg in terms of the research on this. We hired a historical fashion researcher to do the groundwork for many periods. As always, if you want to know more about this, head over to Kieron's Tumblr (kierongillen.tumblr.com) and see his writer notes.

ISSUE 36, PAGE 11

11.1

Scene: Standard Ananke Murder.
History: It's the First Crusade. In fact, it 100% starts when this Pantheon is going on.

https://en.wikipedia.org/wiki/First_Crusade

My gut says Ananke in Frankish Pilgrim garb and the Persephone in something akin to Arab clothes in the area would be the way to go.

{92} (EDITOR NOTE: C added this to note the length of each pantheon. Kieron has them all in a spreadsheet already)
LOC CAP: Syria, 1095AD.
SFX: Kllk!

11.2 — Jerusalem

(EDITOR NOTE: When there were multiple options in the original script, C included which decision we made in the final script.)
Scene: Ananke Welcomes Persephone.
History: Well, the previous one was Crusaders. This is actually Saladin kicking the Crusaders out. We could just reverse the previous one — Ananke in Arab gear, Persephone in Frankish Jerusalem state. There's something there, clearly.
The alternative is doing Cambodia, as this is the high point of the Angkor Empire:
https://en.wikipedia.org/wiki/Khmer_
Empire#Suryavarman_II_%E2%80%94_Angkor_Wat
Angkor Wat was constructed in the period around here...
https://en.wikipedia.org/wiki/Angkor_Wat
So that period could give a bunch of stuff.
{92}
LOC CAP: Jerusalem, 1187AD.
SFX: Kllk!

11.3

Scene: Standard Ananke Murder.
History: Kublai Khan conquers China, which is obviously a huge deal, and I don't think we can avoid doing it.

https://en.wikipedia.org/wiki/Kublai_Khan
https://en.wikipedia.org/wiki/Mongol_conquest_of_
China

Honestly, what I've actually read about the Mongols vs the Chinese is pretty amazing.

I feel Ananke should be in Chinese garb. I suspect Persephone should be a Mongol. I feel this was a VERY mongol dominated Pantheon in this time. Definitely lean into the Steppes people of this. The alternative is the Mali Empire, but I'm going to work that in a little later.

{92}
LOC CAP: Northern China, 1279AD.
SFX: Kllk!

11.4

Scene: Standard Ananke Murder... of a sort. Ananke is in bed. She has the plague. Persephone is visiting her. This is likely where I'm going to set the final Special, with Lucifer Nun visiting the bedridden Ananke.

History: this is the Black Death in Europe. It peaked earlier, but could still be going on — and I like the idea that Ananke is STILL suffering it for a long time and just not dying.
https://en.wikipedia.org/wiki/Black_Death

{92}
LOC CAP: France, 1371AD.
SFX: Kllk!

11.5 - Africa

Scene: Standard Ananke Murder — though we can see injuries here. The last Pantheon was hard on Minerva. Possible scarring. Gods are pretty much immune to disease... except when they're not.

History: God, so much here! But I'm going to go with...
https://en.wikipedia.org/wiki/Mali_Empire
(with a little...)
https://en.wikipedia.org/wiki/Songhai_Empire

This guy is earlier, but certainly should be on our mind...
https://en.wikipedia.org/wiki/Musa_I_of_Mali
He is basically the richest dude of all time.

I'm putting as West Africa for now — depending on your choices, I'll tweak to an actual country if we go that way.

This is one of the two places we could do an Incan empire — though I am loathe to lose one of the only West African ones though.

{92}
LOC CAP: West Africa, 1463AD.
SFX: Kllk!

11.6 — Inca Persephone / Florence Ananke

Scene: Standard Ananke Murder.
History: The Renaissance, so this is a European one, probably has to be Florence.

In passing, this is when Bathony would have been born, so this is the Pantheon where one of the gods ended up bathing in blood. We're not showing that, but good for us to know, and so Katie can turn it into a vampfic inside her head.

However, this is the OTHER place we could do an Incan one. The Incan empire fell during this period. Clearly, also giving up a Renaissance Pantheon is a big deal, but the PERSEPHONE could be Incan. If we go this way, it should be very clear that Ananke is dressed like a Western Renaissance figure and so imply much of the rest of the Pantheon was there.

{91}
LOC CAP: Cusco, 1554AD.
SFX: Kllk!

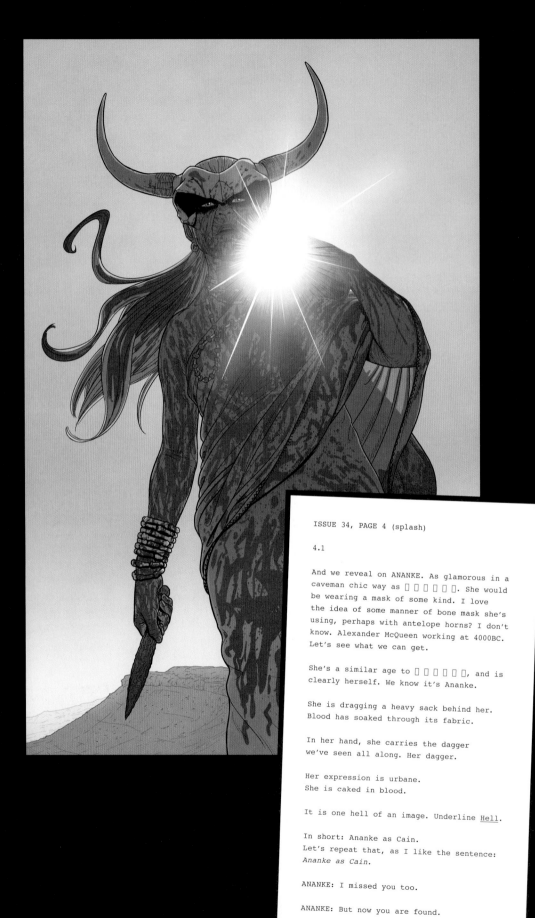

ISSUE 34, PAGE 4 (splash)

4.1

And we reveal on ANANKE. As glamorous in a
caveman chic way as ⬚ ⬚ ⬚ ⬚ ⬚. She would
be wearing a mask of some kind. I love
the idea of some manner of bone mask she's
using, perhaps with antelope horns? I don't
know. Alexander McQueen working at 4000BC.
Let's see what we can get.

She's a similar age to ⬚ ⬚ ⬚ ⬚ ⬚, and is
clearly herself. We know it's Ananke.

She is dragging a heavy sack behind her.
Blood has soaked through its fabric.

In her hand, she carries the dagger
we've seen all along. Her dagger.

Her expression is urbane.
She is caked in blood.

It is one hell of an image. Underline <u>Hell</u>.

In short: Ananke as Cain.
Let's repeat that, as I like the sentence:
Ananke as Cain.

ANANKE: I missed you too.

ANANKE: But now you are found.

ISSUE 34, PAGE 15 (3 panels)

15.1

And we're on Woden's lab. All is quiet
there. It's dark. The cage is the only
light. If there's any route you can see to
Woden's lab upstairs, it would have a light
on in it.

Just reestablish the room, really...
The added line here is basically to make it
clear there hasn't been much talking since
shit went down — I suspect I may try and
lose all the lines if I could. My original
intent was the CAPs to only drop at the end
of the page with the eye-flick to reader,
but when I reworked 16 to get a "Luci is
alive" beat, I had to push captions back
to here.

CAP: No one's speaking here now. A little
shouting and then we slumped. So...

CAP: ...I think it's time **we** started
talking again, right?

15.2

And inside the cage. Everyone sitting down.
I sort of see Persephone and Cass with
their backs against the throne. Perhaps
Mimir's head is in the lap of one of them
— I would suspect Cass may be best. Just
still. Heads hanging. Clearly, there's no
hope here.

Cass has taken the faceplate off. We
can see Jon's face there. She plays
with the faceplate throughout the scene
intermittently. Here, I can almost imagine
her holding it up and looking through its
opening.

We may imply there hasn't been much talking
when we've been away.

We could add other panels here — 3 panels
is good, and the minimum, but part of me
thinks we could do some kind of aspect-
to-aspect kind of storytelling here, to
really extend the moment in the cage. Just
decompress it. Make it live sadly.

But three panels would do it. I mean, it's
been 4 months IRL since our readers will
have seen our cast. They've been trapped
here for a while — an hour, tops.

CAP: It's been a while. Do you hate me?
I've done terrible things. You should hate me.

CAP: I hope you hate me. It'd be terrible
if it was all for nothing.

15.3

And Persephone, glances up, looking
directly at us. Perhaps slightly raising
her head, glancing to one side towards us,
confessional. Conflicted. Not really wanting
to start talking, but doing it anyway.

CAP: It's easier to be in hell if everyone
agrees it's where you deserve to be.

ALSO BY THE CREATORS

THE WICKED + THE DIVINE

VOL. 1:
THE FAUST ACT
#1–5 COLLECTED

VOL. 2:
FANDEMONIUM
#6–11 COLLECTED

VOL. 3:
COMMERCIAL
SUICIDE
#12–17 COLLECTED

VOL. 4:
RISING ACTION
#18–22 COLLECTED

VOL. 5:
IMPERIAL PHASE 1
#23–28 COLLECTED

GILLEN McKELVIE WILSON COWLES
THE WICKED + THE DIVINE
THE FAUST ACT

VOL. 6:
IMPERIAL PHASE 2
#29–33 COLLECTED

GILLEN McKELVIE WILSON COWLES
IMPERIAL PHASE PART 2

BOOK ONE:
#1–11 COLLECTED

GILLEN McKELVIE WILSON COWLES
THE WICKED + THE DIVINE
1

BOOK TWO:
#12–22 COLLECTED

GILLEN McKELVIE WILSON COWLES
THE WICKED + THE DIVINE
2

ALSO BY THE CREATORS

PHONOGRAM

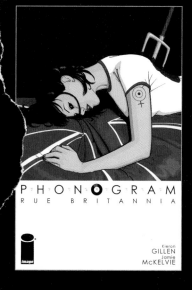
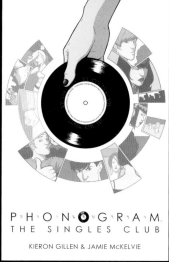
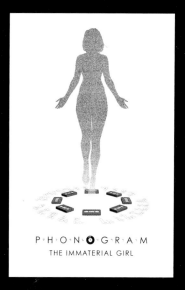

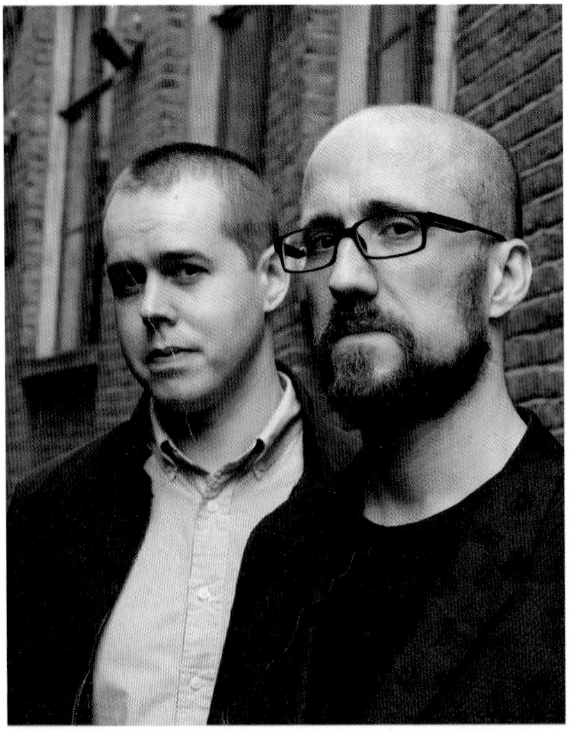

Kieron Gillen is a writer who lives in London.

Jamie McKelvie is an artist who used to live in London.

Matt Wilson is a colourist who needs to come to London so we can get a good photo of all three of us, as this perpetual running joke about Matt not being in the photo is getting silly. It's been four years! We are useless.

Photograph by Lindsey Byrnes